Cambridge Studies in Islamic Civilization

Sex and society in Islam

Cambridge Studies in Islamic Civilization

Other titles

ANDREW M. WATSON, *Agricultural innovation in the early Islamic world*
ELIAS SAAD, *Social history of Timbuktu*
G. H. A. JUYNBOLL, *Muslim tradition*
SURAIYA FAROQHI, *Towns and townsmen of Ottoman Anatolia: Trade, crafts and food production in an urban setting*

Sex and society in Islam

Birth control before the nineteenth century

B. F. MUSALLAM

The right of the University of Cambridge to print and sell all manner of books was granted by Henry VIII in 1534. The University has printed and published continuously since 1584.

Cambridge University Press

Cambridge
London New York New Rochelle
Melbourne Sydney

Published by the Press Syndicate of the University of Cambridge
The Pitt Building, Trumpington Street, Cambridge CB2 1RP
32 East 57th Street, New York, NY 10022, USA
10 Stamford Road, Oakleigh, Melbourne 3166, Australia

First published 1983
Reprinted 1986, 1988

Printed in Great Britain at the University Press, Cambridge

Library of Congress catalogue card number: 82–23539

British Library Cataloguing in Publication Data
Musallam, Basim
Sex and society in Islam.—(Cambridge studies in Islamic civilization)
1. Birth Control—Islamic countries
I. Title
304.6'6'0917671 HQ766 5.1/

ISBN 0 521 24874 4 hardcovers
ISBN 0 521 33858 1 paperback

Contents

Tables

Preface

The difference between man and the other animals is that only man practises contraception.* Jahiz made this distinction in the ninth century when he discussed human and animal sexuality in his *Book of Animals*, a classic of medieval Arabic literature. Some of his readers may not have shared his belief in the primacy of the distinction, but they would have understood it, for they lived in a society where contraception was viewed as an ordinary part of life.

Medieval Arabic discussions of contraception and abortion in Islamic jurisprudence, medicine, materia medica, belles lettres, erotica and popular literature show that birth control was sanctioned by Islamic law and opinion. The sanction had wide distribution and was articulated in terms of social, economic, personal and medical needs. Knowledge of effective methods of birth control was also available throughout pre-modern times, in scientific and popular literature alike. All of these categories of material reflect the same historical reality, each in its own way.

Birth control evidence in the pre-modern Arabic sources presents an embarrassment of riches, and a major problem of this study was one of selection. This book does not pretend to deal with all the problems which the evidence raises. Its principal task is to establish birth control as a pattern in medieval Islam. But even where the book argues against historical demographers who posit that pre-modern populations did not practise birth control, it relies heavily on the vividness of the picture it has drawn of a society which expressed its involvement in birth control through almost every medium except the statistical.

The first two chapters rely heavily on Islamic jurisprudence (Arabic *fiqh*). This literature was the most characteristic achievement of classical Muslim civilization. Jurisprudence dealt with everything relevant to

* "Among the animals that mate, only man practises withdrawal when he does not want children . . . A donkey does not discharge into the she-ass because he seeks progeny, nor does he avoid offspring by practising withdrawal as men do. His only desire is to satisfy the sexual appetite. It never occurs to him that anything can be created from that semen." Jahiz, *Hayawan*, vol. 1, p. 110.

religious and social life, from religious obligations such as fasting and prayer to the organization of the market place.

When we identify a certain society as Muslim, if we do not mean that Islamic law has informed to a recognizable extent its social institutions, we mean nothing at all. It was jurisprudence which gave Islamic religious practice its form and guaranteed its continuity and coherence. Jurisprudence regulated the most material aspects of religion in society: marriage, divorce, birth, death, inheritance. The attempts of Muslims to come to terms with the problems of their society and history are reflected in it throughout.

The association between contraception and modernity is very strong, and may lead some to belittle the medieval juridical evidence. We should remember, however, that our evidence for medieval marriage or divorce is not any better than that for contraception. The evidence for all of these practices exists in the same sources, and to the same extent or limit. There is no more reason to believe that a medieval Muslim had more than one wife or could divorce her at will, than to believe that he practised contraception.

Many of the sources for Chapters 4 and 5 were in manuscript form, and had to be edited and translated before they could be used. These texts are central to my argument; they will be published in a separate monograph now being prepared ("Contraceptive Medicine in the Medieval Middle East"). The essential information on birth control techniques of some texts is included in tables which accompany their discussion below (pp. 77–88, 101–4).

The Introduction considers the major ideas in historical demography regarding pre-modern fertility and the place of birth control in history. It is my attempt to integrate the findings of this book into the body of current knowledge. Chapter 6 explores the extent to which birth control evidence can be integrated into what is known about Middle Eastern demographic history in general.

Without statistical data, it is difficult to gauge the impact of birth control as a factor in demographic change. But the absence of such data for pre-modern times should not make us abandon the effort. I believe that mortality was the more important factor, *grosso modo*, in determining population size in the medieval Middle East. But even if birth control had a very small impact on the ultimate numbers (we cannot tell for sure), it deserves special attention in social history, simply because it is the most directly volitional factor. Observations made by some individuals in medieval Middle Eastern society, to the effect that birth control was a proper reaction to the perilously shifting conditions of life, reveal a temperament which must have affected behaviour in other areas of social and economic life. Factors like death by war or plague can never have this kind of reach.

In the years of work on this book I have received much help and support, and it is an honour to acknowledge it. David S. Landes and Roger Revelle convinced me to begin my study and, together with Joseph Fletcher, Jr, Albert Hourani, and Sharon A. Lefevre, made me realize that it was possible. Ansley Coale, John T. Noonan, Jr, Etienne van de Walle, and Michael Cook read various versions of the whole manuscript and made generous and valuable criticism.

I am indebted for support in the period of writing this book to the Harvard Center for Middle Eastern Studies and its Director, Muhsin Mahdi; the Harvard Center for Population Studies and its Director, Roger Revelle; the Princeton Office of Population Research and its Directors, Ansley Coale and Charles Westoff, and the Center for Middle Eastern Studies at the University of Pennsylvania and its Director, Thomas Naff. I am grateful to the Ford Foundation for an Individual two-year grant to study population and Middle Eastern history, and to the American Philosophical Society for a grant to study medieval biological theory.

To ALBERT HOURANI *and* ROGER REVELLE

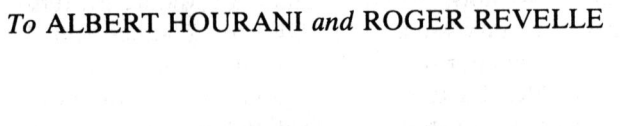

Introduction

Birth control and pre-modern populations

The study of past populations, although it has only recently come into its own, has been flourishing, nurtured as much by scientific and historical curiosity as by the grave anxieties of our time. Economic historians, demographers and family planners have all contributed to our knowledge of past populations. Nevertheless, this knowledge is still very sketchy, and what is known has not always been used with precision. Some of the confusion doubtless results from the disparate interests and perceptions of the varied groups of scholars who have studied population questions.

Aside from formal demography, there have been two major currents of interest in population studies. One is historical: research into the past of *European* populations. The other is political, in the widest sense of social and economic planning: the solution of the problems posed by the growth of non-European, *third-world* populations.

European economic historians have dealt with population, but they have had their own axe to grind. Their work, though important, has dealt primarily with the relationship between industrialization and demographic change. Did the Industrial Revolution create its own labour force, or was an expanding population one of the causes of the Revolution?[1] In other words, the work of economic historians was restricted mainly to the eighteenth century in Europe, which was characterized by the decline in mortality rates; they have done less work on the later, and, with reference to the present-day problem of world population growth, more relevant phase, when the European birth rates adjusted themselves to the lower mortality rates.[2]

The demographers, of course, have been interested in population *per se*. Demography is "the statistical study of population",[3] and historical demography is the same endeavour applied to past population.[4] Both of these concerns are "formal demography", the study of the data necessary to account for population size, nature, and movement. As we move to the study of causes, effects, and interpretations of population movement or change, we enter the realm of demographic history (as opposed to historical demography). Demographic history is historical writing that narrates and explains demographic events.[5]

Demographers have achieved near-miracles, creating new and impressive methodologies based on limited and difficult data (family reconstitution, for example). They have paid less attention to the ideas that help form their views on the character of past populations. And of all the different aspects of population studies, demographic history has prospered least.

In its genesis and concerns, historical demography is pre-eminently a Western, or more accurately, a West European discipline.[6] Nowhere is this more apparent than in the theory of "demographic transition" which has been historical demography's most comprehensive and pervasive idea.[7] The theory of demographic transition holds that (1) all human populations in pre-modern times maintained themselves or slowly expanded under conditions of high mortality balanced against high, essentially uncontrolled fertility – that is, fertility which is free from the volitional control of birth within marriage; (2) mortality started to decline during the Industrial Revolution, while fertility remained high and "traditional", as above, with the result that populations in the West experienced rapid growth; and (3) during the nineteenth and early twentieth centuries fertility declined in the West as a result of the deliberate control of birth within marriage. The "demographic transition" was a movement from a condition of high mortality and fertility to one of low mortality and fertility.[8]

As an attempt to order our information about European population change over the last two hundred years, the theory of transition has been very useful. But there is no historical foundation for the assumption that pre-modern populations did not practise birth control to any significant extent. Nevertheless, it was generally believed that *all* pre-modern populations, not just Europeans, had high, essentially uncontrolled fertility, and that the impact of modern Western science, medicine, and public health has lowered mortality while fertility has remained "traditional". Population growth in underdeveloped lands today has been viewed as essentially a repetition of the same process that occurred in the West a century or so ago.

Some early formulations of the theory (Notestein (1953), for example) did not deny the presence of pre-modern contraception.[9] Still, in the last two decades, the theory of transition with its implicit denial of pre-modern contraception has been an unfortunate and rarely questioned orthodoxy.

Some historical demographers have recognized that the theory of transition has serious limitations. David Glass, for example, has explicitly challenged its relevance for the study of contemporary societies:

> The theory of transition does not, in its present form, provide an adequate framework for the study of contemporary societies. It could hardly do so, since it is

rather mechanistic and, in addition, is beset by too many apparent deviations as well as by gaps in essential information.[10]

Glass has, furthermore, devoted a valuable paper to the development of these criticisms.[11] In a review of the facts relevant to an explanation of the population increase in eighteenth-century Europe, he discusses critically the questions of changing marriage patterns and mortality and fertility trends. He makes reference to Hollingsworth's work on the British peerage, Hajnal's on the "European marriage pattern", McKeown and Brown's on medical factors, Irish demographic developments, and French demographic history.[12] But even in questioning the relevance of the transition theory for the study of contemporary societies, and by these he means the underdeveloped countries, Glass' criticism and modifications of the theory rest on exclusively European evidence. Although Glass' effort is valuable within the framework of European demographic history as such, in the final analysis the theory of transition has little relevance for third-world populations unless it is tested by information about *their* past and experience.

It is perhaps no accident that interest in historical demography showed remarkable vitality in the period following the Second World War, when the population problems of the underdeveloped world thrust themselves upon Western consciousness. In any case, a major argument used by the demographers for the utility of their research on historical (European) populations has been the urgency of present-day (third-world) population problems.[13]

The discovery of the third world's "population explosion" has resulted in the creation of important national and international agencies to deal with it. The "family planners", that is, all those who have applied themselves to checking the "population explosion", whether demographers, social and behavioural scientists, biologists, physicians, statisticians, international public servants, or public health workers, have drawn upon the historians' and demographers' findings about European populations for their ideas about population in general. There has been an anomalous situation where would-be managers of the Egyptian or Indian populations knew more about the past trends of British or French populations than about the history of the third-world populations they were trying to change.

Perhaps it is fair to say that since the present condition of the non-European populations lies at the root of much of the interest and planning, then the past of these populations themselves also requires investigation. It would be wrong to assume that the past of third-world populations is not relevant to understanding their current problems. All those who have applied themselves to the solution or understanding of population problems in the third world have held ideas about the character and behaviour of "traditional", "pre-modern", "pre-industrial", or "agricultural" populations. Such ideas have always influenced their questions and approach and have thereby affected and will continue to affect population planning and policy. Moreover, these ideas are rooted in historical knowledge, for they mostly originate in the work of historical demographers on *European* populations. As long as we cannot escape using ideas rooted in historical knowledge, there should be agreement about the importance of the past. In any particular context the question should be: which is the more relevant past?

A priori there is not a sound basis for believing that European population experience has universal applicability and meaningfulness, and there is good evidence to suggest the opposite – that the past of the Europeans may very well have been unique or different, with no necessary relevance to population behaviour elsewhere.[14] In any case, historical information about Europe is no substitute for historical information from the third world.

The fundamental element which is used, both implicitly and explicitly, to explain the modern movement from high to low fertility in the West is volitional birth control within marriage.[15] In the same way, the high fertility rates of pre-modern and "traditional" populations are assumed to result from the absence of birth control. To follow Louis Henry's definition, pre-modern populations had a regime of "natural fertility", unaffected by volitional factors. Henry contrasted natural fertility with modern, "controlled fertility":

> We can term as natural the fertility which exists or has existed in the absence of deliberate birth control . . . Control can be said to exist when the behavior of the couple is bound to the number of children already born and is modified when this number reaches the maximum which the couple does not wish to exceed.[16]

As a description of fertility behaviour, Henry's definition is very precise regarding certain modern populations whose fertility is governed by the practice of birth limitation within marriage linked to parity (the number of children already born). This means that contraception is systematically used after the desired number of children is achieved; it is also used meanwhile to space births. Demographers have found in Henry's distinction between natural and controlled fertility a useful tool for identifying populations with a "modern" (that is, controlled) fertility behaviour.

The spacing of children, and the systematic prevention of pregnancy after the desired number is achieved, produces an easily identifiable statistical pattern: "Control is indicated, crudely, by a steeply declining age-schedule of marital fertility, and more precisely by such clues as a substantially earlier age at the birth of the last child for women who married under age 25 than for those who married over 30."[17] If the statistics show, for example, that women married at age 25, had their first child at age 26, a second child at age 29, and a third and last child at age 33, then demographers can safely assume that birth control had been practised to space children and to prevent pregnancy after the birth of the last child. One of the great virtues of Henry's model, and the source of its great appeal to historical demographers, is that it dispenses with the need for non-statistical evidence to establish the presence of birth control. In most cases such evidence is absent or difficult to interpret.

But the distinction between natural and controlled fertility is not entirely satisfactory to the historian, for the statistical pattern of controlled fertility can be produced by means completely different from the one (birth control) which Henry assumed. Japanese demographic data from the Tokugawa period produce a statistical pattern which fits Henry's model most accurately:

> The childbearing span was short; i.e., in Fujito, it covered no more than a dozen years on the average. In this village, the mean age at which women, who married between 1825 and 1841 and whose marriages lasted until they were 44, bore their last child was 35.7 (average age at mid-year). For women married after 1841, the average age was 35.1. With a three-year birth interval, the result was a mean completed family size of just over three children . . . and this family size seems to have prevailed . . . for other areas in Tokugawa Japan.[18]

Can we surmise, because both European and Japanese fertility behaviour in the nineteenth century produced the same statistical pattern, that the two populations achieved it the same way?

Literary, non-statistical, evidence (the only true reliable evidence on the question of means and ends) shows that the Japanese used *infanticide* to limit their families (Susan Hanley, who studied the demography of Tokugawa Japan, called infanticide "post-partum birth control").[19] The demographer, as statistician, may not be disturbed by linking contraception and infanticide together as instruments of control. The historian must distinguish between them for the sake of complete accuracy. The distinction may also be important in showing differences between the lives and ideas of different societies.

There is also a question of demographic methodology. "Infant mortality" has been a major element in all demographic analysis. Demographers place data relating to live birth under "fertility", and that relating to deaths after birth under "mortality". To accept the Japanese data as indicating the same pattern of fertility behaviour, following Henry's model, is to measure fertility by data which are used normally to measure mortality. Susan Hanley has anticipated this objection, and has forcefully argued that "babies who were deliberately killed at birth, or 'returned' as the Japanese put it, should not be confused with babies who were intended to live but died in the early days or months of life".[20] The first go under "fertility", the second go under "mortality".

This argument is based on the *intentions* of the parents, and derives from literary evidence. The statistics as such do not reveal any difference between the infant who died naturally and the one who was killed in the first days after birth.

But Henry's model has been powerful precisely because it promised to dispense with the need for arguments about intentions and means, which can only be based on treacherous literary evidence. European demographic historians would be truly at a loss if they were to be burdened with the requirement to support their statistical procedure with direct, literary evidence about the means of control and the intentions behind it.

While Henry's model assumes contraception and perhaps also abortion as the instruments of control, he does not name them explicitly. The definition of "controlled" fertility skips over this important element because everyone in Europe knows that the modern secular decline in Western fertility has been the result of contraception within marriage. Putting culture-bound historical experience and literary evidence aside, if one were to look at a European statistical pattern of controlled fertility from a purely Tukugawa Japanese perspective, would not one assume that the Europeans limited their families by using infanticide?

"Natural fertility" is a concept which attempts to describe the fertility behaviour of the largest possible number of human populations – that is, all the historical populations before modern times, and most of them during the last two hundred years. It is different from controlled fertility in this very important sense: it does not claim that populations which are characterized by natural fertility have the same fertility pattern. On the contrary, there are significant variations among the fertility rates of pre-modern populations, sometimes as great as those between "controlled" and "natural" fertilities, and all fertility rates fall below the rates biologically possible.[21] Demographers, until recently, have avoided suggesting that birth control may have had something to do with these variations.

How, then, to account for the variations? Henry was aware of this rich variety and has attempted to take (nearly) full measure of it, attributing these differences to a long list of biological and institutional restraints. Biological restraints are factors like the age of menarche, lactation length, the duration of post-partum amenorrhea, relative fecundity, sterility, and pregnancy wastage. Institutional restraints include a variety of social customs and regulations which determine the probability of exposure of women to sexual intercourse, such as taboos against intercourse during lactation or the so-called "European marriage pattern", observable in Western Europe from the sixteenth century on, in which late marriage was the norm and a large percentage of the population remained unmarried.

All fluctuations and differences in birth rates between pre-modern populations were explained away by the institutional and biological factors mentioned above. Contraception was conspicuous by its absence, and has been reserved for "modern" populations.[22]

The only thing that populations with natural fertility have in common is the *absence* of modern fertility behaviour – that is, they lack the pattern which shows control linked to parity. This does not mean anything more than that, in their fertility behaviour, fourteenth-century French or ninth-century Syrian, or nineteenth-century Indian, or eighteenth-century Chinese populations are different from the twentieth-century French population (and from each other). This is important to recognize, but it does not begin to say something meaningful about the nature of these populations. "Natural fertility" has been nothing more than a negative definition which has served to provide a background for "controlled fertility", the modern pattern which was Henry's primary interest.

Theoretically, there is nothing in Henry's definition that precludes the possibility that contraception was practised among populations with natural fertility. That is, practised now and then, haphazardly, inconsistently, and practised by a minority. Such practice would of course influence fertility, but not enough to produce the modern pattern of control linked to parity.

The demographer might object that such behaviour is not important enough to take seriously in demographic analysis. Nevertheless, it is important enough for the historian if he wants an accurate description of a particular population, and it is important in historical demography when we address the question of how the modern pattern evolved. Was contraception present before modernity or was it a modern invention?

Whatever validity the notion of a regime of "natural fertility" has, it has for pre-modern Europe, and even there it has been challenged, as we shall see below. The truth is that we know next to nothing about pre-modern populations outside Europe, and the idea that pre-modern populations did not practise birth control was simply part of the equipment of European scholars, whose own historical experience taught them that "the control of marital fertility by contraception, as we know it today in the Western countries, is without doubt a fairly recent development".[23] Louis Henry himself became interested in historical populations as a result of "his need to estimate the levels of fertility in populations in which birth control was not practised to any sizable degree".[24] To find what he needed he went to pre-modern populations.

Later research on some pre-modern European populations has cast doubt on the theory of natural fertility. Demeny, Livi-Bacci, and Goubert have questioned it, their main argument being that biological and institutional factors are not enough to account for contemporaneous variations in birth rates between different regions or for fluctuations occurring in the same region over time. The data can be explained, they add, only if one posits birth control within marriage.

It should be borne in mind that these "revisionist" views are meant to apply not to pre-modern Europe proper – that is, Europe before the eighteenth century – but to the period of transition to lower fertility (the eighteenth century in France, the eighteenth to nineteenth century in Spain, and the nineteenth century in Austria–Hungary). In the first place, they argue that the transition from high to low fertility occurred a few years or decades before the accepted dates, but that it nevertheless occurred among populations considered by the transition theory to be pre-modern, with a regime of "natural fertility".[25] This has led at least Livi-Bacci and Demeny to a tentative revision of the theory of transition by suggesting that the movement from high to low fertility may not have been as revolutionary and sudden a phenomenon as is generally believed, but that it may have involved to a greater degree the diffusion and spread of old contraceptive habits as populations adjusted themselves to new conditions.[26] In other words, births in at least some pre-modern European populations were checked not only by biological and institutional restraints, but also by contraception.

These scholars based their conclusions solely on data which show marked differences in fertility, and they have posited birth control as an explanation even though they have no direct evidence of birth control itself. On birth control European sources are remarkably silent: "The possibility of fertility control within marriage was hardly ever mentioned, even in France, before the second half of the nineteenth century."[27]

Some demographers have voiced doubts as to whether birth control was absent in pre-eighteenth century populations:

> It might be thought that, before the age of general use of contraceptives, fertility was always high and always about the same, at a level close to the maximum physically possible. This is much too naive a view. It seems probable that births have been controlled in practice by one means or another since the dawn of civilization, and there is an unanswered question of how it was done and how much, in every historical society and at every period.[28]

On the whole, although these doubts have sometimes been seriously expressed, they have not been seriously pursued. On that score we are still where Norman E. Himes, in his classic *Medical History of Contraception* (1936), left us.

Middle Eastern birth control evidence has serious implications for population studies, for it is doubtful that the idea of a "natural fertility" applicable to all pre-modern populations would have been formulated had Christianity, for example, permitted contraception. If Christian theologians had rationalized birth control within marriage in terms of economic, social, and personal needs and motives; if every pre-modern European medical book had included a sound discussion of contraceptive and abortifacient methods; if popular erotic books written by churchmen and other estimable leaders of European society, and published in the vernacular languages of Europe, had included chapters on birth control; if the pharmacological lists of medicines sold by druggists in medieval European towns had included contraceptive and abortifacient recipes: and if, in addition, there were evidence for the actual use of birth control, and Europe had experienced a population depression lasting several centuries, then the idea would surely have been held that birth control was a significant factor in pre-modern populations.

That every condition mentioned above is true of the pre-modern Islamic Middle East may be difficult to accept, for the association between birth control and modernity is very strong. Demographers, armed with knowledge about the high fertility rates of pre-modern Europe on the one hand, and the high fertility rates of contemporary third-world populations on the other, have associated "pre-modern" with "traditional" and have not suspected that the high fertility rates of some of the underdeveloped countries may be as recent as the low fertility rates of the modern West. For fertility rates in "traditional" societies may not have always been the same, and we cannot pretend that such populations were always static. We know that European populations have changed, and we should seriously entertain the possibility that third-world populations may have changed also, and in more ways than the decline in mortality rates which they so obviously manifest. How, when, and why are questions to which historical research can seek answers.

Birth control is not simply an aspect of modernity, nor is it necessarily alien to pre-modern societies. It is known that the remarkable secular decline in Western birth rates in the nineteenth and twentieth centuries was first achieved through the use of traditional, that is "medieval", contraceptive methods, such as coitus interruptus, which any motivated male can use, whether in nineteenth-century France or fourteenth-century Damascus.[29]

CHAPTER 1

Why Islam permitted contraception

> We rode out with the Prophet to raid Banu al-Mustaliq, and we captured female prisoners . . . We desired women and abstinence became hard. [But] we wanted to practise coitus interruptus; and we asked the Prophet about it. He said, "You do not have to hesitate, for God has predestined what is to be created until Judgement Day."
>
> *Hadith* from the Prophet

Birth control and sexual morality

The use of birth control by any given population is always part of the wide complex of its ideas and social institutions. Knowledge of the biology of reproduction is one important factor affecting attitudes on birth control. Ideas on the nature of human life are another important factor. When does life begin? Is the semen protected by religious law? Is the foetus a human being? Placed in a larger context the question is: under what conditions may human reproduction be controlled?

Most directly, attitudes on birth control are part of the cluster of ideas that constitute a society's sexual morality. Noonan has shown convincingly how Western Christian ideas on sexual morality "combined to encourage both sexual restraint and postponement of the serious step of entering marriage and raising a family".[1] These Christian ideas confined sexual intercourse to marriage, treated marriage as monogomous and permanent, justified sexual intercourse within marriage by procreative purpose, condemned contraception and abortion, and emphasized the education of children. Christian sexual morality shaped the development of the "European marriage pattern" (a norm of late marriage with a large percentage of the population remaining unmarried), a pattern which curbed population growth in Western Europe from the sixteenth to the nineteenth centuries. Contraception served the same end in modern times, so that the "European marriage pattern" lost its social function and the age of marriage dropped.

That Islam's sexual morality differed from Christianity's, and that the Muslim view of birth control was therefore likely to differ, should have been no secret. Islam and Christianity have shared the same Mediterranean universe, facing each other for centuries at the two shores of the ancient sea, always touching, in war or trade. Medieval European Christians, to whom Islam was a profound threat and challenge, worried about it. Two aspects of the Muslim phenomenon obsessed them: power and pleasure.[2] Islam's conquests and might terrified them, and its sexual ethics fascinated them. Roger Bacon, in his survey of the world of the thirteenth century, classified the nations of the world according to their pursuit of one of six possible ways of life: pleasure, riches, honour, power, fame, or the felicity of a future life. For the Muslims, he said, it was pleasure.[3]

Medieval Christian obsession with sex in Islam often manifested itself in prurient ways. The Christians believed that Islam encouraged sodomy and that Muslims habitually practised it; their interest in the sexual life of the Prophet was boundless. But it is to their credit that they also recognized that the major difference between the two medieval societies lay in the most important of sexual institutions, that of marriage.

The nature of the institution of marriage is the key to many related issues, including contraception. Medieval Christians considered marriage a permanent relationship, to be dissolved only by death; they "simply understood indissoluble monogamy by the word 'marriage'".[4] The term could not be applied to any other kind of sexual relationship, including those defined as marriage by modern European laws. The medieval Europeans knew that there was polygamy in Islam, and "polygamy" only begins to describe the differences between two pre-modern societies' institutions of marriage.

Using Noonan's list of the cluster of Western Christian ideas of sexual morality as a model, and putting aside the education of children, also emphasized in Islam, the following were the major elements of Islam's sexual morality:

1. Marriage was treated as polygamous.
2. Legitimate sexual intercourse was not confined to marriage, but extended also to the institution of concubinage.
3. Marriage was not viewed as a permanent relationship; easy divorce could end it at any time.
4. Marital intercourse needed no justification by procreative purpose, and was also based on the right to sexual fulfilment.
5. Contraception was permitted and abortion tolerated.

While Christianity confined legitimate sex to permanent monogamous marriage, Islam did not confine sex to marriage, and Islamic marriage was polygamous and subject to termination by easy divorce. The theoretical impermanence of marriage in Islam and the risk inherent in concubinage of fathering children who, following their mothers, could be slaves, were *prima facie* indications for the utility of birth control. One of the reasons for birth control cited by Muslim jurists was that a man might wish to divorce his wife in the foreseeable future,[5] and an argument most frequently used was the fear of begetting slave children.[6]

Islam, Christianity and Judaism

Judaism, Christianity, and Islam have a common origin and share many religious assumptions; their attitudes and laws, whether they agree or diverge, always shed light on one another. Because it permitted birth control, the Islamic attitude is of unique significance for understanding the nature of religious reaction to the problem within the broad Jewish–Christian–Muslim Mediterranean tradition. The Muslims, from their side, were aware that Jewish attitudes were different; and some medieval Churchmen knew of the Islamic permission of contraception, and added it to their list of the sexual "horrors" of Islam.[7]

Recent scholarship on Christian and Jewish attitudes regarding birth control exhibits no awareness or interest in the Islamic tradition. John T. Noonan's excellent study of contraception in Christianity has an intrinsically Islamic background which, however, is not fully exploited.[8] His central argument that the Catholic doctrine on birth control was promulgated in the face of contraceptive practice that marked the period 400–1600 is supported mainly by reference to contraceptive recipes "which came almost wholly from the Arabs".[9] The basic medical text of medieval Europe was the *Canon* of Ibn Sina (Avicenna): "The scholastics sought a standard treatise in every learned field. What the *Digest* was in law and the *Sentences* in theology such was the *Canon of Medicine* in medicine. For Europeans it was the main textbook until the middle of the seventeenth century."[10] Given the central role that the contribution of Arabic culture played in Noonan's interpretation, it is unfortunate that Ibn Sina's intellectual and religious background, at least on the matter of contraception, was not considered.

It is more surprising that D. M. Feldman's book on the Jewish tradition also neglected Islam, even though he relied on the work of rabbis in close proximity to Islam, many of whom were Arabic-speaking themselves.[11] The centres of much of Jewish learning from the eighth to the eighteenth centuries were in Arab or Muslim lands (Babylonia, Palestine, Egypt, Spain, North Africa, and Turkey). The name of the great Maimonides alone compels one to consider twelfth-century Spain and Egypt. Feldman used comparative material from Christianity and Noonan used comparative material from Judaism; comparing the work of the Jewish and Christian authors to that of their Muslim contemporaries is at least as necessary.

Islam and Christianity were, in the medieval Middle East and Europe respectively, dominant world and social views. Because Christianity regarded contraception as wrong, it became an untouchable subject for European medicine down to the nineteenth century, even though Europeans had access to good information from Arabic and Greek sources.[12] Because Muslim jurists permitted contraception, it was possible for Arabic physicians to deal with it to the fullest possible extent, limited only by their medical resources and experience (Chapter 4). This was even true of Arabic-writing Christian and Jewish physicians, whose own religious traditions condemned contraception, but who apparently were more influenced by the attitudes of the dominant Muslim culture and its medical tradition than by the attitudes of their own religions.[13]

Scientific knowledge in turn influenced law and morality. There is a clear relationship between the Islamic view of contraception and the medieval scientific knowledge of human reproduction and birth control techniques. The Islamic argument for the permission of contraception is an illuminating case where biological knowledge directly influenced ethical attitudes.

The authors of the Islamic attitude: jurists and 'ulama

The Islamic attitude toward contraception consisted only of the opinions of Muslim jurists, both individually and in terms of the schools of legal interpretation to which they belonged (pp. 29ff.). Since the Quran said nothing about contraception, and there was nothing like the Christian concept of the "Church" in Islam, there existed no "Islamic" attitude independent of or above that of the jurists.[14] The opinions of these private but specialized individual Muslims defined the attitude of Islam.

Who were the Muslim jurists? The jurists were 'ulama, learned specialists in the religion and traditions of Islam, a category of persons which was common to all historical Muslim societies. They were always one element of the population which specialized in studying Islam and strove to live the Islamic life. The 'ulama were the custodians of the community's traditions, keeping and passing on what in their judgement was worthy of historical record, and in this way deciding what was important to Islamic life. They were the authors of most of the written records of Muslim societies.

This last circumstance creates serious problems for the historian of the Muslim Middle East, especially in social and economic history, for the 'ulama were mostly an urban phenomenon. While it is proper to say that the evidence which they have handed down to us reflects, in one way or another, urban conditions, it would be misleading to treat this evidence as a window to society as a whole, that is, both urban and rural.

Unfortunately, there is little evidence bearing directly on rural life in the Middle East. This does not mean that evidence from the cities has no relevance for conditions in the countryside; but it is necessary to underline an essential reservation about the possibility of making generalizations regarding society as a whole. Given the city-centred nature of the records that the 'ulama have bequeathed to us, it is important to bear in mind that the discussion below is valid only as a description of urban conditions.

The 'ulama came from all social and economic classes of urban society. There were 'ulama who were merchants, workers, or craftsmen, and being one of the 'ulama did not change a person's social and economic class, his occupation, or place of abode and livelihood. However, it gave him the additional respect and status which urban Muslim society invested in the learned. The 'ulama came from all levels of urban society and deeply influenced all of urban society.[15]

We know much about the 'ulama and their activity, for we have detailed information regarding the origins, education, occupations, and writings of thousands of them in the medieval biographical dictionaries. The biographical dictionary was a unique creation of Muslim societies; in it the 'ulama immortalized themselves.

> The conception that underlies the biographical dictionaries is that the history of the Islamic community is essentially the contribution of the individual men and women to the building up and transmission of its specific culture; that is, it is these persons (rather than the political governors) who represent and reflect the active force in Muslim Society in their respective sphere; and that their individual contributions are worthy of being recorded for future generations.[16]

In going through any of the universal biographical dictionaries, it soon becomes clear that the education, activity, and contributions of the 'ulama lay essentially in the field of jurisprudence (*fiqh*, the science of the *shari'a*, the sacred law of Islam), or in fields subsidiary to it. The 'ulama shared one universe of concern (Islam), and applied themselves to it in one way (learning). More than anything else, this learning meant jurisprudence.

Early Islamic opinion on contraception: the hadith

One of the basic analytical principles of the classical theory of Islamic law was the *sunna*, that is, the example of the Prophet as incorporated in the recognized *hadith* (the reports of his words and actions). The classical theory of law was adopted by the majority of the Sunni Muslims by the tenth century, and will be stated below where it serves an important purpose in analysing the Islamic doctrine on contraception.

Islamic jurisprudence lacked this principle before the development of the classical theory. The jurists of the first two Islamic centuries (also called "the ancient schools of law") claimed either that their *own* living tradition as scholars of the orthodox community represented the example of the Prophet, or that their opinions were based on the teachings of the Prophet's Companions. Opposition to these opinions developed during the second Islamic century into the so-called "Traditionist" movement, and this was a decisive development in the history of Islam. "Traditionists" insisted that formal *hadith* deriving from the Prophet superseded the living tradition of the jurists and the teachings of the Companions:

> The Traditionists produced detailed statements or "traditions" which claimed to be the reports of ear-or-eye-witnesses on the words and acts of the Prophet, handed down orally by an uninterrupted chain (*isnad*) of trustworthy persons. Hardly any of these traditions, as far as matters of religious law are concerned, can be considered authentic; they were put into circulation, no doubt from the loftiest of

motives, by the Traditionists themselves from the first half of the second century onwards.[17]

The basic thesis of the Traditionists triumphed and became an integral part of the classical theory of Islamic law. Medieval Muslims developed an important critical method to distinguish between authentic reports and what they took to be fabrications and untrustworthy accounts. Their principal concern, as believers, was to ascertain the authenticity of the statements which were attributed to the Prophet. Remarkably enough, modern scholars have also concentrated mainly on this issue, as in the quotation above from the best modern work, and found that very few *hadith* can be traced back directly to the Prophet. Arguments about the origins of *hadith* have diverted attention from their true historical value: regardless of whether these *hadith* can be traced back to the Prophet or not, they *are* authentic documents of the first two Islamic centuries. That is, someone at that time reported, remembered, or fabricated them.[18]

First of all, the *hadith* embodied the earliest legal reasoning of Muslims on contraception. Secondly, the *hadith* were essential instruments of argument in later Islamic thought on contraception. Even in cases where it is clear that the jurist was exercising independent judgement, the relevant *hadith* were usually marshalled as additional evidence for his point of view. There is a large number of *hadith* on contraception (specifically on *'azl*: coitus interruptus);[19] the following are the ones which recurred most often in jurisprudence.

1. According to Jabir, "We used to practise coitus interruptus in the Prophet's lifetime while the Quran was being revealed." (There is another version of the same *hadith*, "We used to practise coitus interruptus during the Prophet's lifetime. News of this reached him and he did not forbid us.")
2. According to Jabir, "A man came to the Prophet and said, 'I have a slave-girl, and we need her as a servant and around the palm groves. I have sex with her, but I am afraid of her becoming pregnant.' The Prophet said, 'Practise coitus interruptus with her if you so wish, for she will receive what has been predestined for her.'"
3. According to Abu Sa'id, "We rode out with the Prophet to raid Banu al-Mustaliq and captured some female prisoners . . . We desired women, and abstinence became hard. [But] we wanted to practise coitus interruptus; and we asked the Prophet about it. He said, 'You do not have to hesitate, for God has predestined what is to be created until Judgement day.'"
4. According to Abu Sa'id, "The Jews say that coitus interruptus is minor infanticide, and the Prophet answered, 'The Jews lie, for if God wanted to create something, no one can avert it [or, divert Him].'"
5. According to Judhama bint Wahb, "I was there when the Prophet was

with a group saying, 'I was about to prohibit the *ghila*,[20] but I observed the Byzantines and the Persians, and saw them do it, and their children were not harmed.' They asked him about coitus interruptus, and the Prophet answered, 'It is hidden infanticide . . .'"

6. According to 'Umar Ibn al-Khattab, "The Prophet forbade the practice of coitus interruptus with a free woman except with her permission."
7. According to Anas, "A man asked the Prophet about coitus interruptus, and the Prophet said, 'Even if you spill seed from which a child was meant to be born on a rock, God will bring forth from that rock a child.'"

The obvious points made in the *hadith* are, first, that the Prophet knew about the practice and did not forbid it (no. 1), and second, that the Prophet himself permitted the practice (nos. 2 and 3). These two *hadith* share with a number of others (4 and 7) the emphasis on predestination and God's infinite power. *Hadith* no. 6 was considered weak by the medieval jurists; it introduces the provision, important for later discussion, that coitus interruptus may not be practised without the free woman's permission. The *hadith* reflects too accurately the specific regulation on contraception of the later schools of law.

The *hadith* after Judhama (no. 5) where the Prophet was quoted as saying that coitus interruptus was "hidden infanticide", was the closest approximation in the whole Islamic discussion to the "homocide" of the Jewish and Christian traditions. This *hadith* was the basis for Ibn Hazm's minority argument that coitus interruptus was prohibited by the Prophet. Medieval jurists used the *hadith* about the Jews (no. 4) to refute the argument for prohibition. The question has been asked how the Prophet could have maintained that the Jews lied by calling coitus interruptus akin to infanticide and then have maintained the same opinion himself.

The rationale of the permission

Muslim jurists determined whether an act was allowable or forbidden on the basis of a theory of law which, in the classical form adopted by the orthodox from the tenth century AD on, comprised four principles or sources (*'usul*). Only two of these were strictly religious sources (1) the Quran and (2) the example of the Prophet (*sunna*) as incorporated in the recognized *hadith*. The other two principles were analogical reasoning (*qiyas*), and the consensus of the 'ulama, the religious experts (*'ijma'*).[21]

The Quran, in contrast to the Bible, had no reference to contraception and never figured directly in the legal discussion. But there were the *hadith* of the Prophet on coitus interruptus.

Did Muslim jurists, in their arguments for the permission of contraception, simply repeat a teaching of the Prophet? The *hadith* were important but not decisive; while most were permissive, some were open to other interpretations. Ibn Hazm used one of the latter as a basis for his argument that coitus interruptus was prohibited; his position reminds us that general Islamic views could have been different from what they actually were.

With the absence of an explicit religious provision, Muslim jurists were able to argue to their own satisfaction that contraception was proper. In their argument for permission the jurists employed the *hadith* together with the biological knowledge available to them. Specifically, they interpreted the fundamental Islamic belief in God's providence and infinite power, as far as contraception was concerned, in the light of their understanding of coitus interruptus. Their method was grounded in the third source of Islamic law: *qiyas*, reasoning by analogy. Finally, as the overwhelming majority of jurists reached the same conclusion on contraception, the permission was supported by the definitive principle of the law: *'ijma'*, the historical consensus of the religious experts.

The argument for permission: Ghazali

The most thorough statement of the Islamic permission of contraception was made by the great Shafi'i jurist Ghazali (1058–1111). In one of the most remarkable documents in the history of birth control, Ghazali stated explicitly the grounds of the permission that were mostly implied elsewhere.[22] In view of the absence of a religious text on contraception, he discussed it from premises rooted more in profane biology and economics than in the strictly religious sources of the law. He did employ the *hadith*, but only at the end, after he had completed his argument, and used it as supporting evidence.

Ghazali began by pointing out that there was no basis for prohibiting coitus interruptus. For prohibition in Islam was possible only by adducing an original Text (*nass*, an explicit provision in the Quran or *hadith*), or by analogy with a given Text. In the case of contraception there was no such Text, nor was there any other principle on which to base prohibition.

The correct opinion, in his view, was that coitus interruptus was permitted absolutely (*mubah*), and that there was a principle on which to base permission, namely, reasoning by analogy. A man could abstain from marriage; or marry, but abstain from sexual intercourse; or have intercourse, but abstain from seminal emission. Although it was better to marry, have intercourse, and complete intercourse, abstention from these acts was by no means forbidden or unlawful. Furthermore, all these abstentions produced the same result, for pregnancy had four related causes: (1) marriage, (2) intercourse, (3) emission of the semen, and (4) allowing the semen to reach and settle in the womb. As far as procreation was concerned, abstention from the fourth was like abstention from the third, which was like abstention from the second, which in turn was like abstention from the first.

Ghazali's cardinal argument was the lawfulness of the act of withdrawal itself. He demonstrated this by a proof based exclusively on his understanding of the biology of reproduction (he appealed to no authority higher than *ahl al-tashrih*, "anatomists"). He argued that while abortion and infanticide were crimes against an existing being, contraception was different.[23] This was so because a child did not begin to be formed merely by the emission of the male semen, but by the "settling" of semen in the womb; for children were not created of the man's semen alone, but of both parents together.

In the process of conception the two (male and female) emissions are analogous to the two elements "offer" (*ijab*) and "acceptance" (*qabul*) which constitute a legal contract in Islamic law. Someone who submits an offer and then withdraws it before the other party accepts is not guilty of any violation, for a contract does not exist before acceptance. In the same manner, there is no real difference between the man's emission or retention of the semen unless it actually mixes with the woman's "semen".

Ghazali emphasized equally the contribution of both parents to the formation of the embryo. For "formation" he used the word *in'iqad*, meaning either (1) coagulation, thickening, or (2) meeting, coming together. It was from this double meaning that he realized the possibility of his analogy on contracts. Both *in'iqad* (formation) and *'aqd* (contract) come from the same root *'aqada*: to tie, put together, join. On the basis of Ghazali's argument it is possible to see how all methods of contraception which stopped the semen from reaching the uterus could be permitted.

The exception that proves the rule: Ibn Hazm

In all the Islamic writing on contraception, only one jurist condemned coitus interruptus absolutely. This was the Spaniard Ibn Hazm (994–1063) who belonged to the Zahiri school of law, a short-lived movement whose legal thought has survived mostly in Ibn Hazm's own writings.[24] Ibn Hazm's opinion is an important exception that proves the rule.

Had the Quran or *hadith* contained an explicit provision on contraception, then later Islamic thought could have been simply determined by this provision. In Ibn Hazm's view, there was such a provision.

Ibn Hazm argued that the numerous permissive *hadiths* were early and reflected the fact that in Islam everything was permitted until the Prophet issued a specific prohibition. He claimed that the Prophet had *abrogated* these permissive *hadith* when he later said that coitus interruptus was "hidden infanticide". Since the Quran prohibited infanticide in the strongest possible terms, and the Prophet called coitus interruptus hidden infanticide, Ibn Hazm maintained that coitus interruptus was prohibited also.[25]

Running counter to the general Islamic opinion on the subject, Ibn Hazm's absolute prohibition of contraception became a cause célèbre in

Islamic discussions of birth control.[26] He failed to convince later jurists of his argument, and many refutations of his position existed, the most telling of which was by the Damascene Hanbali scholar, Ibn Qayyim (1291–1351). Ibn Qayyim showed that the argument of Ibn Hazm required an exact historical dating to prove that the "abrogating" *hadith* was subsequent to the permissive *hadith*, and that such an exact dating was impossible. Ibn Qayyim added that, in any case, it was generally agreed in Islamic law that infanticide applied only after the foetus was formed and the child born. Infanticide thus defined was prohibited; coitus interruptus was clearly something else.[27] Another jurist later explained that the Prophet called coitus interruptus *hidden* infanticide because it shared with true infanticide the same motive, that is, escape from additional dependants. But true infanticide was not prohibited because of this motive, which in itself was proper, but because it involved murder.[28]

Contraceptive experience and Islamic law

While there were more *hadith* tending to permit contraception than to prohibit it, Muslim jurists did not settle their arguments simply by counting *hadith*.[29] All of our jurists, Ibn Hazm, Ghazali, and Ibn Qayyim included, accepted these various *hadith* as authentic statements of the Prophet. Because the relevant *hadith* as a group gave conflicting messages, the Muslim jurists could not have arrived at a consensus of opinion regarding contraception, nor could the consensus have been sustained over centuries of argument, had it not also been shaped by weighty influences extrinsic to the *hadith*. The actual contraceptive experience of medieval society informed the interpretation of *hadith* and the fate of the argument.

The medieval Muslims believed as strongly in the possibility of birth control through the practice of withdrawal as in the possible failure of the practice to stop pregnancy. Their experience of withdrawal was a major factor in their justification of contraception. These particular texts in Islamic jurisprudence are the only source for the study of pre-modern knowledge of the effectiveness of withdrawal.

Withdrawal was practised, and some women conceived regardless. This is the significant context of all these discussions, and it adds to the evidence of actual practice of birth control in the medieval Middle East. In the passage below, Ibn Qayyim discussed the contraceptive practice of some of his Damascene fellow townsmen in the first half of the fourteenth century:

> Those who practise coitus interruptus generally deposit their semen close to the vagina. A man begins withdrawal when he feels that he is about to ejaculate, but often some semen would have already seeped out without his awareness. So even though in withdrawal he deposits his semen outside the vagina, that which had earlier seeped out into the vagina will mix with the woman's semen. More than one among those I trust have told me that his wife became pregnant even though he had been practising withdrawal on account of a nursing [infant] or some other reason.[30]

Some men attempted to repudiate and disown children by claiming that they had practised coitus interruptus with their mothers. The issue was posed in this way: "In situations where withdrawal was practised and the woman conceived anyway, is it legal for the man to repudiate the child?"[31] Most jurists thought that it was not legal to do so. The following was a typical opinion: "Fatherhood is legally established by the fact of sexual intercourse, and ejaculation as such is not a consideration. Vaginal intercourse could result in emission of semen which the man may not feel."[32] This opinion singled out one way in which withdrawal could fail, namely, involuntary pre-emission of semen preceding ejaculation. Because of the possibility of failure, the jurists argued that withdrawal by itself cannot serve as the basis for repudiation.

Only jurists belonging to the Hanafi school of law found repudiation possible: if the man had practised withdrawal consistently, and did not repeat intercourse, or repeated it but only after washing first, and consistently practised withdrawal again, then there was some legal justification for disowning a resulting child. It was by no means possible to disown the child if any of these steps were neglected, such as repeating intercourse without having urinated and washed first, "because a remnant of the semen on the man's penis can then be deposited in the woman" and may result in pregnancy.[33]

But even the acceptance of the man's claim that he had practised withdrawal properly and consistently was not sufficient. Legal repudiation of children required, in the final analysis, hard evidence that the woman had had sexual relations with another man, because without such evidence the suspicion remained that "even though he had practised withdrawal, some of the semen may have dropped on the outer vulva which then entered her".[34]

This was strict enough, but all other Muslim opinion was even more rigid on this issue. The Shi'is rejected specifically the very grounds on which the Hanafis had based their position: "A child cannot be repudiated because of coitus interruptus, not even with an accusation of adultery."[35]

The medieval Muslims knew that the proper practice of withdrawal required special care. Yet there was no mystery when the practice failed: pregnancies occurred when semen reached the uterus despite withdrawal, a perfectly reasonable explanation. It is difficult to see how anyone can improve on this medieval knowledge of coitus interruptus: there can be involuntary pre-emission of semen; in situations of repeated intercourse, there can be a remnant of the semen on the glans; even if the man should urinate and wash before repeating intercourse, and practise withdrawal again, there is the possibility that in withdrawal some semen is dropped on the labia.

Medieval knowledge of coitus interruptus was not part of the corpus of revealed truth that the Muslims followed. In the absence of Quranic legislation, this secular knowledge shaped the Muslim religious attitude toward contraception.

That God is all-powerful, and that ultimately no human act can avert a creation He truly intends, was the dominant reason in the *hadith* which the jurists employed to permit contraception. Asked about coitus interruptus in one representative *hadith*, the Prophet answered, "Do as you please, whatever God has willed will happen anyway, and not all semen results in children."[36] Two elements were present in this *hadith*, and were repeated in others. First, the concept of predestination – God has willed everything already. This concept was used in a very interesting way. When withdrawal was successful it meant that God had not intended to create a new life. A pregnancy, in case of failure, simply indicated the opposite. The second element was the observation that "not all semen results in children", obviously based on the common experience that not every act of intercourse resulted in a pregnancy. Some jurists argued that since "semen may spoil and not result in progeny", and there was no sure way of knowing whether God intended a particular emission to cause pregnancy or not, withdrawal should be permitted without qualification.[37]

Other *hadith* repeated and emphasized the same ideas: "Practise coitus interruptus or do not practise it. If God wanted to create a human life He will anyway."[38] "Spilling the seed on the ground" struck moral horror in Jewish and Christian minds as a sinful defiance of God's laws and commandments; the very same image was used in *hadith* in a totally different manner, simply to show how insignificant man's actions were in comparison with God's awesome power: "Even if you spill the seed from which a child was meant to be born on a rock, God will bring forth from that rock a child."[39]

The Muslims were aware that Judaism prohibited coitus interruptus.[40] Muslim jurists thought that the Jewish prohibition rested on the erroneous assumption, which Muslims rejected, that coitus interruptus was foolproof: "Coitus interruptus does not stop pregnancy altogether as abstention would, but it is effective in reducing it."[41] Arguments which were prevalent in Jewish and Christian circles that contraception was a defiant act against God did not gain ground in Islam. Even with the most conscientious and expert practice of contraceptive methods known to medieval Middle Eastern populations, unwanted pregnancies must have occurred frequently enough. To the Muslims, this gap between intention and achievement left ample room for God's will to operate. Ibn Taimiya discussed divine providence, procreation, and contraception this way in the early fourteenth century:

> God creates children and other animals in the womb by willing the meeting of parents in intercourse, and the two semens in the womb. A man is a fool who says, "I shall depend on God and not approach my wife, and if it is willed that I be granted a child I will be given one, otherwise not, and there is no need for

intercourse." [This is] very different from having intercourse and practising withdrawal, for withdrawal does not prevent pregnancy if God wills a pregnancy to occur, *because there can be involuntary pre-emission of semen.*[42]

Reasons for birth control

Ghazali turned his attention to the reasons that motivate men and women to practise contraception only after he had established its lawfulness. The permission was not dependent on these reasons. While Ghazali approved of some motives for birth control, he found others quite objectionable. But even here in the latter circumstance he emphasized that contraception remained lawful. The clarity and force of his argument made it very unlikely that the basic permission would be overturned by objections directed at the reasons themselves. Contraception was lawful in Islam in precisely the same sense that marriage or abstention from marriage were lawful. A person could abstain from marriage for the wrong reason, another could practise contraception for the wrong reason, but under no circumstance would the wrong reason effect the legality of his behaviour.

Ghazali supported contraceptive practice with one's wife or concubine to protect her from the dangers of childbirth, or simply to preserve her beauty. He especially favoured the economic motives for birth control. When practised with concubines, the intention was to safeguard one's property, for slave-women could not be sold after becoming mothers to their master's child. In his opinion, the taking of measures against alienating property was lawful.

A more general economic motive that he also supported was the wish to limit the family to a manageable size. He argued that the increase in the number of dependants multiplied material difficulties, led to extra toil in order to earn a living, and tempted men to engage in immoral or illegal transactions to meet their responsibilities. No doubt it was true, he said, that there was perfection and nobility in total reliance on God, and that, therefore, contraception fell short of absolutely perfect behaviour. But he added that to consider consequences, and to save money, although contrary to total reliance on God, was not forbidden. On the contrary, "material well-being is an aid to religion (*qillat al-haraj mu'in 'ala al-din*)".

Ghazali strongly disapproved of people who practised contraception through fear of having daughters. He cautioned men not to express glee over the birth of sons, or show sadness over the birth of daughters: "there is no way of knowing who will prove to be good. There are many fathers of sons who wished they had daughters instead." He also disapproved of contraception by women for purely personal reasons. He reported that some women practised contraception because they disliked pregnancy, or because they had a fetish for absolute cleanliness, or simply because they did not want to bother with childbirth and nursing. To him these attitudes were an "innovation" (*bid'a*), alien to Muslim custom. Here, however, he was careful to add that it was the intent that was objectionable, not the actual prevention of pregnancy. It is difficult not to notice that Ghazali approved of a man's wish to preserve the physical appeal of the woman, but disapproved of a woman's wish to avoid pregnancy for her own personal convenience.[43]

Ghazali explicitly separated the legal permission of contraception from the sentiments that people held regarding the practice. In historical Islam, different feelings about the wisdom of contraception did not confuse the issue of its legality; after Ghazali this was due in no small part to his elegant distinction. For the modern historian his text has great additional value; it is an inventory of the reasons behind contraceptive practice in Ghazali's own time, the late eleventh and early twelfth centuries.

In contrast to Islamic opinion, which permitted contraception and advanced good reasons for family limitation, the Jewish law codes condemned coitus interruptus absolutely. Maimonides stated the prohibition as follows: "It is forbidden to destroy seed. Therefore a man may not practice coitus interruptus." The other Jewish law codes followed Maimonides without deviation.[44] The Jewish prohibition applied, properly speaking, to all so-called "destruction of seed" (*hash hatat zera*), and was not simply limited to coitus interruptus. Talmudic and post-Talmudic literature was unanimous in its view of "destruction of seed" as an offence to be condemned absolutely. The condemnation was so severe that even a radical procedure like sterilization would have encountered fewer legal difficulties from the rabbis than any contraceptive "which may thwart the normal course of seminal emission".[45] To the rabbis, the destruction of seed was "a repugnant moral offence", a sin with two aspects, homicide ("He kills his own children") and self-defilement. In the Jewish mystic tradition, the Zohar, it was "a sin more serious than all the sins of the Torah".[46]

Only in modern times did the rabbis permit the (restricted) use of contraception—when there is a mortal danger to the woman in case of pregnancy. Contraception in this case was permitted provided that the method employed was not covered by the absolute prohibition against all methods which involved "destruction of seed".[47] Although the rabbis had based their permission on the Jewish legal principle of "avoidance of hazard", they did not allow the principle to include personal and economic hardship:

> The question must arise: . . . if support of another child will incur a hardship – a severe hardship, let us say, not just an ordinary one – do not the same principles of attention to self and its legitimate interests come into operation? This question is answered with . . . unanimity of legal opinion . . .: the economic motive is simply not admissible. . . . Here the Jewish and Christian spiritual traditions meet: both

would underwrite the essential religious message implied hereby, that material considerations are highly improper in the connection with something as spiritual and selfless as the bearing and raising of children.[48]

Christianity condemned contraception no matter what the reason or need. The Church's attitude toward contraception has a long and complex history. By Augustine's time, Christian preoccupation with original sin had placed sexual intercourse in a suspect position, "stained by concupiscence, forced to justify itself by a procreative purpose".[49] Augustine pushed the procreative rationale to its limit and condemned contraception absolutely. His beliefs about procreation and contraception remained dominant in the Catholic Church until modern times. The Church believed contraception to be homicide. Specifically, it condemned coitus interruptus as mortal sin, and Thomas Aquinas taught that to "depart from the inseminating use of the sexual act is to offend God directly".[50] Although Aquinas was not as important as Augustine in formulating the historical Christian attitude, it was he who introduced the argument from natural law, and after him the Church saw the act of contraception as a sin against nature. In Thomistic terms, "reason itself appeared to condemn contraception".[51]

The question of therapeutic contraception was posed only twice in Christian literature, once in the twelfth century and another time in the seventeenth. Peter Cantor put the case first: "The doctors say that if she bears another child, she will die. May she 'procure sterility' for herself? Peter resolved this difficult case brusquely: 'This last thing is not at all lawful, because this would be to procure poisons of sterility; that is prohibited in every case.'"[52] The Jesuit Paul Laymann brought up the case again in the seventeenth century, and again answered no: "Contraception is contrary to the principal end of marriage."[53]

The contrast with Muslim attitudes is sharp. The motives for birth control that Ghazali advanced included the medical indication for therapeutic contraception permitted by Judaism. But he went far beyond that, and his opinions were quite representative. Shawkani was even more comprehensive: "Some of the reasons for the practice of coitus interruptus are the attempt to escape having too many dependants, or to escape having any dependants at all."[54] The explicit use of economic motives for birth control is remarkable. The first known use outside Islam of an economic motive in support of birth control was Jeremy Bentham's advocacy of the contraceptive sponge to reduce the English Poor Rates (1797) and the Mill–Place birth control propaganda in the 1820s.[55]

Because of Islam's basic permissiveness towards contraception, the jurists did not cite extreme cases – there was no need for special pleading. The only medical indication (fear for the woman's life) that the religious literature discussed was the one, already noted, from Ghazali. Arabic medicine was different, and there medical indications were consistently advanced, and only medical indications. The physicians were free to discuss only the reasons proper to their profession.

Islam permitted contraception in the case of need (*haja*); but did not prohibit the practice in the absence of need: "In case he practises coitus interruptus without need, the act is blameworthy (*karuha*), but not prohibited (*lam yuharram*)."[56] As noted earlier, economic reasons loomed large in the medieval Islamic understanding of "need". One of the indications most often cited was the desire to protect property, as in the case of concubines.[57]

Another cluster of motives for contraception had to do with the well-being of children. The presence of a nursing infant was a major indication for birth control. Medieval Muslims believed that the effect of a new pregnancy on a nursing infant was sure death. A new pregnancy set an upper limit on lactation length, resulting in palpable harm to the child being nursed. We know from studies of Indian villages in the Punjab in the 1950s (where public health conditions were probably comparable to those in the medieval Middle East) that "virtually any child not established on breast milk died. Conversely, if the infant survived longer than a month, it meant that nursing had been established and usually continued longer than a year."[58]

In the first half of the fifteenth century Ibn Hajar thought that people practised contraception for three reasons: in fear of fathering slave children, in fear of having a large number of dependants, and in fear of the ill-effects of pregnancy in the case of a nursing infant. This last was the only reason that met with Ibn Hajar's personal approval, for "experience" showed that "such pregnancies are generally harmful".[59] Another motive was the need to provide for the education and proper upbringing of children. Bujairimi maintained that "if contraception is practised for an excuse (*'udhr*), such as the raising (*tarbiya*) of a child, it is not even blameworthy (*lam yukrah*)".[60]

The medieval jurists also expressed concern for the unborn. In case the wife was a slave of another party, fear that one's children would be slaves was reason enough to practise contraception.[61] Fear for the enslavement of children was also behind the recommendation to practise contraception in enemy territory (*dar al-harb*). The Hanbalis went so far as to insist that in such a circumstance birth control became *mandatory* (*yu'zalu wujubann bi dar harb*).[62] In Islamic jurisprudence this was the one reason for birth control that had a direct social, rather than personal, basis, the one instance where birth control was legislated. This Hanbali position was probably related to the historical conditions in the northern Syrian territories contested for centuries by the Muslims and Byzantines. Huge border areas passed from Christian to Muslim hands and back again seasonally. The hold of Islam on populations that had earlier been Christian for centuries was still relatively weak. The jurists were afraid that an Islamic community could be lost through the conversion of its own children.

The one most significant reason that the later medieval jurists used for the *unconditional* permission of contraception was that of "bad times" (*fasad al-zaman, su' al-zaman*). Chapter 6 discusses the extent to which birth control was part of the response of Middle Eastern populations to the manifold ravages that enveloped the area in late medieval times.

Contraceptive method and religious permission

The Muslims were able to think about contraception in a way quite different from that of Christians and Jews, and this was due in no small part to the absence of a Quranic reference to contraception. The Bible, in contrast, had the story of Onan in Genesis 38:

> But Er, Judah's first-born, was wicked in the sight of the LORD; and the LORD slew him. Then Judah said to Onan, "Go in to your brother's wife, and perform the duty of a brother-in-law to her, and raise up offspring for your brother." But Onan knew that the offspring would not be his; so when he went in to his brother's wife he spilled the semen on the ground, lest he should give offspring to his brother. And what he did was displeasing in the sight of the LORD, and He slew him also.[63]

The "sin of Onan" has not been by itself the basis for the Christian condemnation of contraception, although it was often used as a capsule argument for an otherwise complex prohibition. The Jews also based their prohibition of contraception on weightier considerations. Nevertheless, the Bible contained a reference to contraception, and the reference was unfavourable. Even when not invoked directly, the story of Onan was always present as a limit to the possibility of permissive views. The Muslims were free from this limitation. But like the Jews and Christians, the Muslims were not free to legislate independently of their fundamental beliefs concerning God and revelation.

The Muslims had employed biological knowledge to rationalize their permission of contraception, and they did so in the context of their fundamental religious beliefs. Two ideas informed their argument: the first was their belief in God's infinite power; but this was interpreted, as far as contraception was concerned, in the light of the second, secular understanding of coitus interruptus as a contraceptive method. Knowledge about coitus interruptus fitted well the belief in God's power. Conception resulted from the union of the male and female semens, and coitus interruptus often succeeded and sometimes failed to prevent this union. Accidental pregnancies continuously proved that when God wanted a child to be born, he was. With this kind of understanding it was difficult to argue that contraception was an act of defiance against God.

The use of biological knowledge to solve the problem of contraception was by no means limited to the Muslims. It was later to be repeated by others. When the Catholic Church relaxed its prohibition by permitting the Rhythm method in 1951, this development followed new biological knowledge.[64] The Ogino–Knaus findings of the 1920s on the sterile/fertile cycle of the human female which made Rhythm a practical possibility, do not by themselves explain the Catholic permission. The critical factor was how the Catholics used this information, and like the Muslims, they used it in the context of their fundamental religious beliefs.

With the spread of information about the Ogino–Knaus method from the 1930s on, many Catholic priests found in it an answer to the pressing problem raised by contraceptive practice among Catholics despite the Church's condemnation. Abstention had always been favoured by the Church; the Rhythm method required abstention during the fertile period, while during the sterile period intercourse is carried to completion without doing anything by which conception is prevented. There was at once no possibility of pregnancy and no departure from God's natural laws as the Catholics understood them.

On 29 October 1951, Pope Pius XII spoke out publicly approving the Rhythm method as one open to all Christian couples. The pope taught that to have intercourse and avoid the duty of procreation without a reason was still sinful, but the Rhythm method used to control birth for a reason was licit. He further taught that reasons for licit birth control were "present in the so-called 'indications' – medical, eugenic, economic, and social".[65]

The rabbis too, faced with the formidable prohibition against "destruction of seed", found no method of contraception which they could wholeheartedly support. Their opportunity came even later than that of the Catholics, for it was the development of the oral contraceptive pill that finally seemed to provide the orthodox rabbis with a method that appeared to skirt all of their legal problems. The Jewish prohibition was against destruction of seed, that is, the male semen, and the Pill appeared to do nothing directly to the male sperm.[66]

Within the broad Jewish–Christian–Muslim religious tradition the chief touchstone to the permissibility of contraception has been the *method* itself. The Muslim recognition of economic, social, personal, and medical reasons for contraception does not explain the Islamic permission. At the same time that Jewish and Christian literatures condemned contraception, they also were keenly aware of these reasons. Such reasons are generally recognized to be present; they become acceptable as *indications* for birth control only when a certain contraceptive method becomes acceptable.

CHAPTER 2

Contraception and the rights of women

> The Prophet forbade the practice of coitus interruptus with a free woman except with her permission.
>
> *Hadith* from the Prophet

Muslim jurists, in treating contraception, were principally concerned with coitus interruptus. Historically, this has been the most common contraceptive method known to man; well into the twentieth century the history of contraception was to a significant extent the history of coitus interruptus. It was the medieval experience of this particular method of birth control that sustained the general Islamic permission of contraception (Chapter 1) and, at the same time, coitus interruptus was also the source of the legal problems which Muslim jurists faced in their justifications of contraception.

There was a remarkable unanimity among Muslim jurists concerning this technique. Apart from Ibn Hazm (pp. 18–19), I have searched in vain for opposition to the basic permission of contraception among the writings of Muslim jurists of all the historical Sunni and Shiʿi schools of law spanning the period from the birth of Islam to the nineteenth century.

Agreement on the sanction of contraception was so general that the permissive view became a cultural cliché. Rare was the legal book that did not deal with it and repeat the permission. The sanction of coitus interruptus for birth control was a constant fact of Islamic law in the same sense that its prohibition was a constant fact of Jewish law and Christian teaching. One can therefore speak of a "classical" Islamic opinion on contraception generally and consistently adopted in Islamic jurisprudence, regardless of school. *This classical opinion was the sanction of coitus interruptus with a free woman provided she gave her permission*. Furthermore, this was the basic but "minimal" position, for some opinions permitted more and none permitted less.

The Muslim jurists generally based their permission of contraception on the free woman's consent because she had a right (1) to children, and (2) to complete sexual fulfilment, which withdrawal was judged to diminish. Contraception became an issue in Islamic law because coitus interruptus was an act of male volition in conflict with these basic female rights. Remove the specific context of women's rights and there remains no apparent occasion for the discussion of coitus interruptus in Islamic jurisprudence. Once contraception was deemed legitimate, and the above regulation was formulated to protect these rights, both the Arabic term for coitus interruptus (*'azl*) and the ethical permissibility were extended by analogy to include other known contraceptive techniques.

The historical schools of law

In the first Islamic century the Muslim community split over the issue of succession to the Prophet and the nature of political sovereignty in the Islamic state. One group, the Sunnis (orthodox), recognized the authority of the Medinan, Ummayad, and Abbasid caliphs. The other major group, the Shi'is, came to maintain that sovereignty was a matter of divine right, residing in the descendants of the Prophet. A third group, the Kharijites, maintained that the leader of the Islamic community should be elected by the entire community of believers.

Four main schools of jurisprudence developed among the Sunnis: the Shafi'i, Hanafi, Maliki, and Hanbali schools. These took definite shape in the third century of Islam and were the only surviving orthodox schools after the seventh century (1300). Similarly, the main Shi'i groups (the Twelver Shi'is, the Isma'ilis, and the Zaidis) each developed its own school of jurisprudence, and there was also a Kharijite school (the Ibadi).[1]

Most orthodox Muslims from the tenth to the thirteenth century, and all of them after 1300, observed the religious law by following one of the four Sunni schools. Within the orthodox camp all the different opinions were deemed legitimate – that is, variant but equally proper Islamic views – and they were recognized as such by all orthodox jurists: "their alternative interpretations are all equally valid, their methods of reasoning equally legitimate, in short, they are equally orthodox".[2]

Since, on the subject of contraception, both Sunni and Shi'i opinions were in substance the same, I have included both in the same discussion. There has been some controversy as to whether the Shi'i and Ibadi schools differed more from the four Sunni schools than these latter differed from one another in terms of positive doctrine. On the problem of birth control it is apparent that they did not.

Because I have summarized the major opinions and main themes within a limited space, the reader may gain the false impression that opinions which were uniform in substance were also uniform in detail. This was by no means so, nor was it true that all jurists belonging to a given school of law adopted the views of that school to the exclusion of other opinions. Whenever possible I have referred, either in the body of the text or in the notes, to different and rival opinions mentioned by the jurists. The first mention of any of the schools of law is coupled with a reference to jurists who adopted or cited the majority opinion of that school. The discussion then proceeds to show where opinions have differed.

Ethical status of contraception

Islamic law assessed all human acts by a scale of religious qualifications, the essential function of which was to determine whether an act was allowable or forbidden. This was the most important feature of Islamic law, the central principle which guaranteed it unity in spite of its great diversity.[3] While the concept "forbidden" (*haram*) was simple, the concept "allowed" was complex and encompassed acts which ranged from "obligatory" (*wajib*, *fard*), such as prayer and fasting, to "blameworthy" (*makruh*), such as coitus interruptus. Between these two were the concepts of "recommended" (*sunna*, *mandub*, *mustahabb*) and "indifferent" (*mubah*).

The Muslim jurists viewed contraception as an allowable but "blameworthy" (*makruh*) practice. They ranked it "blameworthy" because it was not a simple, unmixed good. Since procreation was a good, abstention from it was an abstention from a meritorious deed – but such abstentions were by no means forbidden. As Ghazali explained, it was a *makruh* in the same sense that it was a *makruh* for a believer to sit idly in the mosque without engaging in prayer or meditation. It is essential not to extrapolate from the English sense of "blameworthy", but to understand the Islamic legal conception. *Makruh*, as the jurists applied it to coitus interruptus, meant an allowable act which, however, was not recommended unless there was a need to prevent pregnancy, although it was *not* prohibited even when practised without a need.

In addition to the scale of religious qualifications, there was another scale which Muslim jurists applied concurrently to the same acts, that of legal validity. A deed was (1) "valid" (*sahih*) if both its nature and its circumstance agreed with the religious law, (2) "blameworthy" (*makruh*) if both aspects also agreed with the law but something forbidden was connected with it, (3) "defective" (*fasid*) if its nature agreed with the law but its circumstance did not, or (4) "invalid" (*batil*) if neither aspect agreed with the law. Deeds or transactions which were judged to be *sahih* or *makruh* (1 and 2 above) had the same degree of legal validity, and therefore *sahih* (valid), in its more general sense, was a term usually applied to both.[4]

In the light of this scale of legal validity, the Muslims believed that since the act of contraception was proper in itself, and there were good reasons to control births, contraception was lawful: both its nature and its circumstances agreed with the religious law. But it was "blameworthy" (*makruh*) because the act impinged the free woman's rights to complete sexual fulfilment and progeny. The jurists were quite flexible in their application of these concepts, and contraception was viewed, sometimes by the same jurist, and depending on the circumstances, as either "blameworthy" or not. There were circumstances that even pushed some jurists to view contraception as "obligatory", in the sense of a religious duty, *fard*, equal to that of prayer or fasting, the highest possible recommendation.

Islamic jurisprudence treated coitus interruptus under three main headings: (1) with a wife who was a free woman; (2) with a wife who was a slave of another party, man or woman; and (3) with a man's own female slave, or concubine. These divisions were based on the varieties of sexual intercourse which were deemed legitimate by Islam: marriage and concubinage. A man could marry a free or slave woman. He could not marry his own slave. Therefore, a wife who was a slave was always the slave of someone other than her husband. A man could legitimately have sexual intercourse with his own female slave, but only as a concubine, not as a wife.

The right to sexual pleasure: contraception with a wife who was a free woman

The Shafi'is, among the orthodox, were the only jurists who tended to permit coitus interruptus without any condition, that is to say without the woman's permission.[5] They reasoned that since withdrawal itself was not a forbidden act, no condition should be attached to its practice. The other schools normally took other matters such as women's rights into consideration. Most Shafi'is adhered to this absolute permission, but a few adopted the classical position that the practice was licit only with the free woman's consent.[6]

Although jurists belonging to a given school were generally inclined to adopt the view peculiar to that school, there were always some jurists who felt free to adopt opinions from rival schools. The Shafi'i jurist Shirazi, for example, adopted the classical opinion, and was then faced with the problem of a wife who refused to grant permission. He offered two alternative judgements without committing himself to either: first, that coitus interruptus was illicit without her permission; and second, that it was licit, because she had a "right to intercourse, but not to ejaculation".[7]

Those Muslim jurists who argued that coitus interruptus may be practised without the woman's permission (primarily the Shafi'is, but some others too) found it possible to bypass the woman's right to children. They never denied, rejected, or overruled her right to sexual fulfilment, but faced with both the necessity of contraception and woman's basic right to sexual pleasure, they defined the latter as *intercourse and female orgasm*, without necessarily including ejaculation of the male sperm.[8] As a result coitus interruptus was not seen to infringe on the woman's sexual rights.

In contrast to the Shafi'is, the Hanbali school insisted on the woman's permission.[9] They reasoned that (1) children are the free woman's right, and (2) that she may suffer harm as a result of the practice of withdrawal.[10] The harm was specified as a reduction of her pleasure in intercourse.[11]

Here, sexual fulfilment for the woman was understood to depend on the completed act of intercourse, something which coitus interruptus obviously was not.

Despite the Hanbali schools' strict views, a few of its jurists, notably Ibn Qudama al-Maqdisi, also argued that coitus interruptus was licit without the woman's permission, similarly basing their opinion on the understanding that the woman did not necessarily have the right to male ejaculation.[12] Nevertheless, Maqdisi maintained that it was preferable to ask the woman's permission anyway for the sake of convenience and amity.[13] The only allowance which the Hanbalis, as a school, made for the practice without the free woman's permission was the duty to practise contraception in enemy territory (*dar al-harb*) for fear of Muslim children being enslaved.[14]

The Hanafis' original position was as strict as that of the Hanbalis: they too sanctioned coitus interruptus with a free woman only with her permission, for, in the Hanafis' view, she had a right to her own progeny.[15] In later centuries, Hanafi jurists argued that since "the times are bad" coitus interruptus with a free woman was licit without her permission. "Bad times" and related indications were judged to take precedence over a free woman's right to withhold consent.[16] When the later Hanafi jurists adopted this view they were aware of the school's stricter traditional attitude, but they argued that "regulations change when the times change".[17]

The Maliki school, like the Hanbalis and early Hanafis, also permitted coitus interruptus with a free woman only on condition that she give her consent,[18] but some Maliki jurists added a new twist by granting the woman the right of demanding and receiving monetary compensation as the price of her permission.[19] The woman was to give her permission for a specified period of time, the compensation being a set amount of money, and she could change her mind and withdraw her permission before the end of the period. Malikis disagreed as to whether, if she did change her mind, she had to refund the whole amount or only an amount proportional to the remainder of the period, but the latter alternative was preferred.[20]

The Twelver Shi'i position was essentially the same as that of the orthodox schools of law: coitus interruptus with a free woman was licit only with her permission.[21] But Shi'i jurisprudence differed from that of the four orthodox schools by allowing for the establishment of the woman's consent as a precondition in the marriage contract.[22] After such a pre-condition, a husband could practise coitus interruptus without his wife's immediate consent.

The concept of monetary compensation, which had originated among the orthodox Maliki jurists, became, among the Twelver Shi'is, "blood money" to be paid to the woman in the event that coitus interruptus was practised against her wishes without a stipulation authorizing it in the marriage contract. The sum was sizable – ten dinars each time coitus interruptus took place under these conditions.[23] Some Shi'i authorities insisted on the payment;[24] others rejected it, and still others argued that although the man did not have to pay, it was better if he did.[25] Essentially the division seems to have been between those who saw coitus interruptus without the free woman's permission as prohibited (*haram*) and those who saw it as merely blameworthy (*makruh*). The former demanded payment. The latter did not. Those who completely rejected the idea of payment based their opinion on early Shi'i authorities who maintained that coitus interruptus was the man's right and prerogative.[26]

The Isma'ilis sanctioned coitus interruptus with the free woman's consent and, like the Twelver Shi'is, favoured the establishment of her prior consent in the marriage contract.[27] The Ibadi position was the classical one stated above.[28] Zaidi jurisprudence recommended seeking the woman's permission but did not prohibit the practice when she refused. They reasoned that coitus interruptus "is not worse than complete abstinence".[29]

We notice that one of the last rights to be tampered with, given the necessity of contraception, was the right to sex, albeit *legitimate* sex. But the range of legitimate sex in Islamic religious morality was wide: within marriage it was not bound by procreative purpose, and it encompassed concubinage as well. The point can be driven home most economically, however, when we appreciate the fact that certain Muslim jurists, including some of the most "orthodox" Hanbalis, were able to permit masturbation (*al-'istimna' bi al-yad*).[30] It is true that they permitted it only because of their greater fear of *zina*, that is, illegitimate intercourse. They believed masturbation to be lawful in the absence of a legitimate partner to satisfy sexual lust. Ahmad Ibn Hanbal, the founding authority of the school of law that bears his name, taught that masturbation was licit especially for the prisoner, the traveller, and the indigent, lonely persons who did not have access to a lawful sex partner.[31] Jurists who followed him permitted a woman alone without a husband to resort to masturbation to satisfy her needs.[32]

For jurists who thought along these lines, masturbation was licit even during Ramadan, the great month of fasting when believers abstained during daylight from the pleasures of the flesh, primarily food and sex. The medieval culture and its medical authorities believed that the accumulation of semen in the testicles could result in serious injury to the body if not released.[33] The jurists who discussed this problem clearly stated that it was better for a person to masturbate than perish, and they likened his condition to that of the believer who, in case of illness, was allowed to eat and break his fast.[34]

No doubt the permission of masturbation belonged to the outer reach of legitimate sexual morality in Islam. A great number of jurists viewed the practice with distaste and repugnance, although this was not the same thing as prohibition. Still others, such as the strict Shafi'i jurist Nawawi, whose opinion is typical of the Shafi'i jurists as a whole, said that masturbation was absolutely forbidden (*haram*). But then we find that he, as well as the other Shafi'is, permitted masturbation when it was performed by the hand of a man's wife or concubine, "for he has a right to the enjoyment of her hand as he has to the rest of her body".[35]

Masturbation is akin to coitus interruptus in its "spilling of seed", as the English use of "Onanism" sometimes to mean the first, sometimes to mean the second, shows.[36] The fact that no special sanctity was attached to the semen as such is an important implication of Islamic attitudes. Muslim jurists viewed "spilling the seed" as a natural, even necessary function of the body. This point of view was shaped and continuously sustained by certain underlying ideas about human reproduction which profoundly influenced Islamic sexual legislation (Chapter 3).

Sex versus property: contraception with a wife who was a slave of another

In cases where the wife was a slave (*ama*) of another (someone other than her husband),[37] a different set of legal opinions applied, but these opinions were generally based on the same principles as the opinions regarding free women. The primary object of coitus interruptus was the prevention of children. Since a free woman had a right to her own children, her permission for coitus interruptus was generally deemed necessary, but in the case of a slave wife, the children would belong to the master; so incomplete intercourse did not infringe her right to them. Still, withdrawal was judged to reduce the woman's pleasure in intercourse, and sexual fulfilment was a woman's right as a *wife*, regardless of her legal position as free or slave. The jurists, in their elaboration of the rules governing coitus interruptus, had to choose between these two conflicting principles. Some based their opinions on property rights to children and required the master's permission; others argued on the basis of a woman's right to sexual fulfilment, and insisted on her permission.

The Shafi'is, who found it possible to set aside even the free woman's right to children, and to interpret her right to sexual fulfilment so as to permit coitus interruptus unconditionally, found no difficulty in sanctioning coitus interruptus with a slave wife absolutely. For the Shafi'is neither her own nor her master's permission was needed.[38]

The majority of the Hanbali jurists based their position on the primacy of property rights to children, so the master's permission, and not the slave wife's, was required.[39] But the freedom of the children could be included as a precondition in the marriage contract. With such a precondition, the master's permission became superfluous and was dropped.[40]

The conflict between property rights to children, which resided with the master, and marital rights to sex, which resided with the slave wife, soon became apparent. The important Hanbali jurist, Ibn Qudama al-Maqdisi, rejected the view that the master's consent was necessary and argued that since it was the slave wife, and not her master, who had the right to sexual intercourse, the master could have no say as to how intercourse was to be performed.[41] In other words, Maqdisi regarded coitus interruptus as nothing more than a sexual technique, a coital method.

Such an opinion is possible only when one separates the sexual act within marriage from its procreative end, which Muslim jurists were inclined to do. They believed that women had two distinct rights, one to children and another to sexual fulfilment, so that the very concept that Muslims held of sexual fulfilment was alien to the idea that sex within marriage was legitimate only for the purpose of procreation. This contrasted sharply with Christian views, and nowhere was the contrast more clearly expressed than in the Zaidis' unconditional permission of coitus interruptus "because it is not worse than complete abstinence".

Although the majority opinion among the Hanbalis remained based on property rights, some Hanbali jurists, insisting on the position of the slave woman *as wife*, argued that it was her permission, and not her master's, that was needed.[42] Others agreed with this opinion but put it in slightly different terms. When it was felt that a slave wife "suffered" as a consequence of coitus interruptus, then her permission became necessary.[43] Even Maqdisi, who rejected the need for the master's permission and who did not feel that the slave wife's consent was necessary, hastened to add that it was better to ask her permission anyway.[44]

Hanafi jurists further eroded the position based on property rights, namely, the need for the master's permission. Although the school's founder, Abu Hanifa himself, argued from property rights and insisted on the master's permission,[45] two other early authorities of the school, Abu Yusuf and Shaybani, stressed the woman's right to sexual fulfilment, and insisted on the slave wife's and not the master's permission. Although a small number of Hanafi jurists chose one or the other of these opinions,[46] the majority cited both opinions without committing themselves to either.[47]

The primacy of property rights over marital rights seems to have disappeared completely among the Malikis. Although there were some Maliki jurists who adopted the view that coitus interruptus with a slave wife was licit only with her master's consent,[48] many Malikis permitted the practice only with the consent of the slave wife and her master together, and the master's consent was needed only if the woman was fertile. If she was sterile, her permission alone sufficed.[49] This last was a bit of sophistry, for it is difficult to see the need for contraception in the case of a sterile woman. Nevertheless, the legal sophistry helps to shed light on the principles involved: if the slave wife was fertile, both property rights (children) and marital rights (pleasure) were involved, and both had to be met by seeking the permission of both master and wife; if she was sterile, only marital rights were involved, and only her own permission was needed.

In the final analysis, the slave wife's permission took precedence over that of her master, for in situations where the master granted his consent and she refused, her husband was forbidden to practise coitus interruptus with her, and she could take him to court and seek redress on the basis of harm done to her by his withdrawal against her wishes.[50]

The Twelver Shi'is[51] and the Zaidis[52] sanctioned coitus interruptus with a slave wife unconditionally. The Isma'ilis permitted the practice only with the master's consent,[53] and the Ibadis permitted it with his or with the slave wife's permission.[54] All these points of view were essentially parallel to those of the orthodox jurists.

Sex as property: contraception with a man's own slave

Since the requirement to ask anyone's permission for the practice of coitus interruptus was based either on property rights to children, or on marital rights to sexual fulfilment, the permission of those who had neither right was obviously not needed. All Muslim jurists absolutely agreed that coitus interruptus might be practised with a man's own slave or concubine unconditionally.

Marriage of pleasure: contraception in **mut'a**

In contrast to the other schools, Twelver Shi'i law sanctioned still another form of legitimate sex, the *mut'a* union between a man and a free woman (or a slave with the permission of her master). This so-called "temporary marriage" (the literal meaning of *mut'a* is "marriage of pleasure"), involved a legal agreement of sexual partnership for a certain financial recompense and a fixed time, which could vary from a day to months, or even years. The *mut'a* contract provided the Shi'is with an extremely flexible legal instrument. *Mut'a* was a legal and socially acceptable alternative for what elsewhere would have been regarded as prostitution: at a price a woman would provide sexual services for a short period of time. The man had no legal obligation to provide her with food and shelter, a basic assumption of the Islamic law of ordinary marriage, nor could the two inherit from each other, another basic assumption of the law. But in theory a *mut'a* contract could serve a radically different purpose, for it was possible to stipulate a period of one hundred years, and also make provision for inheritance rights. Under these conditions *mut'a* could become the most binding form of marriage that was available in Islam, for with a *mut'a* contract divorce, otherwise so easy in Islamic law, becomes impossible.[55]

Coitus interruptus was deemed absolutely licit in *mut'a* because its basic purpose, like the basic purpose of concubinage, was "pleasure without progeny".[56] It was taken for granted that withdrawal would be a normal practice in *mut'a* unions – so much so that a man who *wanted* children had to make special provision (in the original agreement) so as "*not* to practise withdrawal".[57]

However, few men sought their children in short-term *mut'a* arrangements. The more typical problem for men was to avoid being burdened by the issue of such sexual unions. For in what was perhaps the firmest feature of the law governing *mut'a* (a provision which served to protect the interests of the child), children always belonged to the man: "The child of *mut'a* belongs to his father, regardless of whether he had inserted a condition to preclude that [responsibility]. He cannot deny the child, regardless of the fact that he had practised withdrawal."[58]

Female use of contraceptives

As we saw when we discussed the reasons for birth control, and in particular the emphasis on economic motives for the limitation of family size, in a society where the economic burdens of family and livelihood fell on the man, it is clear that medieval Muslim men desired to control births. Male interest in contraception was equally evident in medieval popular literature, which discussed mainly male contraceptives (Chapter 5).

But men were not alone in their desire to control births, and it is clear from jurisprudence itself that some women practised contraception.[59] Furthermore, in Arabic medicine, references to female contraceptives in the form of intra-vaginal suppositories and tampons outnumber by four to one references to male contraceptives.[60] But when the jurists discussed the female use of contraceptives, they did so mostly as an afterthought. Evidently, they were not concerned with female contraceptives as a legal problem, and their occasional references to them were primarily a reflection of social practice.

Ibn Taimiya, the great Hanbali judge and theologian, dealt in one of his legal opinions with the case of a woman "who inserts a suppository (*dawa*) during intercourse, thereby stopping the semen from entering the uterus [literally "channels of conception", *majari al-habal*]".[61] The Hanafi jurist Ibn Nujaim maintained by analogy with the classical opinion on coitus interruptus, that the blocking of the *os uteri*, "as women do", to prevent pregnancy should be subject to the husband's permission.[62] Another Hanafi jurist, Ibn 'Abidin, disagreed and suggested that women's practice of inserting suppositories and tampons "to block the *os uteri*" was permissible without the husband's consent. He added that the difference between this practice and coitus interruptus was obvious.[63]

'Ulaish, a Maliki jurist, argued in his collection of legal opinions that the practice of "placing something like a rag in the vagina during intercourse to stop the semen from reaching the uterus is permitted, along with coitus interruptus, but with the husband's permission".[64]

Twelver Shi'i opinion held that, although the practice is better done with the husband's permission, it was not prohibited without it. The Twelvers argued that "there is no tradition" (in the sense of precedent) concerning the female use of contraceptives.[65]

It should be noted that the evidence cited above from both Ibn Taimiya and 'Ulaish comes from their *fatawa*. *Fatawa* are opinions on points of law, delivered for the benefit of private individuals,[66] and both jurists mentioned female use of contraception because actual cases came before them. These are not theoretical discussions of fine points of law or imaginary legal problems, and the very language used by the jurists bears this out. For example, Ibn Nujaim, as mentioned above, speaks of blocking the *os uteri* "as women do to prevent pregnancy".[67] Ibn 'Abidin uses the same language.[68] Significant too is the fact that the one form of female contraception reported or in any way discussed in Islamic jurisprudence was the use of intra-vaginal suppositories and tampons to stop the semen from reaching the uterus; in other words, only direct and relatively effective methods were mentioned.

CHAPTER 3

Conception theory in Muslim thought

> "From what is man created?" The Prophet answered, "He is created of both, the semen of the man and the semen of the woman. The man's semen is thick and forms the bones and tendons. The woman's semen is fine and forms the flesh and blood."
>
> *Hadith* from the Prophet

What is the precise contribution of male and female parents to conception? Why do children resemble their parents? What is the course of the foetus' development? These questions about generation defined a scientific field of inquiry which informed Islamic attitudes regarding the sexes generally, and had direct bearing on the legal regulation of contraception and abortion. Until the discovery in the last one hundred years of genes, chromosomes and DNA, it was very difficult to answer these questions – or, at least, the answers were very different (the female contribution to conception, the ovum, was not discovered and accurately described until the third decade of the nineteenth century).

The Quran and *hadith*, by their emphasis on God-the-Creator, frequently referred to sexual generation, the creation of new individuals. Thus the Islamic religious sources contained statements on reproduction and the development of the foetus that believers considered binding. How binding these statements actually proved to be depended on their degree of explicitness and clarity. When medieval Muslims interpreted them, they relied directly and heavily on their scientific tradition.

The scientific sources of biological knowledge in the pre-modern Middle East were medicine and natural philosophy, two clearly defined disciplines with their own literatures and leading authorities, primarily Hippocrates and Galen for medicine, and Aristotle for natural philosophy. This scientific tradition was native to the Middle East for centuries before Islam, and by the tenth century the whole of this heritage had become available in Arabic. Hippocrates, Aristotle, and Galen were as much part of Arabic Middle Eastern culture as anything else in it. This was so much the case that it would be possible to write a decent history of ancient Greek biology from medieval Arabic sources alone.[1]

The last two chapters reconstructed the rationale for the Islamic permission of contraception on the basis of the arguments which were internal to jurisprudence itself. Only reasoning which the jurists had linked directly to their regulation of contraception was considered; for what ultimately mattered in society for the majority of Muslims were the regulations themselves – that a man can legitimately marry more than one woman, that he can divorce her by a solemn repudiation pronounced three times, that withdrawal is licit with her permission, etc. Behind these regulations there were always deeper layers of religious thought and considerations, and these are our focus in this chapter. To demonstrate the relevance of these deeper layers to the outward practice of religion in society is never easy. Inevitably, the attempt involves movement away from the aspects of Islam which touched all Muslims directly, to the metaphysical and theoretical concerns that occupied only some of them in any given generation. Yet the medieval Muslim scholars themselves related biological theory to specific legal regulation, and, in doing so, have made our task possible.

Hippocrates, Aristotle, Galen, and their medieval students agreed in substance on the problem of foetal development, but disagreed radically on the question of parental contribution to generation. Hippocrates (supported by Galen) maintained that both male and female contribute equally to the formation of the embryo, that both have "semen". Aristotle categorically rejected this theory, maintaining that only males have semen, and that females provide only the passive material which the male semen, as carrier of the soul, fashions into the new individual.[2] Muslim religious thinkers, for reasons we shall discuss, sided with Hippocrates and rejected Aristotle, with important consequences generally for Islamic legislation regarding the sexes. More specifically, the Hippocratic theory provided Muslim thinkers with the ultimate theoretical underpinning for their permission of contraception.

Attitudes towards abortion depended even more directly on ideas regarding the stages of foetal development. The fundamental question for the religious law was: at what point of development is the foetus a human being? The Muslims believed that point to be the end of the fourth month of pregnancy, when the foetus was ensouled. As a consequence, many Muslim jurists permitted abortion until that stage. It was a matter of great consequence to the relationship between religion and science generally, and to medieval biological thought specifically, that the Quran described the development of the foetus in the language of the biological sciences of the time. There was little difference between the language of the Quran and that of Galen on the stages of foetal development. This circumstance did not surprise the medieval Muslims, who were generally convinced that God spoke to humanity in a language it could understand.

Quranic and *hadith* exegesis, Islamic jurisprudence, Arabic medicine, natural philosophy, and other secular literature all discussed sexual generation and contained cross-references to each other. Apparently it was as difficult to interpret the relevant statements of the Quran and *hadith* without reference to science, as it was to write a medical or philosophical treatise free of their influence. When the evidence as a whole is surveyed, it becomes clear that whether one begins with philosophy, medicine, historical writing, or religious literature, one is likely to find oneself participating in the same discussion.[3]

My choice of material below is in part the result of considerations which are tangential to the medieval evidence itself. Nineteenth- and twentieth-century scholarship has managed to construct a certain image of medieval Islam. I have in mind the notion of a fateful struggle between science and religion, reason and superstition, that resulted (by about the twelfth century) in the triumph of religious orthodoxy and the downfall of the spirit of rationality in Islam. In the light of this influential idea, even Ibn Sina's *Shifa'*, the central document of medieval biology, can be viewed as belonging to a limited tradition that became irrelevant to the future development of Muslim culture. The same judgement, unfortunately, can be applied also to the authors of Islamic theology (*kalam*), such as Fakhr al-Din Razi. Razi's great commentary on the Quran, *Al-Tafsir al-kabir*, represents the basic textual link between natural philosophy and Islamic religious thought. But the most "orthodox" of Muslim thinkers, that is, the Hanbalis, took the position that theology itself was "un-Islamic". The Hanbalis were the fierce guardians of the primacy of the religious sources of Islamic life, and were deeply suspicious of speculative theology whose dependence on metaphysics and science could erode the primacy of the Quran and *hadith*.

Therefore it is particularly interesting that by the fourteenth century, the two greatest Hanbalis of the age, Ibn Taimiya (1263–1328) and his student Ibn Qayyim (1292–1351) proved to be quite capable of holding fast to their insistence on the primacy of the Islamic religious sources, and at the same time engage in theological debate. It matters little whether or not we view this development as the triumph of theology in the orthodox heart of Islam. The presence of philosophy and the sciences even in this most orthodox quarter of historical Islam, dispels any doubt about the importance of our material for the culture as a whole. Opposition between different traditions existed in the Middle East, but as a feature of their presence together in the same large, cosmopolitan civilization. When some medieval Muslims, in their efforts to combat their *internal* opponents or rivals, called certain attitudes un-Islamic, they had no idea that moderns would accomplish for them what they had not been able to achieve in their own time.

This chapter is organized primarily around the work of Ibn Qayyim. There are at least four separate treatments of generations in Ibn Qayyim's published work. The two most important are: (1) *Kitab al-tibyan fi aqsam al-qur'an*, a commentary on "oaths in the Quran", and (2) *Tuhfat al-mawdud bi ahkam al-mawlud*, a book which deals with the bringing up of infants from the viewpoint of Islamic law and the popular customs of the community (he wrote it on the occasion of the birth of a grandchild). The *Tuhfat* concludes with a long chapter that takes man from his origins as semen to his final destiny in the afterlife.

The *Tibyan* contains a similar chapter that addresses the following questions: What is the nature of semen? Do females have semen? Is the foetus formed of both male and female semens equally? Do the two semens mix until they become one, or does one of them provide the matter, and the other the form? What are the causes of sex-differentiation? How do twins occur? Can a foetus result from two separate acts of intercourse (that is, can the child have more than one father)? How does the foetus develop? Which organ is formed first? When is the foetus ensouled? Does the foetus have volitional movement or sensation before ensoulment? Why do pregnant women stop menstruating? Why do they crave strange foods early in their pregnancy? What is the duration of pregnancy? What is the position of the foetus in the womb? What causes spontaneous abortions? How does the foetus emerge during childbirth?

All of these questions are important, but unfortunately only a few of them can be discussed below. Arabic discussions of generation are a neglected part of the history of biology. Between Galen in the early centuries of Christianity, and Malpighi and Harvey in early modern times, there are about fifteen centuries during which the basic contributions to biology were made in Arabic. Historians of science have studied above all else the immediate background to modern embryological research, the period since the sixteenth century.[4] There has also been important work on the ancient Greeks.[5] But for the middle period between Galen and the early moderns, we encounter a serious gap in our knowledge.[6] No attempt can be made within the confines of this book to give more than a sketch of Arabic biological investigations. In a separate study I will deal with the subject more fully; here I will confine myself to the essence of the argument regarding generation (the problem of semen) and its relevance to religion and society.

As we shall see, the essence of the argument is theoretical. That is, it consists of more or less abstract hypotheses which ancient and medieval scholars constructed to make sense out of various observations of biological life. But while I will, of necessity, concentrate on the theories themselves, it would be a mistake to assume that detail and observation were not equally important to the ancient or medieval thinkers. In the first place, their speculations were always based on observation. Then, ultimately, the test of whether a hypothesis was correct was the extent to which it explained the phenomena of the senses. Yet, without microscopy and the other advanced techniques of modern biology, pre-modern scientists were severely limited to what could be observed with the naked eye.[7]

The problem of semen

1. Hippocrates

Disciplined speculation about generation began in the Hippocratic writings with attention to the facts of resemblance. Since children resembled both of their parents, Hippocrates argued that both male and female must contribute similar reproductive material to the foetus. What defines the material as similar is precisely that both seminal contributions equally have the ability to pass inheritance.

According to Hippocrates, semen is formed during sexual excitation, when the heat of lust causes all the fluids and organs of the body to release particles from their essence which represent, and can duplicate, their likeness in the child. It follows that semen is a complex, heterogeneous substance, made up of all those different particles that the organs have released. Semen comes from all parts of the body of each parent, and goes to all parts of the body of the child:

> [The child] must inevitably resemble each parent in some respect, since it is from both parents that the sperm comes to form the child. The child will resemble in the majority of its characteristics that parent who has contributed a greater quantity of sperm to the resemblance, and from a greater number of bodily parts.[8]

The Hippocratic hypothesis seemed to explain the general similarity of the child to its parents, as well as the specific similarity to particular organs, such as the shape of nose or hand. In the nineteenth century Charles Darwin proposed essentially the same theory to explain inheritance, and gave it its name: *pangenesis*.[9]

2. Aristotle

The physiological mechanism Aristotle conceived to explain the transmission of resemblance was, in certain respects, strikingly similar to that of Hippocrates. Aristotle believed that semen was a residue of nutriment in its final form – that is, blood. Blood begins as food which the digestive system transforms until it becomes suitable for the nourishment of the body. To nourish each organ meant "to become part of it", that is, to become "like" it. Because semen is concocted of such blood, it contains that similarity we call inheritance.[10] Aristotle conceded that either his theory or pangenesis can account for the resemblance equally well, "since it comes exactly to the same thing whether we speak of being drawn from every one of the parts [pangenesis] or passing into everyone of the parts [Aristotle]".[11]

A very thin line indeed separated the substance that was already part of the organ (pangenesis), and that substance (Aristotle's "ultimate residue of nourishment") so similar to the organ that it can become a living part of it instantly. But it is a line that Aristotle did not wish to cross. He fixed the source of semen at that moment before the blood joined the organs because he wanted to argue that only males, by virtue of their adequate vital heat, can transform it into semen. Females lack this ability because they are not "hot" enough. A female, according to Aristotle, was by definition a "deformed" or "incomplete male": "A woman is as it were an infertile male; the female, in fact, is female on account of inability of a sort, viz., it lacks the power to concoct semen out of the final state of nourishment . . . because of the coldness of its nature."[12] As a result, the female discharges her substance in the form of menstrual blood, "the analogous thing in females to the semen of the male".[13]

When considered independently, Aristotle's mechanism suggests a tendency towards admitting a similar contribution of male and female in reproduction. At least the difference between them should be one of degree only, since both semen and menses are different stages of the same physiological process. But other considerations, ultimately stemming from Aristotle's need to explain embryological development (below, p. 45), forced him to formulate a radical distinction between the two, which sharply disavows this expectation. He asserted that the male contributes absolutely nothing to the body of the foetus, but instead "the male provides the 'form' and the 'principle of movement'". He also asserted, with equal finality, that the female contributes only "matter" to the foetus, and no "form" whatsoever. Menstrual blood, as passive matter, is the only original contribution of the female to generation.[14]

The male semen fashions the female menses into a new individual very much as a carpenter fashions wood into a bed, or a builder bricks into a house. This Aristotelian formulation is the most radical statement of the difference between male and female in the history of biology, the strongest statement on record for the biological inferiority of women:

> The female always provides the material, the male provides that which fashions the material into shape; this, in our view, is the specific characteristic of each of the sexes: that is what it means to be male or female . . . Thus the physical part, the body, comes from the female, and the Soul from the male, since the Soul is the essence of a particular body.[15]

The dichotomy of form and matter was central to Aristotle's metaphysics and, since he considered it a primary example of how his system was supposed to work, there was much at stake in whether his hypothesis could explain the observed phenomena of sexual generation.[16] But Aristotle, unlike Hippocrates, was not primarily interested in explaining heredity. Rather, he was principally concerned with solving the central problem of embryology: how does the foetus develop?[17]

Aristotle's belief that the foetus passes through different stages of growth and differentiation, that the organs are not all formed at once, but one after the other, is called *epigenesis*. Because Aristotle believed in epigenesis and at the same time vigorously rejected pangenesis, historians of the subject too readily assume that these two are mutually exclusive hypotheses. It is not always recognized that they are attempts to solve two different, though related, problems. Pangenesis tries to explain genetic inheritance (why does the child resemble its parents?). Epigenesis deals with embryological development. While all theories of generation deal with both issues, it is fair to say that different theorists were more absorbed by one or the other. While the Hippocratic writings deal with embryology, their primary concern was genetic inheritance. Aristotle's primary concern was embryology. He set about to answer such questions as: what is it that tells the foetus to develop into dog, or human, or horse?[18] How does the foetus know how to form the organs? How does it know the order of their development and differentiation? In brief, what is the organizing principle?

The special role Aristotle gave the male semen was to be precisely the principle of organization, the Soul that would guide and determine embryological development. As a substance, the male semen is nothing but water and *pneuma*, literally "hot air" (or spirit). In the uterus, the water content of the semen evaporates and it is the *pneuma* which performs the task of forming, differentiating, and organizing the new individual. At the crucial point in his argument Aristotle suddenly reveals that *pneuma* is akin to *aither*, the divine element of the stars – the higher and eternal intelligences.[19] Because it is literally out of this world, *pneuma* can do all the miraculous things Aristotle needs it to do.[20]

Thus the role that Aristotle gives to the male semen is a solution to his most pressing problem. But the fact that he located his solution in the male semen and not the female menses, or that he considered that form and matter should originate exclusively in either sex rather than be equally shared by both sexes, is the result of considerations which were extrinsic to his essential problem.[21]

What about resemblance? When the male principle – the form – is able completely to master the matter (matter invariably resists formation, in the same way that stone resists the sculptor, much more so than clay, and hard metal more than stone), the child will be a male and will look like his father. A male who looks like his mother, a female who looks like her father, a female who looks like her mother, or one who looks like a distant ancestor, or a monstrosity, are all gradations reflecting the relative failure of the male form to master the recalcitrant female matter. In this, Aristotle's ultimate explanation of resemblance, his physiological theory concerning resemblances (that is, semen's origin in blood so much like the organs that it potentially transports the likeness to the child) seems to play no role whatsoever.[22]

3. *Galen*

Aristotle's severe rejection of the theory that both sexes equally contributed semen was energetically criticized by Galen who, otherwise profoundly influenced by Aristotle, reaffirmed the original Hippocratic thesis, and supported it with new evidence. This new evidence was the discovery of the ovaries, which Galen called "female testicles". Aristotle had had no notion whatsoever of these organs and, to complicate matters, had also denied that the male testicles had anything to do with the actual production of semen. By analogy with mechanical devices, Aristotle had argued that the testicles served as "weights" to keep the seminal passages steady during intercourse, much to the amusement of some later writers.[23] Galen reaffirmed the direct relevance of the testicles to generation and was now able to point to the organs in both sexes where the semen collects and is finally concocted.[24]

Galen placed great emphasis on the Hippocratic argument from resemblance: if females did not contribute semen, or conversely if the male semen did not contribute materially to the substance of the foetus, then children would not resemble their parents. He argued that the female semen, just like the male semen, contributes both to the matter and to the form of the foetus. Galen's insistence that the male semen contributes to the formation of the *body* of the foetus was the issue over which he departed most radically from Aristotle, and where his criticism of Aristotle was harshest in tone.[25]

In Galen's case we see clearly that whether semen was derived from the organs (pangenesis) or from blood that was "ready" to join the organs (Aristotle), it was possible to believe that women could produce it as well as men. For Galen was thoroughly Aristotelian in his notion of *how* the semen was formed: it is a residue of the final state of nourishment. Galen had become the great champion of Hippocrates against Aristotle even though he had adopted Aristotle's own mechanism for semen formation.[26]

By Galen's time the two scientific disciplines of medicine and natural philosophy had become clearly distinct. After Galen, the "natural philosophers" and the "physicians" formed opposing camps, and for centuries to come generation remained at the centre of their dispute. When Islamic religious thought confronted scientific ideas regarding generation, it did not face a monolithic, generally accepted body of scientific theory. On the one side were Hippocrates and Galen, undisputed authorities for medicine; on the other side was Aristotle, the fountainhead of natural philosophy. One of these two sciences, namely medicine, provided strong support for the basic Islamic ideas on generation.

4. *Ibn Sina (Avicenna)*

For the pre-modern Middle East as well as Europe, it was the biology of

Ibn Sina (980–1037) that had the widest currency. Ibn Sina highlighted the basic scientific and philosophical issues of Aristotle's biology, and defined conclusively the manner in which Middle Eastern and European natural philosophy was to approach them for centuries to come. His *Hayawan* (the title of the biological section in the *Shifa'*) was, quite deliberately, a grand apologia for Aristotle's *Generation of Animals*. After Galen's criticism of Aristotle, and in a context where Galenism was reigning supreme,[27] Aristotelians were on the defensive. It was Ibn Sina's historical role to restate the Aristotelian arguments convincingly for a new age. His principal task was to integrate the post-Aristotle biological observations, which had given Galen his most effective evidence against Aristotle, into the Aristotelian system.

The *Hayawan* contains in Books 15–19 a masterly abridgement of the *Generation of Animals*,[28] but in Book 9, right in the middle of the *Hayawan*, Ibn Sina was forced to depart from his plan to follow Aristotle's arrangement of subjects, "to discuss here the controversies concerning semen and the foetus – not according to Aristotle's arrangement, but following what we consider more appropriate in our own time".[29]

By Ibn Sina's time, the discovery of the ovaries had been incorporated into the body of scientific knowledge. It was the most important fact about human reproduction that was not known to Aristotle, and that Ibn Sina was obliged to accommodate, without, however, retreating from Aristotle's central hypothesis.[30] He did so, in the first instance, by accepting flatly the argument of Hippocrates and Galen that females produce semen, and that it is the female semen, and not menstrual blood, which represents the basic female contribution to generation. Ibn Sina says that because the female semen has undergone further concoction than simple menstrual blood, "it is more fit than the menses to aid in the formation of the embryo. Otherwise a woman would not emit it, or have nocturnal dreams, or experience pleasure as a consequence of its flow, in contrast to simple menstrual blood whose flow does not produce pleasure."[31]

The acceptance of the ovaries and the female semen was a critical departure in Aristotelian biology, for without it the Aristotelian theory remained behind the times, in the sense that it was contradicted by generally accepted scientific observation. Ibn Sina argued that Aristotle himself believed in the existence of the female semen *in addition* to the menstrual fluid. While he based his contention directly on his reading of a rather difficult passage in the *Generation of Animals*, more generally it fulfilled the logic of Aristotle's mechanism for the common origin of semen and menses.[32] Ibn Sina reasoned that some of the menstrual blood is more concocted than the rest, and that this can be called the "female semen".

But while Ibn Sina has accepted the existence of the female semen, he defined its *role* in a manner that did not depart at all from Aristotle's original scheme:

It is clear that the seed of women is fit to be matter, but not fit to be the principle of movement. The seed of men is the principle of movement, for there is no doubt that the female semen is like menstrual blood, and menstrual blood is fit to be matter and not the principle of movement.[33]

Ibn Sina has given the female semen exactly the same role that Aristotle had assigned to the menstrual blood.

His solution shows the extent to which it was possible, given the limits of biological knowledge at the time, to incorporate even important new elements into an original system and still keep its basic structure intact (this was equally true of the opposite camp).[34] There were purists among the Aristotelians after Ibn Sina – I am thinking principally of Ibn Rushd (Averroes, 1126–98) – who were not ready to accept the role of the ovaries, and who held fast to the letter of Aristotle.[35] The truth of the matter is that it was very difficult to agree on the identity of the female substance before the discovery of the mammalian egg in the nineteenth century (even then it was not an easy discovery).

In Europe scientific biology was introduced through the writings of Albert the Great (1206–80), principally in *De Animalibus*.[36] Albert's *De Animalibus* was, for all practical purposes, a paraphrase of the Latin translation of the biological section from Ibn Sina's *Shifa*', the comprehensive statement of Aristotelian logic, natural philosophy, and metaphysics that became the standard text of medieval times. It is difficult to overstate the importance of Ibn Sina as a scientific and philosophical authority for the pre-modern Europeans. His importance for the history of biology was succinctly stated by Sarton: "The real fountainhead of Aristotelian zoology, East and West, from the eleventh century on was the summary of the nineteen books by Ibn Sina . . . for every serious treatise on zoology naturally took the form of a commentary on Aristotle, i.e., on Ibn Sina."[37] Sarton was right about the intimate connection between Aristotle and Ibn Sina, but the explanation as to why medieval Aristotelians chose to view their biology through Ibn Sina, and not directly (Aristotle's original *Generation of Animals* was available in both Arabic and Latin), is that Ibn Sina's version of Aristotle was much less vulnerable to Galenic attack than the original.

While both natural philosophy and medicine dealt with generation, it was understood, at least in principle, that the first responsibility of medicine was the maintenance of health and the cure of disease. The more theoretical or abstract problems, such as the nature of life and change, were the domain of natural philosophy. Ibn Sina himself, who was also the most important *physician* of the Middle Ages, illustrates this segregation of responsibilities well. In the *Canon*, his great medical work, he discussed generation but maintained that as a subject it belonged to philosophy.[38] (Ibn Rushd made the same point in his own medical book, the *Kulliyat*.)[39] He explained that the theories of generation and the controversy surrounding them do not concern the practising physician, who could neglect them without any harm. But even more interesting is the structure of his discussion in the *Canon*. Here, there was no massive criticism of Galen as in the *Hayawan* ("Let us then look at Galen's contradictions, and show that he did nothing and said nothing well, that even when he thought he presented proof he did not convince; and that he is extremely weak in the principles [of philosophy], even though he is very productive in the branches of medicine").[40] In the *Canon*, Ibn Sina briefly stated the different theories of Hippocrates, Aristotle, and Galen with admirable neutrality. He also quoted Hippocrates directly – something which he did not do in the *Hayawan*. Surprisingly, he even approved of Hippocrates' ideas about resemblance and made a strong statement in support of pangenesis: "[Semen] must include a representative sample from each of the principal organs. The other organs must also secrete [their own contribution] to it, and it is by this [process] that resemblance is caused."[41]

The treatment of generation in the *Canon*, which showed an eclecticism that was shunned in the *Hayawan*, was not the result of confusion or carelessness, but of sensitivity to the nature of medicine as an independent art with different requirements than those of natural philosophy.[42] Medicine also had its own authorities, namely Hippocrates and Galen, and it was the ideas of these two which generally dominated Arabic medicine from its beginnings.[43] Even Ibn Sina's *Canon* is testimony to this fact.

5. *Ibn Qayyim and Islamic religious literature*

While Ibn Sina's influence in the Middle East was vast, he never achieved among the religious thinkers of Islam the status of supreme authority that he did among the pre-modern Christian thinkers of Europe. Still, all biological discussion in natural philosophy, which remained for centuries an important part of Middle Eastern scientific activity, depended heavily on his *Hayawan*.[44] Thus the Aristotelian interpretation continued to have great vitality in the medieval Middle East. But it also faced formidable opposition, and not only from Galenic quarters.

The most formidable opposition came from the Islamic religious sources where, to put it mildly, all the cards were stacked against Aristotle; for the statements about parental contribution to generation in the *hadith* paralleled the Hippocratic writings, and the view of foetal development in the Quran agreed in detail with Galen's scientific writings. A Muslim religious thinker who wished to deal with the religious texts head on, and at the same time remain committed to Aristotle, faced an impasse – as in the case of Fakhr al-Din Razi.[45] In contrast, someone like Ibn Qayyim, who was not an Aristotelian, was able to take full advantage of the agreement between revelation and medicine. Ibn Qayyim welcomed the opportunity to support revelation with evidence from an independent secular source and, significantly, moved ahead to express the relationship between revelation and science in a new and surprising way.

Ibn Qayyim's primary sources in the *Tibyan* are the Quran, *hadith*, Hippocrates, Aristotle, Galen, Ibn Sina, and Fakhr al-Din Razi. Some of the significance of the discussion below will be lost if we forget Ibn Qayyim's own place in the Islamic tradition – as a Hanbali; or his date – the fourteenth century; or the textual location of his discussion – in Quranic commentary rather than in medicine or natural philosophy.

He begins with a description of semen that follows closely that of the Hippocratic treatise *The Seed*. He is quick to acknowledge that his hypothesis (that semen comes from all parts of the body) is one alternative in a debate in which the other side contends that semen is a homogeneous substance, a residue of the final nourishment.[46] Thus Ibn Qayyim has plunged himself into the centuries-old debate on generation.

His point-by-point justification of the theory of pangenesis gives essentially the arguments that Aristotle had enumerated.[47] Aristotle's objections immediately follow, in an abbreviated but accurate presentation of the original.[48] Ibn Qayyim's renditions represent the manner in which the arguments usually appeared in medieval scientific discussions.[49] In all this introductory part, there is little reliance on the Islamic religious sources, but in Ibn Qayyim's final rebuttal of Aristotle's objections to pangenesis, there is a quotation from the *hadith*.[50] The form of the discussion is that of Muslim dialectic with its familiar set phrase: "if you say . . . we say . . .".

Ibn Qayyim continues: "If you say, you are stating explicitly that women have semen, and that the female semen is one of the two parts from which God creates the child. Some physicians however believe that women do not have semen." He answers by using both the *hadith* and Galen. 'Aisha and Umm Salama, two wives of the Prophet, asked him the same question, and in his answer the Prophet "established the female semen": "Should a woman wash after a nocturnal emission (*idha ihtalamat*)?" The Prophet said that she should do so if there is a trace of the fluid. They asked again: "Do women have nocturnal emissions?" The Prophet retorted: "How else would their children resemble them?" Ibn Qayyim also quotes another version of the *hadith* with the following addition: "Do you think that there is any other reason for the resemblance? When her semen dominates the man's semen the child will look like her brothers, and when the man's semen dominates her semen the child will look like his brothers."[51]

Immediately after recounting the *hadith*, Ibn Qayyim introduces the scientific debate by reminding us that Galen had attacked Aristotle's scandalous opinion that women do not have semen, and adding "let us now discuss this problem [with evidence] from nature after our argument from the religious law". This part of the argument reflects Galen's language: the semen is one of the residues and humidities of the body, and this is something which both males and females have; from it directly the foetus is formed, and through it resemblance occurs. If women did not have semen, their children would not look like them. The male semen alone does not generate a child; generation happens only when it mixes with another, equivalent semen from the female.[52] In a clear reference to Ibn Sina and his school, Ibn Qayyim adds that some followers of Aristotle have admitted that the female contributes a white and viscid substance which becomes material for the body of the foetus. But they questioned whether it has a formative faculty like the male semen. Ibn Qayyim has a ready rebuttal from the *hadith*, where the Prophet had discussed this issue and said: "The male semen is white and the female semen is yellowish. When the two meet and the male semen overpowers the female semen, it will be a male; when the female semen overpowers the male semen, it will be a female." Ibn Qayyim adds that it is possible to say that the female semen is lighter, more yellowish, and seeps out more slowly, instead of gushing out like the male semen. However, and this is the important point, both have equally the formative faculty of generation – *provided the two semens unite*.[53]

Perhaps it is useful to remember that everyone concerned believed that both male and female were *needed* for generation; the argument revolved around the nature and quality of their contribution. The view that male and female contributions were equal in value and quality was basic to Ibn Qayyim's thinking. In the *Tibyan* he returns to discuss it two more times. "If you say, it is established that the foetus is formed from the semen of both parents. Do the two semens mix until they become one? Or does one of them provide the matter, and the other act like rennet to coagulate it [Aristotle's famous analogy for the action of male semen on female menses]?"[54] Here Ibn Qayyim says that the natural philosophers prefer the second opinion. They claim that the male semen does not contribute to the body of the foetus, but is like the soul (*al-ruh*) that animates the organs; that the body of the child is formed exclusively of the mother's semen; and that once the male semen has coagulated the female semen, it disintegrates and becomes waste. According to him, the natural philosophers claim that there is support for their point of view in some regulations of Islamic law, to wit, that the child will be free or slave depending on the status of his mother, regardless of the status of his father; and that in case the male slave of one man impregnates the female slave of another, the child will belong to the master of the female slave. In their opinion, these regulations support the notion that the child's body is formed exclusively of the maternal contribution.

At this point Ibn Qayyim informs us, correctly, that the Muslim majority disputes the notions of the natural philosophers and maintains that the foetus is formed of both the male and female semina.[55] This is not surprising in view of an earlier point in his discussion where Ibn Qayyim touched on this issue and quoted another *hadith*. In answer to the question "from what is man created", the Prophet says: "He is created of both, the semen of the man and the semen of the woman. The man's semen is thick and forms the bones and tendons. The woman's semen is fine and forms the flesh and blood."[56] The correct view, then, is that the organs, parts, and form of the child are the combined and equal contribution of both, that both semens mix and become one. The fact that the child in some cases resembles the father, and in other cases the mother, confirms this point of view. God's words in the Quran also point this interpretation, when He addresses humanity and says: "We created you of a male and a female."[57]

Ibn Qayyim considers it impossible to decide on the basis of biology whether the father or the mother has more of a right to the child. While the father has precedence and the child takes his name, the child follows the mother in freedom and slavery because, in addition to the original share she contributes, it is formed in her womb and fed by her milk. In case of conflict, Ibn Qayyim suggests that perhaps the more religious of the two should have the child.[58] This is as clear a statement of the biological equality of male and female as Aristotle's was of their biological inequality.

The most important consequence for Islamic law of the theory of generation contained in the *hadith* is very difficult to describe directly, for it has to do with a certain absence. The theory of equal contribution of male and female removed, perhaps completely, the possibility of rationalizing the unequal treatment of women by reference to a supposed biological inferiority of females. Islamic law treated women differently from men in a certain number of important areas, such as inheritance rights. This unequal treatment of women had its basis in Quranic legislation. Islamic jurisprudence shows that the jurists were able to defend and rationalize the discrepancies mostly with reference to social reality, and social reality of course changes.

Biological theory and contraception

The theory of equal contribution of male and female to reproduction was central to Ghazali's argument for the permission of contraception (Chapter 1), and pervaded all Islamic religious thought. The remarkable consensus among all Muslim jurists from the tenth to the nineteenth century that contraception is licit is difficult to understand completely without it. Neither the male nor the female semen by itself amounted to much, and the religious law did not extend protection to either. In Muslim religious thought no special sanctity was attached to the semen as such, and some orthodox jurists were able to permit even masturbation.

Ghazali called the male semen "nothing" unless it united with the female semen and "settled" in the womb. Qurtubi in his commentary on the Quran did not mince his words: "The semen is nothing definite (*yaqinann*), and it is of no consequence if a woman gets rid of it before it settles in the womb; before then it is still as if it were in the man's own body."[59] It would be difficult to pretend that Ghazali and Qurtubi were ignorant of the Aristotelian alternative when they made their arguments.

In the rival theory of Aristotle the male semen had a clear primacy, and for his followers it was nothing less than the carrier of the human soul. Ibn Sina in the *Shifa'* says it plainly – the male semen "is in every organ like the moving principle. From it the soul is formed."[60] Had Muslim jurists followed Aristotle's beliefs, they would have found it difficult indeed to permit the destruction of semen as in contraception (or masturbation).

Development of the foetus

There are two basic elements which can be viewed as the defining characteristics of an Islamic attitude towards sexual generation. The first is that father and mother are equal contributors to the form and matter of the offspring (to use Aristotelian terminology in a radically un-Aristotelian context). The second element is the subject of this section and can be stated simply: the foetus is a new creation which progresses through stages of differentiation and growth.[61] On the development of the foetus Muslim religious thinkers had no quarrel with Aristotle, and both scientific traditions of medicine and natural philosophy emphasized epigenesis as the standard idea of foetal development.[62]

Quranic references left no doubt that the foetus undergoes a series of transformations before becoming human. Generation is the subject of some of the most eloquent passages of the Quran, as a compelling sign of God's majesty and power. In the light of the attention they have received historically in Quranic exegesis and Islamic jurisprudence, the two most important passages are undoubtedly Sura XXII, 4 AND SURA XXIII, 12–14. The first is from the chapter of *The Pilgrimage*:

O mankind! If you are in doubt as to the Resurrection,
(a) [consider] that we have created you of earth;
(b) then of semen;
(c) then of a blood-like clot;
(d) then of a lump of flesh,
(dd) [which is] formed or not formed;
so that we may demonstrate to you [our power];
and we establish in the wombs what we will,
till a stated term;
then we bring you out as infants . . .

The second is from the chapter of *The Believers*:

(a) We created man of a quintessence of clay.
(b) Then we placed him as semen in a firm receptacle.

(c) Then we formed the semen into a blood-like clot;
(d) then we formed the clot into a lump of flesh;
then we formed out of that lump bones
and clothed the bones with flesh;
(dd) then we made him another creation.
So blessed be God the best Creator.[63]

Most interpreters of the Quran understood the creation of man out of earth (a) to refer specifically to Adam.[64] But the same commentators sometimes entertained the possibility that God might be referring to semen's origin as nourishment, since nourishment has its ultimate source in "earth and water".[65] The lines that follow it (b, c, and d) describe the first three stages of the foetus. The first stage of development, a period of forty days from conception, is the *nutfa* (semen). The second, also lasting forty days, is the *'alaqa* ("blood-like clot"). And the third, another forty days, is the *mudgha* ("lump of flesh"). In these three early stages the foetus lacks the human soul and has only the life of plants and animals. But at the end of 120 days from conception the foetus is *ensouled*. Muslims interpreted the lines marked (dd) as a direct reference to ensoulment,[66] an idea that had profound consequences for the legislation in Islamic law on abortion.

The division of these stages into forty-day periods is not Quranic, but first occurs in the *hadith*:

The Prophet said: Each of you is constituted in your mother's womb for forty days as a *nutfa*, then it becomes a *'alaqa* for an equal period, then a *mudgha* for another equal period, then the angel is sent, and he breathes the soul into it.

The stages of development which the Quran and *hadith* established for believers agreed perfectly with Galen's scientific account. In *De Semine*, for example, Galen spoke of four periods in the formation of the embryo: (1) as seminal matter; (2) as a bloody form (still without flesh, in which the primitive heart, liver, and brain are ill-defined); (3) the foetus acquires flesh and solidity (the heart, liver, and brain are well-defined, and the limbs begin formation); and finally (4) all the organs attain their full perfection and the foetus is quickened.[67] There is no doubt that medieval thought appreciated this agreement between the Quran and Galen, for Arabic science employed the same Quranic terms to describe the Galenic stages (as in Ibn Sina's account of Galen): *nutfa* for the first, *'alaqa* for the second, "unformed" *mudgha* for the third, and "formed" *mudgha* for the fourth.[68]

When Ibn Qayyim turned his attention to the development of the young embryo, he gave the standard scientific account of its growth and differentiation as it can be read in Ibn Sina and all manner of medieval Arabic literature.[69] If conception is to begin, when the two semens enter the uterus and mix, the uterus envelops the semen tightly. (1) The seminal mixture turns around itself and becomes spherical. Thus it grows to the end of six days; and as it grows a spot appears in the middle, and that is the place of the heart. Another appears above it, and that is the spot of the brain, and one to the right, the liver spot. (2) These spots start moving apart from each other, and red lines appear between them, for another three complete days. (3) In another six days the blood veins reach all over the embryo, and the three organs become distinct. (4) Then the spine marrow develops for another twelve days (the total of the above is twenty-seven days). (5) In nine days between ages twenty-seven and thirty-six days, the head separates from the shoulders, the limbs from the ribs, and the belly from the sides. (6) Differentiation progresses for another four days until everything becomes clearly visible by observation. The whole process takes *forty days*, at the end of which the foetus becomes recognizable as human – that is, not another kind of animal.[70]

Ibn Qayyim presented this account as a matter of fact and immediately noted its agreement with the *hadith*, "Each of you is constituted in your mother's womb for forty days." He observed that the Prophet said it in a "general rather than detailed way".[71] Apparently the Prophet had left the essential detail to science. Ibn Qayyim's awareness of the "general" and sometimes "vague" nature of many of revelation's statements on scientific questions was a basic insight that informed his view of the relation between revelation and science. This awareness goes a long way towards explaining how he was able to view the relation between religion and science not as a dichotomy but as an intimate continuum.

Ibn Qayyim's other treatment of generation, in the *Tuhfat*, is the most remarkable example of a true symbiosis of science and religion. Here, the words of Hippocrates explain the Quran and the Prophet, and the latter explain Hippocrates, in one continuous discourse.[72] It is here that the agreement between statements of the Prophet and the Quran and those of Hippocrates and Galen, reaches its fullest ramifications. In spite of belonging to the most orthodox segment of the religious community, in interpreting Islamic religious traditions, whose source is the word of God, Ibn Qayyim found it possible directly to involve Hippocrates, a pagan Greek, as one of his major sources of knowledge. The passage below is only a short (but typical) portion of Ibn Qayyim's long treatment. The words of Hippocrates are direct quotations from *The Nature of the Child*; those of Ibn Qayyim and his quotations from the Quran and *hadith* are italicized. Note how Ibn Qayyim moves from Hippocrates (A) to the Quran (B) to his own commentary (C) to other Quranic commentators (D) to Hippocrates (E) to his own commentary on Hippocrates (F) to the *hadith* (G) to Ibn Hanbal (H) to Abu Hanifa (I) to Shafi'i (J) to Ibn Hanbal and Ibn Taimiya (K) to his own commentary on Islamic law (L) to his own commentary about nature (M) to Hippocrates (N) to the *hadith* (O), etc.

(A) Hippocrates said in the third chapter of *Kitab al-ajinna*: . . . The semen is contained in a membrane, and it grows because of the blood of its mother which descends to the womb, and the semen in these membranes draws in the air and breathes it for the reasons we have mentioned . . . As the semen becomes a foetus several other membranes are formed, and grow within the original membrane, all being formed the same way as the first. Some membranes are formed at the beginning, others after the second month, and others in the third month . . . (B) *This is why God says, "He creates you in the wombs of your mothers, by one formation after another in three darknesses (Quran 39:6)."* (C) *Since each of these membranes has its own darkness, when God mentioned the stages of creation and transformation from one state to another, He also mentioned the darknesses of the membranes.* (D) *Most commentators explain: it is the darkness of the belly, and the darkness of the womb, and the darkness of the placenta* . . . (E) And Hippocrates said: The membranes exist once the flesh and body are formed, and when the foetus grows the membranes also grow and form pouches outside the foetus. When blood descends from the mother the foetus draws it and uses it for nourishment, and its flesh increases. The surplus blood which is not used as nourishment descends into the passages of the membranes, which is why these membranes – when they form pouches that collect blood – are called the "chorion" . . . (F) *And I say that this is the reason a pregnant woman ceases to menstruate, and when blood appears it appears as a result of illness, not menstruation.* (G) *This is supported by one of the two* hadiths *after 'Aisha*, (H) *and it is the well-known position of Ibn Hanbal which his followers invariably accept.* (I) *It is also the position of Abu Hanifa.* (J) *Al-Shafi'i, following his own version of the* hadith *after 'Aisha, has maintained that such blood ought to be considered menstrual blood;* (K) *and Ibn Hanbal agrees with him in a tradition which my teacher [that is, Ibn Taimiya] has accepted.* (L) *The rationale for this opinion is apparent, for Islamic law permits women to abstain from fasting and prayer on the basis of the presence of blood; and this is a general rule to which neither God nor his messenger made an exception.* (M) *It is true that the blood is diverted to the nourishing of the foetus, but a surplus can perhaps remain after the nourishment and emerge as menstrual blood* . . . (N) Hippocrates said: The bones become hard as a result of heat, for heat hardens the bones . . . The head projects from the shoulders, and the upper and lower arms from the sides, and the legs separate from each other. The sinews develop around each of the joints to bind and tighten it . . . The mouth opens up spontaneously, and the nose and ears are formed from the flesh. The ears are opened, and the eyes, which are filled with a clear liquid. (O) *The Prophet used to say in prayer, "I worship Him who made my face and formed it, and opened my hearing and eye-sight."* . . ., etc.[73]

According to Ibn Qayyim, religion and true science agree on the nature of parental contribution to generation, and broadly on the development of the foetus through a series of transformations. However, he clearly identifies an area where only revelation, and not science, has meaning. Basing his opinion – an absolutely common Islamic opinion – on the *hadith*'s timing of foetal development, he says that the foetus is ensouled and becomes human "in the fourth of the forty-day periods, after 120 days". He adds, "this can be known only through revelation, *for there is nothing in nature as such which requires it*. As a result, the best physicians and philosophers have been perplexed by this issue and say that it cannot be known except by conjecture (*al zann al-ba'id*)."[74] While ensoulment is a normal part of God's ways in the generation of human beings, its understanding is not open to the methods of science. Ensoulment belongs to a different realm of meaning, outside science but at the centre of religion.[75] The only other problem, besides ensoulment, where Ibn Qayyim applies the same argument is that of sex differentiation. He insists that being male or female is like being human in its divine origin, and also in the sense that it cannot – it should not – be explained by natural science.[76]

Islamic law and abortion

Many regulations in Islamic law depended directly on the religious view of foetal development.[77] If someone hurt a pregnant woman and she aborted, the amount of blood money depended on whether the foetus was "formed" or "unformed"; if the aborted foetus showed any signs of volition the full *diya* had to be paid, just as in the case of an adult person; such a foetus also inherited (the importance of this regulation was that the foetus passed inheritance to its relatives); a slave woman, pregnant by her master, ultimately gained freedom if in the case of a spontaneous abortion the foetus was "formed" – she did not if it was an early embryo. Ceremonies of religious burial were permitted in the case of the "formed" foetus, and prohibited otherwise. The Muslim view of foetal development was also central to the Muslim arguments on abortion.

All Muslim jurists believed that the foetus became a human being after the fourth month of pregnancy (120 days). The majority of jurists, as a result, prohibited abortion after that stage. The Hanafi jurists, who comprised the majority of orthodox Muslims in later centuries, permitted abortion until the end of the fourth month. The Hanafis granted the pregnant woman the right to abort even without her husband's permission, but suggested that she should not do so without a reason.[78] One reason which was often mentioned was the existence of a nursing infant. A new pregnancy put an upper limit on lactation, and the jurists believed that if the mother could not be replaced by a wet-nurse, the infant would die.[79]

Most of the Maliki jurists prohibited abortion absolutely. They agreed with the others that the foetus was not a human being before ensoulment, but maintained that since the destiny of the semen, once it settles in the womb, is ensoulment, it should not be tampered with: "When the womb has retained the semen it is not permitted for the husband and wife, or one of them, or the master [of the slave wife] to induce an abortion. After ensoulment, however, abortion is prohibited absolutely and is akin to murder."[80] Evidently, the Maliki prohibition of abortion was stronger after ensoulment than before it, and a small minority of the Malikis permitted abortion of the young embryo of forty days or less.[81]

Compared to the remarkable agreement on the permission of contraception, on abortion there remained important differences between the jurists. Many Shafi'i and Hanbali jurists agreed with the Hanafis in their toleration of the practice, some putting an upper limit of forty days for a legal abortion, others eighty days or 120 days.[82] The variety of legal regulations blurred the exact religious attitude towards abortion. Not only that, but given the nature of Islamic law, both Hanafi opinion (permission) and Maliki opinion (prohibition) were deemed legitimate by all orthodox Muslims.

The Islamic discussion of abortion was related to that of contraception in two ways. In the first place, some jurists, to strengthen their argument for the permission of contraception, had maintained that it was preferable to abortion.[83] One Hanafi jurist put the case as follows: since a pregnant woman has the right to induce abortion before the foetus is 120 days old, she should also be given the right to use female contraceptives. By removing the necessity for abortion, contraceptives represent a better alternative.[84] Special pleading in this instance resulted from the fact that female contraceptives were only occasionally dealt with in jurisprudence, where the permission of contraception normally referred to withdrawal.

On the other hand, the general permission of contraception strengthened the tendency to legalize abortion. In Islam, conception was the beginning of a new living thing, but it was the separate act of ensoulment that created *human* life. In Judaism, Christianity, and Islam it is not the taking of "life" that is prohibited, for all three religions permit the slaughter of animals – that is, non-human life. Because murder was considered a crime against a human being, and not simply against any living thing, it was essential to decide at which moment the foetus became a person: was it at the moment of conception, of birth, or some point between ? Christian theology recognized that the early embryo was not a true human being, and that it became one only when it was "ensouled" or "formed": "The dominant view in Christianity is that the foetus became a man only when 'formed'. The moment of formation appears to be the forty-day period set by Aristotle for males, and the eighty-day period suggested by Leviticus for females."[85] The Muslim view that the male semen was nothing until it united with the woman's to form an embryo was basic to the permission of contraception. If contraception is permitted because it does not tamper with human life, then abortion of the pre-ensoulment foetus can be permitted on the same grounds. Zaidi Islamic jurisprudence explicitly stated that since the "unformed" foetus, like the semen, had no human life, abortion, like contraception, was unconditionally permitted.[86]

Islamic legal attitudes towards abortion were not as consistent as those on contraception, and there was no simple Islamic religious position. But given the fact that prohibition was not the dominant view by any standard, given the fact that Muslims believed in ensoulment as the crucial event before which the foetus was not a person, and given the fact that the sanction of contraception strengthened the view that abortion should be legalized before ensoulment, perhaps we can say that, on the whole, abortion was religiously tolerated. This conclusion gains indirect support from the contemporary medieval Arabic secular literatures. Medicine, materia medica and popular literature all treated contraception and abortion as if they were two aspects of the same process: birth control.

CHAPTER 4

Arabic medicine and birth control

Arabic medical writers usually devoted special chapters to contraception and abortion, always paying attention to birth control as a normal part of the physician's art. These chapters in medical works represent an additional layer of evidence for medieval contraception, for they do not repeat the information that we have already gathered from religious literature, but lead us into new ground. True to their view of medicine as a practical art, the physicians offered their birth control prescriptions unencumbered by any non-medical considerations. The medical texts are essentially dry and matter-of-fact lists of contraceptive and abortifacient remedies, and contrast sharply with the theoretical discussions of the last chapter. The only other subject they introduce is that of medical indications for birth control.

This degree of professional specialization on the part of the physicians reflected the fact that in their society the moral and social aspects of birth control were being fully argued by those who were more directly concerned with social and ethical practice. A more fundamental point is that the sanction of contraception by religious opinion had removed birth control from the position of a religious or legal problem in medieval Muslim societies. Thus medical and other writers were able to discuss birth control freely, and in a manner that directly reflected their own interests. The physicians did it one way, the writers of erotica another way, but neither group was limited by religion. They were limited only by the extent of their knowledge.

The recent revolution in contraceptive technology which we associate with the IUD and the oral contraceptive pill (the first truly radical departure in the medical history of contraception) has established, after 1955, a new standard of contraceptive effectiveness. From this new and contemporary perspective, the contraceptives of medieval Arabic medicine appear primitive, but by the same token so do the contraceptives of fifty years ago. In the twenties and thirties of this century, modern medicine still concentrated principally on female contraceptives such as the diaphragm, cervical cap, and chemical spermicides.[1] Such techniques, involving the placing in the vagina of a physical or chemical barrier to fertilization, were the direct descendants of the intra-vaginal suppositories and tampons which were the mainstay of medieval Arabic contraceptive medicine.

The means of control in medicine

Knowledge of conception control in Arabic medicine was based on an essentially solid and rational tradition. The medieval physicians knew less than we do today, and their techniques were less effective. Nevertheless, these techniques were often reasonable or functional. The classic authority on the medical history of contraception has found the work of Arab physicians to be work of distinction.[2]

The primary Arabic medical text on contraception and abortion, without any doubt, is Razi's *Hawi* (Rhazes, *Liber Continens*). Abu Bakr Muhammad Ibn Zakariya al-Razi was born about the middle of the ninth century in Rayy in Persia. He achieved the rank of chief physician at the hospital in Rayy, and later administered the great hospital in Baghdad which he helped found. Razi was a philosopher of radical originality, a brilliant clinician, and a prolific author.[3] The *Fihrist* lists about 140 major and minor works by him, the most important of which is the *Hawi*.[4]

The *Hawi* is not an easy book to study, for it is not a finished text published by Razi himself, but a posthumous collection of his private notes.[5] The notes on contraception and abortion are interposed, haphazardly, in a section of Part IX of the *Hawi* entitled: "On aids to childbirth; expulsion of the foetus and placenta; the prevention of pregnancy; the management of women after childbirth; miscarriage; the sickness called *raja'*, that is, false pregnancy; and the sickness resulting from an excess of labour pains."[6] In this section Razi collected virtually all of the medical birth control techniques of antiquity and the Middle Ages, quoting directly seventeen earlier authorities, and relying most heavily on Dioscorides, Galen, and Ibn Masawayh.[7] Razi also added original birth control prescriptions from his own experience as a practising physician.[8] These *Hawi* notes represent nothing less than the common pool of Middle Eastern medical knowledge of birth control technology, from which later physicians departed only rarely.

All told there are 176 contraceptive or abortifacient prescriptions in the *Hawi*. These are systematically classified in Table 1 (pp. 77–82) into five categories (after Himes):

1. Means to be taken by mouth (potions), for female use.
2. Magical means, for female use.
3. Intra-vaginal suppositories and tampons.
4. Techniques used by the man.
5. Miscellaneous techniques, mostly for female use.

Himes believed that the first two categories were more or less "irrational", the magical means self-evidently, and the potions because nothing taken by mouth worked before the invention of the oral contraceptive pill.[9] The three remaining categories he considered more or less rational. It is not necessary to agree with Himes' assumptions about what is "rational" to appreciate that the classification allows a rough differentiation between the contraceptive suggestions which were probably workable, and the less effective techniques. (As to the abortifacient potions, many included vegetable poisons that must have had some effect on the foetus or the pregnant woman.) Perhaps it would be more useful to distinguish between remedies which were applied topically and directly to the organs of generation (to thwart, by chemical or mechanical ways, the passage of semen to the uterus, as in the techniques of categories 3, 4, and sometimes 5), and means which were employed indirectly and at some distance from the sexual organs, like potions and magic.

Of the 176 prescriptions in the *Hawi* there are fifty which are specifically contraceptive (rather than abortifacient). Here the emphasis is on suppositories and tampons, of which there are thirty-one.[10] There are eight potions,[11] and only one magical recipe (cyclamen as an amulet tied to the neck or arm, reported as hearsay).[12] There are three prescriptions for male use, smearing the penis before coitus with ointments of wood tar, dittany of Crete, or balm oil.[13] I have listed seven prescriptions under "miscellaneous" ("spoiling" testicles, jumping backward after intercourse, etc.).[14] Rue occurs twice as a contraceptive without indication of its method of application.[15]

We cannot assume that Razi would have endorsed all the techniques that appear in his copious notes, but a good idea of his criteria of choice may be gathered by looking at the contraceptive prescriptions which he identified as his own in the *Hawi* text. There are six of these, and they do not include potions or magical amulets. Five are intra-vaginal suppositories involving the use of oil from cabbage flowers, pepper, juice of peppermint, leaves of pennyroyal, and dill.[16] In addition, he advanced one male "contraceptive" in the form of rather obscure instructions to "spoil" the testicles with poison hemlock.[17] This apparent reference to sterilization in the context of a birth control discussion is unique in the medical literature. It was not repeated by the later physicians.

The dominant technique in the *Hawi*, and in Arabic medicine in general, was a female method of contraception which involved the introduction into the vagina of a suppository or tampon. These suppositories and tampons achieved their contraceptive results by impeding the entrance of sperm into the cervical os. Many may have worked by simply plugging the vagina, the operative factor being their physical rather than chemical features. Even in the twentieth century, chemical ingredients were often less effective than the physical barrier to fertilization represented by the suppository. In addition, a great number of the medieval suppositories and tampons had ingredients, such as honey or oil, which contributed to the contraceptive effect. Both honey and oil, for example, have a physical clogging capacity. In the twentieth century, greasy substances formed the base of many contraceptive suppositories. As late as 1931, Dr Marie Stopes, the eminent leader of the birth control movement in England, recommended the use of olive oil on a rubber sponge as an "ultra-simple contraceptive" for poor English women.[18] The very early physician Thabit Ibn Qurra (ninth century) mentioned only one contraceptive: "Oil, any kind of oil."[19] Oil gums up the external os and reduces the movement of sperm.

Many more of the ingredients, by changing the alkaline or acid condition of the vagina and uterus, created a hostile environment for sperm. Other ingredients were occlusive agents or astringent solutions (such as alum or natron) which made fertilization much more difficult by contracting the os. Salt, which also figured prominently, is one of the most effective known contraceptives. Even substances which on first reading seem unpromising, like pomegranate pulp or animal dung, turn out to be of some consequence. (The birth control properties of many of the medicines listed in the tables of this chapter can be traced by checking the subject index of Himes, *Medical History of Contraception*.) Yet, even without chemical effect, the mere physical presence of the suppository often provided a more or less effective barrier to fertilization.

From the viewpoint of the historian of medicine, the central importance of the *Hawi* cannot be overemphasized. It quickly became the standard reference work of Arabic medicine, and remained so for centuries. Even in fourteenth-century Spain, at the other end of the Arabic-speaking world, it was still a primary source for medical authors such as Ibn al-Khatib.[20] In contraceptive medicine especially, the vast majority of the prescriptions of later physicians derived ultimately from the *Hawi*.

There was early appreciation of the importance of the *Hawi*, and some puzzlement at the confusion of its arrangement. ‘Ali Ibn ‘Abbas al-Majusi (died 994), the distinguished physician of the generation that followed Razi, devoted a large part of the introduction to his own medical work, *Kamil al-sina‘a*, to a critique of the *Hawi*. He guessed correctly that the book was either a collection of Razi's private notes, or a rough draft of a book meant to represent his life's work, which Razi died before finishing. But Ibn ‘Abbas had no doubt about the scientific value of the *Hawi*:

> Razi mentioned the diagnoses, causes, indications, and cure of every disease according to each and all the ancient and modern physicians, from Hippocrates and Galen to Ishaq Ibn Hunayn, and every physician between them. He left nothing which these physicians had discussed without inclusion in the *Hawi*, to the degree that all the information in all the medical books is collected in this book of his.[21]

But considerations of social history make it difficult to pretend that the *Hawi*, given its confusing arrangement, its bulk and expense, was available beyond the limited circles of distinguished physicians and the libraries of the very rich. Other medical books, more concisely and elegantly written, represent better evidence of wider distribution of medical contraception. We will study five of these books: Razi's own concise *Al-Mansuri*, 'Ali Ibn 'Abbas' *Kamil*, Ibn Sina's *Canon*, Abu al-Hasan al-Tabib's *Khalq al-insan*, and Ibn Jumai''s *Al-Irshad*. All of these books belong to the classical age of Arabic medicine, the period from the ninth to the twelfth century. They are of course direct evidence for the scientific life of the centuries in which they were written, but equally significant is the fact that they remained available and authoritative until the recent past and constitute direct evidence of the available knowledge in the later centuries.

Razi's preference for direct mechanical or chemical means of contraception is confirmed by his treatment of the subject in his *Kitab al-tibb al-Mansuri*, where he did not include any drugs to be taken by mouth, or any magical techniques (Table 2, p. 83).[22] The brief chapter has the title, "On medicines which prevent pregnancy and abort the foetus", and offers six contraceptive prescriptions. Three are female suppositories involving the use of wood tar, rue, and pepper. Two are methods to be used by the man: the first is an ointment of tar on the penis, and the second is a recommendation to avoid simultaneous orgasms: "if the man hastens to ejaculate before the woman reaches her own climax, she will not conceive".

This is one of the very few suggestions, if not the only one, where we can detect the direct influence of biological theory on medical practice. It was not based simply on the idea that the female contributes semen like the male, but on the additional refinement of that idea, the notion that the female, by analogy with the male, also releases her "semen" during orgasm. Thus the assumption that pregnancy could be prevented by separating the two emissions or by completing intercourse before female climax. Although Ibn Sina and Abu al-Hasan al-Tabib adopted this suggestion from Razi, the other later physicians dropped it. We know that experience had taught many to doubt the theoretical basis of this contraceptive technique. For example, Ibn Rushd, who was of course eager to support Aristotle's thesis that women did not contribute semen, argued from direct experience that women became pregnant whether or not they achieved climax:

> Aristotle has argued that a woman can get pregnant without ever experiencing emission. I too have pursued this matter by observation and found it to be true . . . I have also asked women about it, and they tell me the same. That is, they often become pregnant without experiencing pleasure.[23]

No one ever doubted the more common idea, obviously underlying the use of female suppositories and male ointments, that conception can be prevented by destroying the male semen or blocking its passage to the uterus.

There is one last contraceptive method in the *Mansuri*, the suggestion that the woman try and eject the semen by jumping backward violently after intercourse. This notion goes back directly to the famous passage in the Hippocratic treatise *The Nature of the Child*, also very important for Arabic medical attitudes towards abortion:

As a matter of fact I myself have seen an embryo which was aborted after remaining in the womb for six days . . . A kinswoman of mine owned a very valuable danseuse, whom she employed as a prostitute. It was important that this girl should not get pregnant and thereby lose her value. Now this girl had heard the sort of thing women say to each other – that when a woman is going to conceive, the seed remains inside her and does not fall out. She digested this information, and kept a watch. One day she noticed that the seed had not come out again. She told her mistress, and the story came to me. When I heard it, I told her to jump up and down, touching her buttocks with her heels at each leap. After she had done this no more than seven times, there was a noise, and the seed fell out to the ground, and the girl looked at it with great surprise.[24]

Razi had quoted this passage three separate times in the *Hawi*.[25] Both in the *Hawi* and the *Mansuri* he turned the Hippocratic suggestion of violent jumping into a contraceptive technique, probably because Hippocrates had used it to induce abortion in a very early pregnancy (six days). Ibn Sina and al-Tabib also adopted this suggestion from Razi, but the other physicians did not.

The emphasis on female contraceptives, and the reliance on direct physical or chemical means of control, are the basic distinguishing features of classical Arabic contraceptive medicine. ʻAli Ibn ʻAbbas' contraceptive discussion is contained in a short chapter in his *Kamil al-sinaʻa al-tibbiya* (also known as *Kitab al-malaki, Liber Regius*).[26] ʻAli Ibn ʻAbbas was born in Ahwaz in Persia, flourished under the Buwayhid ruler ʻAdud al-Dawla (949–82), and died in 994.[27] His *Kamil*, which he wrote for ʻAdud al-Dawla, and which was apparently his only publication,[28] is one of the most impressive medieval medical works.[29] The chapter on contraception has seven prescriptions: five are female suppositories or tampons, and two are methods to be used by the man (Table 3, p. 83).[30] Of the seven only one (rennet of rabbit) does not appear in the *Hawi*, at least not as a suppository. The other six are either the exact recipes, or combinations of recipes contained in the *Hawi*. Rock salt, which was an abortifacient in the Razi text (used as a suppository), is a contraceptive in the *Kamil* (as an ointment on the penis).[31]

Another short treatment of contraception is by Hibatallah Ibn Jumaiʻ al-Israʼili (died 1198) in his *Kitab al-irshad li-masalih al-anfus wa al-ajsad (Direction for the Improvement of Souls and Bodies)*.[32] An Egyptian Jew, born in Fustat, he became court physician to Saladin, Sultan of Egypt (1171–98). There are seven prescriptions in Ibn Jumaiʻ's text (Table 7, p. 87). Six go back to Razi's *Hawi*.[33] Of the seven, four are suppositories or tampons, two are to be used by the man, and one is to be taken by mouth. The recipe to be taken by mouth, beans on an empty stomach, appears often in the Arabic discussions of contraception. Like some of the magical recipes that we have come across, it is usually preceded by the phrase "it is said", the physicians' way of introducing hearsay material in which they did not necessarily believe (Ibn Jumai' did not attribute any contraceptive qualities to beans when he discussed them in his materia medica).[34]

Ibn Jumai''s discussion of contraceptives is immediately preceded by one on abortifacients (Table 8, p. 87),[35] where he gives twelve prescriptions: four potions, one magical, six suppositories, and one listed under "miscellaneous". All of the prescriptions go back to Razi's *Hawi*.[36]

The matter-of-fact provision of medical contraception by Jewish Arab physicians, whose own religious law strongly prohibited all "destruction of seed", demonstrates the extent to which birth control was an established element in Arabic medicine. Regardless of how they personally may have viewed contraception, it was a subject that was required by the conventions of their art as physicians, and the expectations of the dominant culture that surrounded them. Maimonides, who followed Ibn Jumai' as court physician (to al-Malik al-Afdal, Saladin's son and successor as Sultan of Egypt), illustrates the case better. It was Maimonides who, in his codification of the Jewish law, condemned absolutely all destruction of seed. Yet, attached to the regimen of health which he prepared for his monarch was this advice:

> Contraceptives [to be used] before intercourse. The things that prevent conception are (1) from the man's side anointing [the penis] with juice of onion, wood tar, or gall-bladder of chicken, and (2) from the woman's side inserting suppositories with juice of peppermint, or pennyroyal, or the seeds of leek after purity.[37]

A much longer treatment of birth control than that of Ibn 'Abbas or Ibn Jumai' is by the Baghdad physician Abu al-Hasan al-Tabib (1044–1101) in his *Kitab khalq al-insan (The Creation of Man)*. Abu al-Hasan al-Tabib was court physician to the Abbasid caliph Muqtadi (1075–94).[38] *The Creation of Man* is a fascinating medical treatise which deals with the single subject of the birth, growth, and decay of man in fifty chapters, the last ten of which deal with psychology. The first forty chapters deal exclusively with the processes of reproduction, gestation, parturition, growth, and decay. There is a long chapter on birth control, with twenty-nine prescriptions for contraception and fifty prescriptions for abortion.[39] Of the twenty-nine contraceptive prescriptions in *The Creation of Man* twelve are suppositories or tampons, eight are potions, five are male techniques, and four are "miscellaneous". We find again that the majority of the techniques already existed in the *Hawi* text.[40] To be specific, twenty-five of twenty-eight recipes had been listed by Razi, twenty-four in the *Hawi* alone, and one in the *Mansuri*.[41] Two other suggestions were taken directly from Ibn Sina (avoiding the form of coitus favouring conception, and quick separation of the partners). There is only one recipe, anointing the penis with juice of watermint, which was not traceable to earlier authorities.[42]

The central medical document of pre-modern times was Ibn Sina's *Canon*.[43] More influential and widely used than any other medical textbook, the *Canon* dominated Middle Eastern medicine between the eleventh and nineteenth centuries, and European medicine until the seventeenth century.[44] Abu 'Ali al-Husain Ibn Sina (980–1037 (Avicenna)) was born near Bukhara and died at the age of fifty-eight in Hamadhan. He became the best known scientist of the Islamic world and the most influential philosopher and physician of the Middle Ages. His *Kitab al-qanun fi al-tibb (Canon)* alone is good testimony to the availability of birth control information throughout pre-modern times. It has chapters on contraception and abortion, and in its materia medica (Book 2), about one out of ten of all the simple drugs listed had some abortifacient or contraceptive application (the majority of these drugs are the same ones that we have come across in the *Hawi*).[45]

Ibn Sina's discussion of contraception is contained in the third book of the *Canon*,[46] where he provides twenty different contraceptive prescriptions (Table 4, p. 84). Ten are suppositories or tampons. Four are male techniques. Five are "miscellaneous". There is only one prescription to be taken by mouth, and there are no magical techniques whatsoever. Of the twenty prescriptions in the *Canon*, seventeen existed in the *Hawi*.[47] The only two prescriptions which are completely new are a suppository made of the leaves of bindweed, and the recommendation to avoid the form of coitus which favours conception.[48]

The *Canon* is a document of the medieval culture of Europe as well as of the Middle East, but it does not follow from this fact that the contraceptive information that was available to the two societies in their scientific and popular literatures was of equal value or diffusion. The Latin version of the *Canon* contains Ibn Sina's original birth control material, and shows no sign of censorship. (In contrast, the medieval Hebrew translation omitted the chapter on contraception.)[49] But in Europe the learned, mostly Churchmen, who read Ibn Sina and based their works on the *Canon*, managed in their own writings to mask his birth control information. When the pre-modern Europeans wrote about contraception, they invariably used the euphemism "poisons of sterility", that is, herbal potions. When they said that Ibn Sina in the *Canon* had a chapter on "poisons of sterility", the medieval Europeans suppressed his techniques quite effectively[50] (Ibn Sina provided twenty specific prescriptions, mostly intra-vaginal suppositories and tampons, and only one potion). The nearly exclusive preference for potions and magical amulets in Church references to birth control may have had something to do with the fact that these means were employed at a decent distance from the sexual organs. In any case, the medieval European writers who used Ibn Sina were unwilling to pass on his specific prescriptions. Albert the Great is a case in point. While Ibn Sina provided specific contraceptives, Albert generalized from them a theory of contraception. Noonan has argued that it could have been possible to deduce from Albert's general notions some practical contraceptives.[51] No such effort was required from a reader of Ibn Sina or any other Arabic-writing physician, druggist, or jurist.

Table 9 (p. 88) reviews only the contraceptive, and not the abortifacient, prescriptions. Over ninety per cent of the recipes mentioned by the physicians who followed Razi, at least the ones we have considered, were traced one by one back to him. One is reminded of Ibn 'Abbas' complaint that Razi had left nothing without inclusion in the *Hawi*. The ratio of direct means (suppositories, male techniques, and "miscellaneous" methods) to indirect means (potions and magical recipes) is better than four to one. The shorter the chapter, the less likely it was to include potions or magical recipes. Razi's *Mansuri* (Table 2, p. 83) and Ibn 'Abbas' *Kamil* (Table 3, p. 83) had none. Ibn Jumai''s *Irshad* had only one potion (Table 7, p. 87). Ibn Sina's chapter in the *Canon* was much longer, but nevertheless it had only one potion (Table 4, p. 84). Al-Tabib's direct means of contraception followed very closely those of Ibn Sina, but he added potions from the general pool of recipes collected by Razi in the *Hawi*. When they had to list a few, the physicians elected to list the more direct methods. Less effective methods and hearsay were dropped.

In *Contraception*, John Noonan was intrigued by the fact that Greco-Roman physicians tended to omit coitus interruptus from their discussions of contraception: "Was this method too evident to need description or too unacceptable to be recommended?"[52] Because Arabic-writing physicians rarely discussed coitus interruptus I was intrigued also. It is not necessary to interpret the ancient and medieval medical silence to mean that the physicians disapproved of withdrawal as a birth control method, or that they were ignorant of it. In the case of the medieval physicians of the Middle East, it is clear that they lived in a society that did not lack interest in or information about coitus interruptus. A more reasonable interpretation is that this male method of contraception did not present a medical problem. The Middle Eastern physicians concentrated instead on *female* contraceptives, the means of control which were less obvious or more problematic. As a result of their effort, Arabic medicine became the primary repository of female contraceptive experience before modern times.

Medical indications: contraception and abortion as birth control

We have paid more attention to contraception than to abortion primarily because modern scholarship has not seriously contested the practice of abortion in pre-modern society.[53] (However, the Tables include both contraceptive and abortifacient information.) Only pre-modern contraception has been subjected to serious doubt. But classical Arabic medicine paid equal attention to abortion and, a significant point, used exactly the same medical reasons to justify both. The medical argument for birth control was usually presented as a brief statement at the beginning of chapters that otherwise contained only methods and prescriptions. The physicians advanced two principal reasons for birth control: contraception or abortion were indicated when the woman was "young", or when they suspected a disease or malfunction of the uterus. All the indications were purely medical – the Islamic religious permission of contraception had left the physicians free to mention only the reasons proper to their profession.

Medieval Middle Eastern physicians used the same medical indications for the prevention of pregnancy and the prevention of birth. They regarded both contraception and abortion as "birth control". Because of its intrinsic value as representative of the best in Arabic medicine, Ibn Sina's introduction to his chapter on abortion is worth quoting at some length:

> At times it may be necessary to induce abortion; that is, when the pregnant woman is young and small and it is feared that childbirth would cause her death, or when she suffers from a disease of the uterus or when a fleshy growth in the uterus makes it very difficult for the foetus to emerge. Also when the foetus dies in the womb of the woman. Know that when labour continues for four days it means that the foetus is already dead. Therefore care for the life of the mother, and not for the life of the foetus. As for the foetus, try and remove it [Ibn Sina gives a detailed procedure for this in the form of instructions to the midwife].
>
> Abortion may be performed by movements, or by medicines. Medicines work by killing the foetus and causing the menses to flow . . . Movements include phlebotomy, starvation, [bodily] exercise, frequent jumping, carrying of heavy loads, provocation of vomiting, and sneezing.
>
> A good procedure is to insert in the *os uteri* a rolled piece of paper, a feather, or a stick cut to the size of a feather made of saltwort, rue, cyclamen, or male fern. This will definitely work, especially if it is smeared with an abortifacient medicine such as tar, the water of colocynth pulp, or some other abortifacient medicine . . .[54]

The medical indications in this passage are essentially the same ones which Ibn Sina used to justify contraception:

> *(Chapter on the prevention of pregnancy)* The physician may be obliged to prevent pregnancy in a young woman in fear of her death in childbirth; or in a woman who suffers from a disease of the uterus; or in a woman whose bladder is weak. In the latter case the weight of the foetus may rupture the bladder, resulting in incontinence of urine lasting all her life.[55]

The same core indications were used by Razi to justify abortion, by Ibn ʿAbbas to justify contraception, and by Ibn Jumaiʿ to justify abortion. Abu al-Hasan al-Tabib elegantly summed up the Arabic medical rationale for birth control. He treated contraception and abortion together in the same chapter, used the same medical indications for both, attributed them explicitly to Hippocrates, and clarified for us what the medieval physicians meant by a "young" woman (a woman under fifteen):

On medicines which abort the foetus before it grows [big] and medicines which prevent conception. The physician needs knowledge of these medicines which prevent pregnancy to use in the case of a woman who becomes pregnant before reaching the age of fifteen. In her case the uterus is too small. It will be difficult for her to give birth, and if she does, it will be under great duress. This is the reason Hippocrates demands the use of abortive drugs before childbirth. So if the pregnant woman was a virgin, prematurely deflowered while still of tender age, she would surely die during childbirth if the foetus was not aborted early in her pregnancy.

Abortive medicines may also be used in the cases of women who are weak of power and sickly of body. In their cases childbirth should be feared. They are also to be used in the cases of women whose uterus or bladder is diseased, for when the child is born it causes weakness of the bladder and incontinence of urine, and as a result the woman will not be able to hold her urine for the rest of her days.[56]

This was the standard view in Arabic medicine which, however, was not universally held by all physicians. 'Ali Ibn 'Abbas represented a group of more conservative physicians, among whom we also find Ibn Hubal (1122–1213), who clearly wished to place restrictions on medical birth control. This is how Ibn 'Abbas began his discussion:

As to medicines which prevent conception, although they should not be mentioned to prevent their use by women in whom there is no good, it is necessary sometimes to prescribe them to those women who have a small uterus, or those who have a disease which, in the case of pregnancy, may cause the woman death in childbirth. Except for women in such predicaments, the physician should not prescribe [these] medicines. Also, he should not prescribe medicines which cause the menses to flow, or medicines which expel the dead foetus, except to women he can trust, because all these medicines kill the foetus and expel it.[57]

Ibn Hubal was even more careful, and wanted to keep birth control medicines under strict medical control:

Contraceptive and abortive medicines should not be mentioned to the common people, but ought to remain restricted to the circles of physicians (*bayna al-atibba'*) for them to use in certain necessary cases [essentially the same cases as those of Ibn 'Abbas].[58]

There is no need to trace this medical conservatism to any Islamic religious source, for, excepting the minority Malikis, many of the jurists were more tolerant of abortion than those physicians. All the jurists, of course, permitted contraception. Rather, the conservative physicians reflected the classical medical attitude which, beginning with Hippocrates and the Oath, had disapproved of abortion. The Hippocratic Oath and its strong condemnation of abortion adorned the introduction to Ibn 'Abbas' *Kamil*.[59] It is true that the Oath said nothing about contraception, but since medieval physicians believed that many of the same medicines could both prevent pregnancy and induce abortion, Ibn ‘Abbas applied his restrictions to both.

But an even stronger influence on the medieval physicians from within the medical tradition itself was the example from *The Nature of the Child*, which had Hippocrates personally giving instructions for abortion (p. 65 above). In addition, Razi, the physicians' physician, had attributed to Hippocrates directly his basic medical indication for abortion:

[Hippocrates] said: Abortive medicines should be used before childbirth if the pregnant woman was a maiden who was prematurely deflowered and became pregnant while of tender age. Abortion of the foetus should be performed before it grows big, otherwise the pregnant woman will die. Any woman the condition of whose *os uteri* was such [that is, small] will die if the foetus were to reach full growth.[60]

These words from the *Hawi*, the fountainhead of Arabic contraceptive medicine, reverberated through all the Arabic medical discussions of birth control. Some physicians, such as Ibn Jumai‘, left the door wide open: "Abortive medicines are to be used when needed; that is, in cases where the pregnant woman is young, or suffers from a disease of the uterus, or there is some other reason."[61] The conservative physicians wished to confine birth control to cases of clear medical necessity.

In a society whose religious law considered birth control licit for the widest range of reasons, is it possible that the argument for restriction by Ibn ‘Abbas and Ibn Hubal constituted censorious, albeit indirect, criticism of the more flexible religious and social standard? Or is there more here than meets the eye? ‘Ali Ibn Nasr al-Katib, the tenth-century lay birth control expert, defined birth control from a wider perspective than that of medicine alone, and in a manner that sheds important light on our problem. He said that "the prevention of pregnancy among women can be achieved in two ways". The first, namely withdrawal, depends on her sex partner, and the second is by means of medicines.[62] The physicians concentrated fully on the second, that is, on medicines mainly for female use, and this was the essential framework of all Arabic medical discussion of birth control. The physicians also excluded withdrawal, the single most important means of control in their time, from their discussions. Withdrawal, and this is the critical point, depended on male volition. Is it possible that the argument of the conservative physicians was not directed at birth control as such (in which male-controlled withdrawal was central), but really had to do with restricting female practice, so that women could not resort to contraception or abortion independently of their men? After all, Ibn ‘Abbas was reluctant to mention birth control medicines because he feared their use by "women in whom there is no good", and strongly advised the physician not to prescribe them except to "women he could trust".

Materia medica

We have already come across pharmacological texts in our reference to Book 2 of the *Canon*, Ibn Sina's own materia medica, where nearly ten per cent of all his medicines had some birth control use.[63] Ibn Jumai''s *Irshad* also devoted considerable attention to medicines, simple and compound.[64] Materia medica were an important part of all medical treatises. Other books on materia medica stand by themselves, written specifically for the use of druggists.[65] The title of an important pharmacopoeia of the thirteenth century was *Manual for the [Drug] Store*, advertising clearly the purpose of these books.[66]

There were drugstores in most cities, towns, and urban centres of the medieval Middle East. It is very likely that only the upper classes consulted the physicians, and the poor must have relied heavily on advice from the druggists.[67] Where there were no drugstores, people must still have been able to buy their drugs from roving peddlers.[68] Ideally, a drugstore's inventory would have included all the drugs mentioned in any of the standard books on materia medica. However, the typical drugstore must have carried a much smaller number of medicines, and the roving peddlers a smaller number still.

We possess some information on the supply of drugs for the hospital in Tabriz in the first part of the fourteenth century. The information is contained in a unique Persian manuscript, a collection of about fifty letters by the physician Rashid al-Din Fadl Allah.[69] Letter no. 18 asked the addressee to supply a long list of medicinal oils: six different kinds of oil from Shiraz, Persia; seven from Basra, Iraq; six from Asia Minor; three from Syria; and three from Hilla, Iraq. The oils included those of violet, jasmine, narcissus, rose, myrtle, orange blossom, absinthe, mastic, camomile, castor oil, and the oil of scorpions.[70] Another letter (no. 21), addressed to an agent in Asia Minor, requested large quantities (50–100 maunds) of six drugs: anise seeds, agaric, mastic, lavender, dodder, and wormwood. Letter no. 42 reported the appointment of a new director to reorganize the hospital "with more regard to the welfare of patients and the supply of necessary drugs and medicaments".[71]

The supply of drugs clearly was not limited to what could be produced locally. It seems that any of the drugs mentioned in materia medica could have been made available. Many of the medicines which were not native to the heartland of the Middle East were imported from the Far East, Europe, or Africa.[72] Drugs – that is, herbs, spices and chemicals – were a large part of the goods which the big merchants handled.[73] In addition to the "international" merchants who dealt in nearly any kind of commodity, there were those who specialized in a particular product. Bynames indicate that many were distributors of fennel, lupine, sesame, or seeds in general; others were specialists in ambergris, camphor, odoriferous woods, rhubarb, saffron, antimony, etc.[74]

The druggists as well as the physicians used as their major source of information a third type of materia medica literature, that is, works which belonged to the herbalistic tradition. Medieval Arab herbalists added significantly to the sum of naturalist knowledge of the Greek tradition, and surpassed by far their European counterparts. The most renowned of the medieval treatises on the subject is the *Treatise on Simples* of Ibn al-Baitar (according to Sarton "the greatest of Islam and the Middle Ages").[75]

'Abd Allah Ibn Ahmad Ibn al-Baitar al-Maliqi (1197–1248) was born in Malaga, Spain, and left for the Arab East about 1220.[76] After visiting North Africa, Asia Minor and Syria, he settled in Egypt where he was appointed chief herbalist to the Ayyubid Sultan al-Malik al-Kamil. He later moved to Damascus, where he died in 1248. The two main works of Ibn al-Baitar are: (1) *Al-mughni fi al-adwiya al-mufrada*, which is still unpublished; and (2) *Al-Jami' li-mufradat al-adwiya wa al-aghdhiya (Treatise on Simples)*.[77] The *Treatise* contains some 1,400 drugs listed in alphabetical order. These are mostly vegetable, although many mineral and animal substances are also included. The book is based on Ibn al-Baitar's own observations and on the work of some 150 earlier authorities including Dioscorides, Galen, Razi, and Ibn Sina. Of the 1,400 entries about 300 are novelties.[78]

In the *Medical History of Contraception* Himes devoted considerable space to Ibn al-Baitar. He used the French translation of the *Treatise* and looked for specifically contraceptive recipes. He found twenty such recipes, eleven of which were potions, four were magical, and only five were suppositories. The overwhelming preponderence of "irrational" means (potions and magic) over "rational" means (suppositories), and the nature of the magical recipes (urinating on urine of wolf, carrying a child's tooth, seed of patience wrapped in linen cloth and worn on the left arm, etc.) convinced Himes that he was witnessing in Ibn al-Baitar "the decline of Islamic contraceptive medicine". These charms were a far cry from the prescriptions in the medical texts of Ibn Sina, Ibn 'Abbas, and the other early physicians.[79]

The decline was confirmed conclusively for Himes and for the scholar who was the source of most of his information about the Arabic medical sciences, Dr Max Meyerhof, by the magical charms of the *Tadhkirat (The Memorial)* of Dawud al-Antaki (died 1599):

> In place of the tampons and pessaries of the earlier writers, this author relies on magical words, letters, and numbers. If Ibn al-Baitar's *Treatise* represents decline in its initial stages, the *Kitab al-Tadhkira* exhibits Islamic contraceptive medicine at its lowest ebb.[80]

A closer look at the works of Ibn al-Baitar and Antaki will show that this interpretation is highly misleading.

In so far as Ibn al-Baitar is concerned, Himes confused Arabic medical literature and Arabic materia medica. Materia medica was a distinct literature which, from its beginnings in the ancient Near East and Greece, always contained the popular lore about medicines and plants. The writings of Ibn al-Baitar were not different at all in this regard from the writings of Dioscorides, who was one of his primary sources in any case.[81] The "superstitions" of Ibn al-Baitar were present all along in the culture, and do not represent a "later" decline from the heights of Razi and Ibn Sina.

In the case of Dawud al-Antaki's *Memorial*, the Himes–Meyerhof interpretation was based on a superficial study of the book. They had located a group of references to contraception, in volume 3 of the printed edition, consisting of preventive measures exclusively in the form of magical words, letters, and numbers. All the printed editions of the book are similar in that they consist of three volumes (all are reprints of the original Bulaq publication).[82] These volumes, however, contain three different books:

1. Volumes 1 and 2 contain Antaki's *Tadhkirat (The Memorial)*.
2. The margins of volumes 1, 2, and 3 contain another book by Antaki, a shorter medical treatise titled *Al-Nuzha al-mubhija.*
3. Volume 3 contains a separate work, not by Antaki himself, but by one of his students. It has the title *Dhayl al-tadhkirat (Appendix to the Memorial)*.

The text which Himes used is from this last work.

In the first place then, the text which Himes used was not by Antaki himself, even though he could have conceivably written something like it – but more about this below. Secondly, the three volumes together contain *four* separate discussions of contraception. Antaki's own discussion in the *Tadhkirat* is in volume 2. His contraceptive prescriptions make his chapter similar to earlier texts, while they exhibit the influence of both the medical and popular traditions (which is studied in Chapter 5). The prescriptions include twelve potions (four of these are recommended for use as suppositories as well); five magical amulets (three to be used by mouth as well); five suppositories and tampons; and instead of specific male ointments, Antaki gave a general statement of the theory behind them and the type of medicine to be used: "Know that oils, salts, and *yatu'at* [the corrosive, irritating milky juice of plants of the genus *Euphorbia*] when used as an ointment on the penis during intercourse prevent semen from impregnating."

What set Antaki's treatment apart from the earlier medical texts were his indications. He mentioned two reasons for contraception. The first was to ensure that a new pregnancy did not follow too soon the birth of a child; and the second was to prevent conception when the man did not consider the woman "fit" enough to bear him children. These indications were more personal and social than medical, and therefore much closer to the kinds of indications which the jurists had used in their own discussions of birth control.[83]

Antaki treated contraception again in his second work, *Al-Nuzha*, where he listed six potions, five amulets, and six suppositories and tampons.[84] His student's chapter on contraception in the *Appendix to the Memorial* was basically a copy of the chapter from the *Nuzha* which, however, omits two of the potions and two of the suppositories.[85] This treatment, which Himes missed, is the only one in volume 3 which has the title "Contraceptives". The passage which Himes used is by this same anonymous author, in the same volume, but it occurs in the treatment of a completely different subject: *ruqan*, magical charms. No wonder the passage included magical means exclusively.

Antaki and his students were men of the sixteenth century who believed in the efficacy of magic, and in this they were not different from the majority of people in the sixteenth century everywhere. The chapter on magical charms in the *Appendix* included instructions for the cure of a number of medical conditions, as well as the remedy of some of the bothersome problems of daily living.[86] These conditions and problems included headaches, haemorrhaging, the endless crying of infants, eye problems, toothaches, paralysis, insomnia, nightmares, love-sickness, difficulty in urinating, difficult childbirth. The chapter also offered charms for ridding the house of ants, mice, flies, and other "harmful insects". For lovers of horse-racing it gave a charm to improve their luck. The fact that contraception figured in this list is important, but its importance is very different from what Himes–Meyerhof took it to be. Clearly some medieval people resorted to magic for the solution of some of their problems. The more interesting question is why the prevention of pregnancy should have merited mention in such a list?

Conclusion

This chapter on the medical tradition has not been the story of scientific progress in medical contraception. Rather, the achievements of medieval medicine were made early and remained standard for a thousand years. During that time Arabic medicine considered birth control a legitimate medical responsibility. When Middle Eastern birth control evidence as a whole is surveyed, medical attention to birth control does not surprise, for jurisprudence and popular literature paid equal, if not more, attention to the subject. But medicine in European societies, for reasons peculiar to them, avoided birth control, even though Europe shared the same Greco-Arabic medical tradition. This medical tradition was, of course, the immediate background from which modern medicine developed. The modern emergence of birth control in the nineteenth and twentieth centuries as a subject of public, and later medical, attention in the West gives the impression of a new departure, an innovation. In the context of European culture this was perhaps the case. In the context of the history of medicine, the story is different. Medical birth control was an integral part of Europe's medical heritage which for centuries it had chosen to neglect.

Our primary task has been to establish the main features of Arabic contraceptive medicine: its emphasis on female contraceptives, its reliance on direct mechanical and chemical means of control, its justification of contraception and abortion together by the same medical reasons. These features of Arabic contraceptive medicine will stand in sharper relief after we study the popular tradition. At that point the picture will be more complete, and we will be in a better position to deal with the texts from the later Middle Ages which, when compared out of context with the earlier classical writings, have given rise to mistaken notions of "decline".

Although the medieval physicians gave extraordinary attention to birth control techniques, the fact remains that the most significant method before the twentieth century was coitus interruptus, and it was Islamic jurisprudence, and not medicine, which contained detailed information on this technique (Chapter 1, pp. 19–22 and note 33). While the pre-modern Arabic medical discussions of contraception were superior to the pre-modern European, in certain respects they were not as good as those in jurisprudence, and jurisprudence was better by virtue of its sharp focus on coitus interruptus. It is not difficult to say that the jurists, dealing as they did with the consequences of actual practice (for example, the problem of disowning the children born despite contraceptive practice), knew as much about contraception as did the physicians. The jurists were not writing technical medical treatises; their careful and detailed knowledge of withdrawal reflected common and current information. Islamic jurisprudence is at once our primary guide to religious and social attitudes, and an indispensable source for the pre-modern means of control.

Table 1. *Razi,* Kitab al-Hawi*: contraceptive and abortifacient methods*

A Means to be taken by the mouth	B Magical means	C Suppositories and tampons	D Techniques used by the man	E Miscellaneous techniques
Razi				
1. juice of cyclamen (5)†	1. cyclamen root around neck or stepping over cyclamen (21)	1. round aristoloch, spurge, cyclamen, cardamom and aloe (2)	1. juice of onion smeared on penis (4)	1. juice of cyclamen smeared on stomach (5)
2. broth of wallflower (6)		2. ammonia, and dorema, mixed with water. Kept overnight with legs raised (3)		2. sitting in broth of wallflower (6)
3. male fern (8)		3. juice of onion (4)		3. fumigation with cardamom (14)
4. cinnamon with myrrh (15)		4. juice of cyclamen (5)		4. fumigation with cyclamen (21)
5. leaves of weeping-willow (17)		5. broth of wallflower with honey (6)		5. smelling scent of luffa plant (22)
6. roots of cyclamen (21)		6. juice of squirting cucumber (9)		*6. "spoiling" testicles with poison hemlock (28)
7. luffa seed with water and vinegar (22)		7. colocynth (10)		
8. wild rue seeds (26)		8. iris with honey (13)		
		9. cinnamon with myrrh (15)		
		10. balm oil (16)		
		*11. oil of flower of cabbage, after coitus (18)		
		*12. pepper, after coitus (19)		
		13. lion's leaf (20)		
		14. root of cyclamen (21)		
		15. root of luffa (22)		
		16. centaury (23)		
		*17. juice of peppermint, before coitus (24)		
		*18. leaves of pennyroyal (25)		
		19. wild rue (26)		
		20. cyclamen, smeared and injected (29)		
		21. rock salt (30)		
		*22. dill in mouth of uterus, before or during coitus (31)		
		23. juice or broth of fresh colocynth (32)		

* An asterisk indicates a specifically contraceptive (rather than abortifacient) recipe.
† Numbers in brackets refer to the location of the recipe in Musallam "Sex and Society in Islam" (Ph.D. dissertation, Harvard University, 1973).

Table 1 (*cont.*)

A Means to be taken by the mouth	B Magical means	C Suppositories and tampons	D Techniques used by the man	E Miscellaneous techniques
Dioscorides				
9. opopanax with honey (33) 10. *Ferula scowitziana* in honey drink (34) 11. galbanum plant (35) 12. savin (37) 13. candy-carrot and myrrh (40) 14. walnut leaves, after menses (42) 15. juice of pennyroyal (48) 16. bark of the root of laurel (51) *17. leaves of weeping willow (52) 18. broth and root of wall flower (53)		24. opopanax with honey (33) 25. galbanum plant as fumigation, then inserted (35) *26. *fami* seeds with honey, before coitus (36) 27. savin (37) 28. roots of yellow gentian (38) 29. roots of wild carrot (39) 30. candy carrot with myrrh (40) 31. spiny cytisus (41) 32. salt (43) *33. sodium carbonate, after coitus (44) *34. cabbage seeds, after menses (45) 35. madder (47) 36. leaves and juice of pennyroyal (48) 37. juice of squirting cucumber (50) 38. black hellebore (54)		7. galbanum plant, fumigation with, then intravaginal insertion (35) 8. fumigation with savin (37) 9. fumigation with cardamom (49)
Ibn Masawayh				
		*39. scammony, colocynth pulp, white bryony, iron-dross, and cabbage seeds mixed with tar. After menses (55) *40. wool impregnated with leaves and fruit in water of weeping willow, after menses (56), and keep (71) *41. wool impregnated with seeds of cabbage, watercress, tar and water of water mint, after menses (57)		

Table I (*cont.*)

A Means to be taken by the mouth	B Magical means	C Suppositories and tampons	D Techniques used by the man	E Miscellaneous techniques
Ibn Masawayh				
19. seeds and leaves of bean clover with wine (59) 20. roots of white bryony (66)		*42. pepper, after coitus (58), (63), (67), (68) *43. cabbage seeds, after coitus (61) *44. elephant dung (62), (70) 45. saltwort, black-cumin, pellitory of Spain, rue, horehound, spurge, myrrh and galbanum plant in white wool (64) *47. elephant dung with henbane (69) *48. seeds of cabbage, and watercress with tar in water of pennyroyal (72) *49. colocynth pulp, scammony, white bryony, black mustard, iron-dross, cabbage, and cabbage seeds with tar. For many days after menses (73)		10. "sitting" in broth of white bryony (66)
Hippocrates				
				*11. jumping and leaping backward (74), (75), (76) 12. phlebotomy causes abortion (77)
Galen				
21. cardamom (78) 22. broth of lupine with myrrh and rue (80) 23. watermint in honey drink (82) 24. broth of great centaury, or centaury (86)		50. seeds of headed thyme (81) 51. water mint (82) *52. dittany of Crete, after coitus (83) *53. camphor with rose water (84) 54. tar (85), (106)	*2. dittany of crete smeared on penis (83) *3. tar smeared on penis during coitus (85), (106)	

Table 1 (*cont.*)

A Means to be taken by the mouth	B Magical means	C Suppositories and tampons	D Techniques used by the man	E Miscellaneous techniques
Galen				
25. fleawort (87) 26. leaves of weeping-willow (89) 27. verdigris (91) 28. dittany of Crete (93) 29. *Ferula scowitziana* with *adrumali* (97) 30. saltwort (100) 31. cardamom (101)	2. wearing or stepping on cyclamen (102) *3. cyclamen tied to neck or arm (102)	55. fleawort (87) 56. flase myrrh gagal (92) 57. dittany of Crete (93) *58. juice of peppermint, during coitus (94) 59. musk rose (95) 60. scammony in piece of wool (96) 61. cyclamen juice in wool (102) 62. juice of squirting cucumber (103) 63. roots of great centaury (104) 64. juice of centaury (105) 65. hellebore (107) 66. christmas rose (108)		13. fumigation with false myrrh gagal (92) 14. fumigation with dittany of Crete (93) 15. cyclamen juice smeared on stomach and side (102)
Ancient medicine				
*32. beans on empty stomach for 76 days (109) 33. water of mugwort (111)	4. bundle of safflower tied to thigh (112)	*67. elephant dung (110) 68. stick of rue (113)		16. smearing navel with gall-bladder of cow (113)
Sarabion				
		69. hellebore, opopanax and ox-gall (114) 70. juice of squirting cucumber with ox-gall (116)		17. fumigation with galbanum plant and sulphur kneaded with ox-gall (115)
Masarjawayh				
34. watercress (117)		71. watercress (117)		
Qalhaman				
				18. fumigation with Arabian costus in a pericarp (119)

Table 1 (*cont.*)

A Means to be taken by the mouth	B Magical means	C Suppositories and tampons	D Techniques used by the man	E Miscellaneous techniques
Rufus				
				19. swings (or seesaws) cause abortion (120)
Bulus				
35. muskrose (121)				
Masih				
		*72. honey and tar, after coitus (126) *73. balm oil, after coitus (127) *74. white lead, after coitus (128) *75. "something wet", after coitus (129) *76. pulp of pomegranates, after coitus (130)		*20. sneezing, after coitus (124) *21. smearing front parts with . . . (125)
Pedigorus				
*36. rennet (132)				
Ibn Dawud				
		77. roots of alexanders (134)		22. fumigation with sulphur (133)
Ishaq				
*37. water of sweet basil (137)		*78. water of rue and dittany of Crete, tar, and savin (136) *79. smearing uterus and penis with balm oil (138) *80. tampon with balm oil, before coitus (139)	*4. smearing penis and uterus with balm oil (138)	*23. water of rue and dittany of Crete, tar, and savin smeared on stomach and back plus intravaginal insertion and drinking water of sweet basil (137), (136)
Anonymous				
*38. mulberry rind, after menstruation (141) *39. fruit of weeping willow, after menses (142)		81. powder of darnel and water of cabbage (140) *82. flowers of cabbage, after menstruation (143)		

Table 1 (*cont.*)

A Means to be taken by the mouth	B Magical means	C Suppositories and tampons	D Techniques used by the man	E Miscellaneous techniques
Kamal *40. water of leaves and the fruit of weeping willow		*83. flowers and seeds of cabbage, after menses (144)		
Yahudi 41. rue for 24 days with hot water (146) 42. juice of rue (147) 43. juice of sesame (148) 44. broth of red beans (149)				
Athorsufs *45. pulp of dog's fennel in white drink after menses (150)				*24. weeping, before coitus (151) *25. fumigation with hoof of donkey (152)

Note:

The following medicines were mentioned in the text without indication of the method of application:

1. asafetida (1) [Razi]
2. German iris (7), (122) [Razi, Bulus]
3. myrrh (11) [Razi]
4. spikes of celandine (12) [Razi]
5. wallflower (27) [Razi]
6. juice of cyclamen (46) [Dioscorides]
7. Macedonian parsley, *kamashir* (60) [Ibn Masawayh]
8. *rue (65), *(99) [Ibn Masawayh, Galen]
9. savin (79), (88) [Galen]
10. colocynth (90) [Galen]
11. roots and seeds of French hartwort (98) [Galen]
12. water of sesame seeds (118) [Masarjawayh]
13. cinnamon (123) [Mihraris]
14. marigold (135) [Ibn Dawud]
15. The method of application of the following recipe is not completely clear; it is probable however that it was to be taken by mouth: birthwort, yellow gentian, seeds of laurel, myrrh, Arabian costus, cinnamon, madder, juice of absinthe, cardamom, pepper, and dittany of Crete with rue. (With intra-vaginal insertion of a stick of rue and smearing of the belly with the gall-bladder of a cow.) (113) [Ancient Medicine]

Table 2. *Razi,* Kitab al-tibb al-Mansuri*: contraceptive and abortifacient methods*

A Means to be taken by the mouth	B Magical means	C Suppositories and tampons	D Techniques used by the man	E Miscellaneous techniques
		*1. tar, after coitus (1)	*1. tar smeared on penis, before coitus (1)	*1. jumping backward (woman after coitus) (4)
		*2. juice of rue (2)	*2. quick male ejaculation before female orgasm (5)	
		*3. pepper, after coitus (3) 4. tar (6) 5. rue (7) 6. pulp of colocynth (8) 7. lion's leaf (9)		

* An asterisk indicates a specifically contraceptive (rather than abortifacient) recipe.
† Numbers in brackets refer to the location of the recipe in Musallam, "Sex and Society in Islam" (Ph.D. dissertation, Harvard University, 1973).

Table 3. *'Ali Ibn 'Abbas,* Kamil al-sina'a*: contraceptive methods*

A Means to be taken by the mouth	B Magical means	C Suppositories and tampons	D Techniques used by the man	E Miscellaneous techniques
		1. rock salt, during coitus (1)* 2. flowers and seed of cabbage, and juice of rue, during coitus; or after coitus (4) 3. rennet of rabbit (5) 4. leaves of weeping-willow (6) 5. fruit of weeping-willow (7)	1. anointing penis with rock salt (2) 2. or tar (3)	

* Numbers in brackets refer to the location of the recipe in Musallam, "Sex and Society in Islam" (Ph.D. dissertation, Harvard University, 1973).

Table 4. *Abu 'Ali Ibn Sina,* Qanun: *contraceptive methods*

A Means to be taken by the mouth	B Magical means	C Suppositories and tampons	D Techniques used by the man	E Miscellaneous techniques
1. water of sweet-basil (18)*		1. tar, before and after coitus (6) 2. pulp of pomegranates with alum, before and after coitus (9) 3. flowers and seeds of cabbage, after menses, or before and after coitus (10) 4. flowers and seeds of cabbage with tar or the juice of pennyroyal or its broth, before and after coitus (11) 5. leaves of weeping willow in a flock of wool, after purity (12) 6. leaves of weeping willow in wool dipped in water of weeping willow leaves, after purity (13) 7. pulp of colocynth, white-bryony, iron-dross, sulphur, scammony, and cabbage seeds with tar (14) 8. pepper, after coitus (15) 9. elephant dung (16) 10. leaves of bindweed, after purity (20)	1. avoiding simultaneous orgasms (2–3) 2. smear tar on penis (7) 3. or balm oil and white lead (8) 4. sesame oil, before coitus (19)	1. woman avoiding form of coition favouring conception (1) 2. avoiding simultaneous orgasms (2) 3. jumping backward (4) 4. sneezing (5) 5. fumigation with elephant dung (17)

* Numbers in brackets refer to the location of the recipe in Musallam, "Sex and Society in Islam" (Ph.D. dissertation, Harvard University, 1973).

Table 5. *Abu al-Hasan al-Tabib,* The Creation of Man*: contraceptive methods*

A Means to be taken by the mouth	B Magical means	C Suppositories and tampons	D Techniques used by the man	E Miscellaneous techniques
1. weeping willow leaves and fruit (10), (20), (22)*		1. juice of watermint, after coitus (5)	1. avoiding simultaneous orgasms (2)	1. woman avoiding form of coitus favouring conception. Safe period? (1)
2. beans on empty stomach for 40 days (13)		2. camphor with rose water in a cotton (6)	2. juice of watermint at coitus (5)	2. avoiding simultaneous orgasms (2)
3. water of sweet basil (14)		3. leaves of weeping willow in wool soaked in water of weeping willow, after menstruation (10)	3. tar during coitus (7)	3. bodily movement to expel semen jumping backward (3)
4. mulberry rind, after menstruation (19)		4. peppermint juice at coitus (11)	4. balmoil (8)	4. sneezing (4)
5. dogs fennel in "white drink", after menstruation (23)		5. cabbage seeds, after coitus (12)	5. juice of onion (9)	
6. water in which sesame seeds had been soaked (25)		6. cabbage seeds, watercress, with tar in water of pennyroyal (15)		
7. savin, round aristoloch and peppergrass alone or together (26)		7. scammony (16)		
8. rue (27)		8. colocynth pulp, iron-dross, cabbage and seeds of cabbage with tar, for many days after menstruation (17)		
		9. . . . flour in cabbage juice (18)		
		10. cabbage flowers after menses (21)		
		11. pomegranate pulp and dill, before and after coitus (24)		
		12. watermint and rue juice (28)		

* Numbers in brackets refer to the location of the recipes in Musallam, "Sex and Society in Islam" (Ph.D. dissertation, Harvard University, 1973).

Table 6. *Abu al-Hasan al-Tabib,* The Creation of Man, *Bodleian MS. Pococke 66, ff. 29–30: "On Medicines Which Abort the Foetus"*

A Means to be taken by the mouth	B Magical means	C Suppositories and tampons	D Techniques used by the man	E Miscellaneous techniques
1. birth-wort, pepper, myrrh in lupine water 2. birth-wort, laurel seeds, myrrh, Arabian costus, cinnamon, madder, juice of absinthe, cardamom, pepper and (. . .) in rue water (plus insertion and smearing) 3. savin, asfetida, dorema, and madder 4. lupine broth with myrrh and rue 5. water mint plus suppository 6. myrrh and cinnamon 7. laurel roots 8. water-cress 9. seeds and leaves of bean-clover and wine 10. candy carrot 11. birth-wort, pepper, and myrrh 12. roots of sweet basil 13. roots of cyclamen	1. stepping on cyclamen plant	1. stem (stick) of rue plus recipe taken by mouth and smearing 2. turbith, myrrh, hellebore, opopanax, gall-bladder of cow 3. squirting cucumber juice and gall-bladder of cow 4. pulp of colocynth and broth of same "injected" (*huqina*) 5. glue (from the *Loranthus europeus*), lousewort, round aristoloch, cyclamen, mezereon seeds, colocynth pulp, and dorema 6. round aristoloch, spurge, cyclamen, and aloe 7. headed thyme 8. water mint 9. tar 10. onion juice 11. myrrh and cinnamon 12. cyclamen 13. hellebore 14. roots of yellow-gentian 15. opopanax 16. opopanax roots 17. roots of wild carrot 18. spiny cytisus 19. birth-wort, pepper and myrrh 20. roots of cyclamen		1. smearing navel with gall-bladder of cow (plus recipe taken by mouth and insertion) 2. fumigation with galbanum plant and sulphur kneaded with gall-bladder of cow 3. fumigation with false myrrh gagal and savin 4. juice of cyclamen smeared on navel 5. fumigation with roots of cyclamen
14. luffa seeds with vinegar 15. seeds of wild rue 16. opopanax with honey 17. *salikh* with honey 18. *salikh*	2. smelling scent of luffa plant, at flowering	21. roots of luffa 22. leaves of pennyroyal 23. wild rue 24. opopanax with honey 25. *salikh*		

Note:

The following medicines are mentioned in the text without indication of the method of application:

1. savin
2. pepper
3. cinnamon
4. gum of *Olea sylvestris*
5. round aristoloch
6. chick peas
7. roots and seeds of French hartwort
8. centaury

Table 7. *Ibn Jumai'*, Kitab al-irshad*: contraceptive methods*

A Means to be taken by the mouth	B Magical means	C Suppositories and tampons	D Techniques used by the man	E Miscellaneous techniques
1. beans on empty stomach, before coitus (5)*		1. juice of peppermint before coitus (2) 2. pennyroyal (2) 3. seeds of leek after purification (3) 4. pessaries made of myrrh, opopanax, rue, and hellebore kneaded with oxgall (4)	Anointing penis with 1. juice of onion before coitus (1) 2. oil of any kind (6)	

* Numbers in brackets refer to the location of the recipe in Musallam, "Sex and Society in Islam" (Ph.D. dissertation, Harvard University, 1973).

Table 8. *Ibn Jumai'*, Kitab al-irshad*: abortifacient methods*

A Means to be taken by the mouth	B Magical means	C Suppositories and tampons	D Techniques used by the man	E Miscellaneous techniques
1. seeds of wild rue (2)* 2. cyclamen (6) 3. wild rue, rue (dried leaves), and myrrh in water boiled with savin (9) 4. cinnamon, cardamom, savin and myrrh (10)	1. stepping on cyclamen plant (8)	1. balm oil (1) 2. seeds of wild rue (2) 3. asafetida (3) 4. madder (4) 5. galbanum (5) 6. cyclamen (6)		1. juice of cyclamen smeared on stomach (7)

* Numbers in brackets refer to the location of the recipe in Musallam, "Sex and Society in Islam" (Ph.D. dissertation, Harvard University, 1973).

Table 9. *Summary*

Author	Potions	Magic	Suppositories	Male	Misc.	Total	Recipes from Razi
1. Razi (Table 1)	8	1	31	3	7	50	
2. Ibn 'Abbas (Table 3)	0	0	5	2	0	7	6
3. Ibn Sina (Table 4)	1	0	10	4	5	20	18
4. Al-Tabib (Table 5)	8	0	12	5	4	28	26
5. Ibn Jumai' (Table 7)	1	0	4	2	0	7	6
Total	18	1	62	16	16	112	56

CHAPTER 5

Birth control in the popular tradition

Medieval Arabic erotica and birth control[1]

The important place of birth control in Arabic erotica is exceptional by comparison with erotic literature in other languages and societies. Pre-modern Chinese and Indian cultures also produced major bodies of erotic literature, but these do not compare well with their Arabic counterpart so far as birth control is concerned. Chinese and Indian writers did not include birth control as one of their important subjects.[2] A single chapter in an Arabic erotic work contained more references to contraception than the whole of Chinese or Indian literature.[3] Bypassing Arabic erotica, Himes was able to ferret out precious little birth control information from other erotic sources, East or West. But he suspected the significance of his omission: "It would seem highly probable that the great Arabic writers on sex devoted attention to it. This literature has not been searched from this point of view, and ought to be a fruitful source of investigation."[4]

Arabic erotica is different from pornography as it has been known in the modern West. In the first place, Arabic erotica is an intermediary form of literature, as much medical as erotic. It is a hybrid which, for the most part, cannot be found outside of Arabic (or Persian) publications, and may therefore be the only literature of that type which could legitimately be dealt with as belonging to the history of medicine.[5]

In the second place, erotica were not written anonymously, and in many cases they were composed by prominent and worthy men. Suyuti, a leading Egyptian religious scholar of the sixteenth century, and probably the most prolific writer in the medieval Middle East, was the author of many books of this type.[6] Erotica were popular books, written and published publicly.

Finally, Arabic erotic literature was popular not only in the sense that it was widely read, but in a deeper, structural sense. Erotic books were, in large part, anthologies of popular material on sex: collections of proverbs on men and women in love, of anecdotes and stories of a smutty nature, and of current erotic poetry. The character of such material as popular literature can be easily seen when compared to the stories and anecdotes in the *Thousand and One Nights*, Arabic popular literature *par excellence*. Both drew on the same folk sources and shared the same popular traditions. When Ibn al-Nadim wrote his *Fihrist*, the tenth-century survey of Arabic culture, he placed erotica together with fables and popular stories in the same group.[7] The inclusion of erotica in the *Fihrist* demonstrates that many were already available in the tenth century; by the sixteenth many more had been written.

Writers of erotica relied heavily on scientific medicine for information which was sexually relevant: the biology of reproduction, diet, aphrodisiacs, venereal disease, etc. Since scientific medicine contained birth control information, this too was used. But there is special significance in the fact that, while other medical information is dispersed throughout a work, in much of erotica birth control commands a separate chapter of its own.[8] Such chapters are at least as long and detailed as the same chapters in medical works proper, and constitute prima facie evidence for the general social interest in birth control.

And yet, it is important to note the degree to which the specific birth control prescriptions in erotica depart from those we have found in scientific writings. It is true that in *The Perfumed Garden* (below) Nafzawi's birth control prescriptions come directly from medicine, even though his discussion as a whole departs from the medical tradition by its disregard of any medical indications. But the other erotic writers appear to draw their prescriptions from some other source, and make it impossible to view the birth control information in erotica as simply diffusion of the same information found in the medical literature.

The relationship among the different medical texts studied earlier is fairly clear. I was able to trace the majority of recipes, one by one, to an original pool of Greek and Middle Eastern medical writings as collected by Razi in the *Hawi*. There is no such close affinity between the texts from erotica on the one hand and the medical tradition on the other. Most recipes from erotica are not traceable to the medical pool, and I have concluded that they were rooted in a tradition of popular birth control remedies.

Birth control chapters in erotica also differed from those in medicine proper by disregarding medical indications. The writers apparently took the positive value of birth control for granted. The only justification or explanation Nafzawi offered was his desire to separate the good from the useless methods. Beyond this, his chapter consisted of a simple, straightforward listing of birth control techniques. Al-Katib, in *The Encyclopedia of Pleasure*, believed contraception could help to protect love and avoid scandal. Another characteristic of erotica, and a likely one given the nature of the texts, was the presence of birth control recipes which were recommended for their additional value as *aphrodisiacs*.[9]

But the erotic and other popular texts below agreed with scientific medicine in treating both contraception and abortion as two sides of the same process. The title of the discussion in *The Encyclopedia of Pleasure* is "the avoidance of pregnancy", but it incorporates recipes which are both contraceptive *and* abortifacient.[10] *The Rejuvenation of the Old Man* has "contraception" in the title and includes several recipes which are contraceptive/abortifacient.[11] The title of the chapter in *The Perfumed Garden* is wonderfully general: "On medicines which expel the semen from the uterus" – before pregnancy, contraception; afterwards, abortion. The chapter lists contraceptive recipes,[12] abortifacient recipes,[13] and contraceptive/abortifacient recipes.[14] Ibn al-Jawzi's title is again "on the prevention of pregnancy", but his brief text includes both contraceptive and abortifacient prescriptions.[15] The same is also true of Nuwairi's discussion of the subject.

The means of control in erotica

To describe birth control techniques in erotica we will look at texts from the tenth, thirteenth, and sixteenth centuries, and from Baghdad, Egypt, and Tunisia respectively. The first, *The Encyclopedia of Pleasure (Jawami' al-ladhdha)* was written by Abu 'Ali Ibn Nasr al-Katib, who was a secretary and a man of letters in tenth-century Baghdad.[16] Ibn al-Nadim knew him personally and remembers that al-Katib often talked about book projects, but adds that he "never finished most of them".[17] *The Encyclopedia of Pleasure* is one of the most original Arabic erotic books by virtue of its rich detail and attention to style.

The second work, from thirteenth-century Egypt, is by the author of one of the best medieval books on jewels,[18] the Egyptian lapidarist Ahmad Ibn Yusuf al-Tifashi who was also a prolific author of erotica.[19] His book is titled *The Rejuvenation of the Old Man (Ruju' al-shaikh ila sibah fi al-quwwa 'ala al-bah)*. While al-Katib's *Encyclopedia* is more literary, Tifashi's *Rejuvenation* is more medical. The difference is one of degree, not of kind. Both works include medical information and popular tales, but in different proportions. Finally, the third work is *The Perfumed Garden (Al-Rawd al-'atir fi nuzhat al-khatir)* of al-Shaikh Sidi Muhammad al-Nafzawi, about whom little is known except that he lived in fifteenth- or sixteenth-century Tunis. This book is available in an English translation (from the French) by Sir Richard Burton.[20]

The Encyclopedia of Pleasure (Table 10, p. 101) contains twelve prescriptions: three are female suppositories; six are male contraceptives; and one is a recommendation to use a particular coital position which is listed in Table 10 under "miscellaneous".[21] The remaining two prescriptions are magical, arsenic in camel or stag leather tied to some part of the body. Al-Katib mentions both together, at the end of the chapter, more or less as hearsay. We notice the tendency in erotica to emphasize male contraceptives: six, compared to only three female suppositories. (However, al-Katib recommends two of the male prescriptions for use as suppositories as well.)[22]

It is impossible to trace the individual recipes from this erotic text back to the medical tradition. There are specific medicines (such as scammony, saltwort, elephant dung, dill, rue, and cinnamon) which can be traced back to Razi and the other physicians, but the complete recipes, as a whole, are quite different. There is also a large number of medicines which appear here for the first time (cypress fruit, camomile flowers, narcissus pollen, soap root, corn poppy, *isqanqur, shabbut*, rough bindweed, and azarole seeds).

In *The Rejuvenation of the Old Man* (Table 11, p. 102)[23] there are sixteen recipes: five potions, one intravaginal tampon, nine male contraceptives, and one "miscellaneous" technique – an early but misguided form of the rhythm method (abstention in the days immediately following menstruation).[24] The tendency in erotica to focus on male contraceptives, which we have already noted, is more pronounced here. There are, in the *Rejuvenation* more techniques to be used by the man than all other methods combined. Tifashi mentioned coitus interruptus only to go beyond it and suggest eight additional male contraceptives in the form of complex ointments to be smeared on the penis before intercourse. All of these prescriptions, except for one, are "new". The exception is tar, which can easily be traced back, and about which more below. It is noteworthy that Tifashi's prescriptions all have different ingredients from the recipes in the *Encyclopedia of Pleasure.*

The *Rejuvenation* has five recipes to be taken by mouth. Again, all are "new". Some smack of the most superstitious and dark folklore (urine of mule with fire-bucket water, and mule dung fed to a woman "without her knowledge").[25] All these "new" recipes suggest strongly that erotica are drawing upon a vast pool of current "popular" recipes which may have varied greatly from one region to another. Tifashi specifically mentions a midwife as his informant for an abortifacient prescription (a potion). It is perhaps significant that the only direct point of contact between the *Rejuvenation* and earlier texts is the intra-vaginal tampon. This is essentially the same as the one from the *Encyclopedia of Pleasure*, indicating a certain continuity in so far as the more efficient female contraceptives are concerned.[26]

Nafzawi's *Perfumed Garden* (Table 12, p. 103)[27] has eight prescriptions (the recipes are six, a couple however are to be used in two different ways: alum, for example, is recommended for intra-vaginal insertion or for smearing on the penis).[28] Of the prescriptions, two are potions, four are suppositories or tampons, and two are techniques to be used by the male. While it was impossible to trace back the recipes from the two earlier texts, in this case tracing was very easy. All of Nafzawi's recipes, with one exception, derive from the medical tradition.[29] Nafzawi's reliance on the medical rather than the "folk" tradition explains his greater emphasis on female techniques of birth control, although he does not neglect the usual male contraceptives of the popular tradition.

Erotica and Islamic jurisprudence

A very important aspect of al-Katib's discussion in the *Encyclopedia of Pleasure* is the notice he took of the religious permission of contraception:

> [Coitus interruptus] has legal conditions . . . In brief, [these are that] in the case of a free woman, withdrawal may be practised with her prior agreement, and in the case of a concubine it may be used unconditionally.[30]

It would have been difficult indeed to have put the core legal regulation governing withdrawal more accurately or succinctly.

In his turn, Tifashi began his birth control chapter in *The Rejuvenation of the Old Man* with a statement of the religious permission of coitus interruptus:

> The religious Law (*Shar'*) has sanctioned coitus interruptus for the man in marital intercourse with his wife's permission. The purpose of this sanction is the prevention of pregnancy.[31]

Tifashi then put this introduction to very interesting use. Perhaps because jurisprudence dealt only with withdrawal, and to a limited extent with female suppositories, while Tifashi was more interested in providing other male contraceptives as *substitutes* for withdrawal, he emphasized that the purpose of the legal permission was "the prevention of pregnancy". It was then much easier for him to argue that his suggestions were, as he put it, "more worthy of sanction", for they served the same end and were not as "harmful" as withdrawal. Be that as it may, the fact that popular writers connected Islamic jurisprudence with popular advice on birth control assures us that the religious permission of contraception was indeed part of the popular consciousness.

Belles lettres (*adab*) proper also made this connection, as in the joke which had great currency and was first told in the eleventh-century *Muhadarat* of al-Raghib al-Isfahani (died 1108):

> The jurists consider coitus interruptus "blameworthy" when practised without the woman's permission. A man asked an adultress, "What would you say about withdrawal?" and she replied, "I hear it is *makruh* ("blameworthy"). He said, "and you have not heard that adultery is *haram* (forbidden)?!"[32]

The means of control in adab

Erotica was that branch of *adab*, belles lettres, which concentrated on sexuality. But even in a larger context, Arabic belles lettres, the general secular literature of the medieval Middle East, referred to contraception frequently enough. The references to birth control were made casually, without surprise, often in passing. The authors took a great deal for granted, and what they took for granted was the background which this book has attempted to reconstruct of birth control as a well-known practice in their society. Jahiz, one of the great founders of Arabic belles lettres, had already said in the ninth century that contraception was a basic human characteristic which distinguished man from the other animals.[33] In that statement, Jahiz was explicitly writing about coitus interruptus, but elsewhere in his widely read *Book of Animals* he also wrote about female contraceptives:

> They say that if a woman used a suppository of elephant dung after mixing it with some honey, she will never conceive . . . Prostitutes in India do so in order to keep their customers.

Significantly, he added,

> Some of our women today use a measure (*mithqal*) of antimony, after purity, because they believe that it will prevent births. But I have seen a woman use it and [nevertheless] give birth to a child.[34]

Female contraceptives were similarly discussed in another of the influential works of ninth-century belles lettres, the *'Uyun al-akhbar* of Ibn Qutaiba (823–89),[35] but Ibn Qutaiba also preserved a delightful little poem in praise of rue, one of the more popular medieval contraceptives:

> Let us praise God and thank Him.
> Were it not for the uses of rue,
> the children of the singer-prostitutes
> would have covered the earth.[36]

In his turn, Isfahani, in his well-known collection of belles lettres, the *Muhadarat* (eleventh century), recounted an anecdote which assumed the widespread use of birth control among prostitutes:

> Abu al-Shamaqmaq used to say to those bent on marriage: "Marry a prostitute!" When a man asked him what he meant, he said, "Listen, a prostitute would be prettier, and more likely to know what pleases men. She would keep herself clean, and if you ever called her an adultress you would not be erring. And then she takes precautions so as not to bear you children . . ."[37]

We shall pay some more attention in the next chapter to similar casual references to birth control in belles lettres, mostly for the light they throw on motivations. But sometimes *adab* dealt with the means of control quite deliberately, by giving them a separate chapter. The emphasis in such chapters on male contraceptives makes them strikingly similar to erotica, enough so to place them in the same popular category.

One such treatment of birth control techniques is by Ibn al-Jawzi (1126–1200), the great Hanbali jurist and historian from Baghdad,[38] in his

Kitab iltiqat al-manafi‘ (The Gleaning of Benefits), a short general work which includes much medical information.[39] Ibn al-Jawzi was a zealous defender of orthodox Islam and a gifted preacher; estimates of crowds addressed by him range from ten thousand to a hundred thousand believers. He was also a prolific author, one of the greatest generalizers in the history of Arabic literature.[40]

There are five different prescriptions in Ibn al-Jawzi's text (Table 13, p. 103): one is a potion, another is a suppository, two are techniques to be used by the man, and one involves fumigation. There are no magical means. While the title of the section is "the prevention of pregnancy", it includes both contraceptive and abortifacient recipes. In line with erotica, there are more male techniques than any other method. All of Ibn al-Jawzi's prescriptions, except for one, are found either in the medical or in the erotic texts.[41]

The exception is the "foam" from the mouth of a male camel in the rutting season (to be taken by mouth). This is the recipe's first appearance in the texts that we have analysed, but it later appears in the fourteenth-century works of Ibn al-Khatib[42] and Sanawbari.[43] The recipe makes its final appearance in early twentieth-century Algeria where an anthropologist reports that "conception is also prevented by . . . *foam* from the mouth of a male camel in the 'rutting season' . . . consumed in water".[44]

Our next birth control text comes from the huge encyclopedia of belles lettres which Ahmad Ibn ‘Abd al-Wahhab al-Nuwairi (1279–1332) wrote in the early fourteenth century in an attempt to sum up all the secular, literate knowledge of his time: *Nihayat al-arab fi funun al-adab*. Al-Nuwairi's text is extremely interesting because of his exclusive attention to male contraceptives. He gives three complex ointments for smearing on the penis before intercourse. In addition to these ointments, he also suggests that the man should avoid simultaneous orgasms, get up quickly, and avoid intercourse in the period immediately following the end of menstruation.[45] All these suggestions, as well as the specific ingredients of his complex ointments, are ones that can easily be traced back to medicine or erotica.

Main features of popular birth control

By the standard which Himes has set, only ten out of the forty-seven contraceptive recipes in the popular texts above are basically "irrational" (Table 14 (p. 104): potions and amulets as compared with suppositories, male contraceptives, and "miscellaneous" techniques. As to abortive potions it is an open question whether some medicines to be taken by mouth may not have been poisonous enough to kill the fetus, but not the pregnant woman.) The rest of the prescriptions are direct "rational" means. Female suppositories account for one out of every five references (9:47), but more than half of all the references are to male contraceptives

(25:47). The pronounced emphasis on male contraceptives in these popular books written by and for men was probably not accidental. This emphasis is in stark contrast to the nearly total absence of reference to male contraceptives in materia medica, the literature which discussed the properties and uses of drugs.

The usual organization of materia medica in the herbalistic and medical traditions was in dictionary form, an alphabetical listing of drugs followed by their description and properties. But the manuals used by the druggists – obviously more relevant documents of social practice – were sometimes organized therapeutically: diseases, ailments, and other complaints were listed first and followed by the medicines to remedy them. One such text, which we shall look at closely now, was originally written by Ibn Tarkhan al-Suwaidi (1203–91).[46] Al-Suwaidi's immense treatise was abbreviated in the sixteenth century by the famous Cairene Sufi, ʿAbd al-Wahhab al-Shaʿrani (died 1565) under the title *Mukhtasar tadhkirat al-Suwaidi fi al-tibb* (*Abbreviation of Suwaidi's "Memorial"*).[47] Because of its popularity and wide use, it is this abbreviated text which is analysed here. In addition to contraceptive medicines, the book has lists of abortifacient medicines, and medicines that aid pregnancy, prevent miscarriage, aid in child birth, expel the dead foetus, etc.

There are fully thirty prescriptions in the *Memorial* text (Table 15, p. 104):[48] thirteen are potions; four are magical; twelve are suppositories or tampons; and only one is a technique to be used by the man. Seventeen of the thirty recipes can be traced back to the medical tradition, although seven of these recipes have a different application (for example, suppositories become medicines to be taken by mouth). One recipe could be traced back only to erotica (Table 15, p. 104, A4). All the magical recipes are "new". In all there are twelve recipes which appear for the first time.[49]

The presence of such a large number of "new" recipes is a characteristic which this text shares with the erotic texts. That many of these recipes belong to popular folklore is a reasonable guess given their nature: blood of menses, urine of ram, parturition blood, ankle of weasel, and skeleton of frog. However, most of the female suppositories are bona fide prescriptions from the medical tradition (ten out of twelve: see note 49). The presence together in a drugstore manual of these two radically opposed types of contraceptives is not really surprising. When drugs were listed in such treatises, those prescribed by the physicians as well as those demanded by popular superstitition were supplied, for the public must have required both kinds from the druggist.

It is noteworthy that there is only one male contraceptive, and that the prescription advanced is the smearing of wood tar (*qitran*) on the penis. Tar comes highly recommended by the physicians as the "strongest" medicine for "voiding" the semen. If the druggist had to prescribe only one such ointment, tar was the likely candidate. Tar made its first appearance as a male contraceptive in the ninth-century *Paradise of Wisdom (Firdaws al-hikma)* of 'Ali Ibn Rabban al-Tabari, the earliest extant Arabic medical book.[50] Although Tabari preceded Razi, I did not include him in Chapter 4 because his book, otherwise very interesting, did not contain a separate chapter on birth control. Nevertheless, Tabari mentions contraceptives and abortifacients here and there in discussing the properties of various medicines.[51] After him, there is scarcely an Arabic discussion of birth control which neglects tar as a male contraceptive. Razi, Ibn 'Abbas, Ibn Sina, Abu al-Hasan al-Tabib, Ibn Hubal, Ibn al-Jawzi, Tifashi, and Nafzawi all recommend it.

So far as I can find, among the hundred or so medicines which Arabic materia medica described as having a contraceptive or abortifacient effect, tar was the single drug which was identified as a male contraceptive. Excepting tar, Arabic materia medica as a distinct literature recognized the birth control properties of medicines for female use exclusively. In other words, the percentage of references to male contraceptives in materia medica was very close to zero.

Materia medica then did not provide the model for the popular writers' fascination with male contraceptives. Nor did scientific medicine pull them in that direction. Male contraceptives were, of course, discussed in medical literature: fourteen per cent of all references to contraceptives in scientific medicine involve methods for use by the man (Table 9, p. 88, 16:112). But in popular literature, fully fifty-three per cent of all the references to contraceptives are to male methods (Table 14, p. 104, 25:47). This is just about the same percentage which female suppositories alone have in medicine proper (fifty-five per cent, 62:112, Table 9, p. 88). It is evident that in their own work popular writers did not follow the model of either materia medica or scientific medicine, but went against them to express strongly the desire to control births among the men of their society.

Classifying Arabic birth control material

Jurisprudence, scientific medicine, erotica–*adab* and materia medica each dealt with birth control in a way that reflected its own preoccupations and concerns. Each of these sources had characteristics of its own which we shall briefly review. Generally we can say that medicine and materia medica were directed towards the female use of contraception, and that jurisprudence and popular literature were directed towards male practice. The analysis which established these differences was made possible only by the richness of the sources – that is, by the nearly systematic medieval attention to birth control. When all is said and done, it is the pervasive presence of birth control information in the pre-modern Arabic material which constitutes our most important fact.

1. Jurisprudence was distinguished by its concentration on coitus inter-

ruptus (and equally by its disregard of indirect procedures such as potions and magical amulets). It contains the best evidence anywhere for male involvement in pre-modern birth control. The only other means which jurisprudence recognized were the female contraceptive suppositories, which in turn dominated the Arabic medical treatments of birth control. Another major characteristic of jurisprudence was its attention to the social and ethical context of the problem; it advanced explicit personal, economic, and medical reasons for birth control.

2. In scientific medicine the ratio of male to female contraceptives was roughly the inverse of that in jurisprudence. Fully eighty-five per cent of all references in medicine were to female contraceptives. The lion's share of these (sixty-three per cent) belonged to intra-vaginal suppositories (references to these in jurisprudence are good evidence as to their actual use). Scientific medicine neglected withdrawal, perhaps because it was an obvious method, but discussed other male contraceptives in the form of ointments on the penis (the kind which erotica–*adab* emphasized). Another important feature of classical medicine was its justification of birth control on purely medical grounds.

3. A great number of prescriptions in erotica–*adab* were independent of the medical tradition, reflecting a separate popular tradition. Erotica–*adab* recognized female contraceptives (references to these were equally divided between suppositories and potions), but this male-oriented literature emphasized above all else contraceptive ointments to cover the penis (fifty-three per cent of all references). Most of the ingredients that went into preparing these ointments were genuine female contraceptives from scientific or folk medicine: paradoxically, the male organ of generation was used to introduce contraceptives into the vagina!

The pronounced fascination with this technique, which could not possibly have been as effective as withdrawal, may reflect the old search for male contraceptives free of withdrawal's shortcomings (Tifashi clearly expressed this need when he called withdrawal "harmful" before offering his substitute ointments). This search was crowned with success in the modern era with the development of the condom.

4. Materia medica shared with erotica the tendency to draw upon the popular tradition. After our study of scientific medicine, we have discovered "new" medicines which made their first appearance in popular literature and materia medica. These, including many magical or fantastic prescriptions, were not new at all. Instead, they were the rejects of scientific medicine. The physicians had selected from the rich but mixed mass of materia medica their own prescriptions, and did so on the basis of a clear preference for direct physical or chemical means of control. Out of the fifty contraceptives in the *Hawi* only one was magical, and Razi reported it as hearsay. The other medical texts that we considered, including Razi's *Mansuri*, had no magical prescriptions whatsoever (this

circumstance was equally true of the material from erotica–*adab*, where Tifashi, Nafzawi, Ibn al-Jawzi, and Nuwairi eschewed magic completely, and only al-Katib indulged in two references, again as hearsay). It is important to raise this issue here because there existed systematic medieval treatises of magical and occult substances, and these treatises figured as one of the independent sources of the later medieval texts discussed below. The most significant of these books on occult substances was *Kitab al-khawass*, and the author of this book was no other than Razi, the same great author of the *Hawi*.[52]

We return to materia medica in order to note their most significant characteristic, namely that, except for one drug (wood tar), materia medica recognized only female contraceptives. Some materia medica (the drugstore manuals) in their turn showed the influence of scientific medicine: most of the suppositories in Sha'rani's manual were genuine physicians' prescriptions. The nearly exclusive emphasis on female contraceptives in materia medica makes one wonder whether most persons requiring this service from the druggists were women.

Later medieval texts

After five centuries and more of the development of Arabic culture in the Middle East, persons who wished to discuss birth control techniques had a wealth of well-established and different sources. Later medieval writers had a pronounced tendency towards the encyclopedic, and were happy to collect all the information possible on a given subject. As a result, later "medical" birth control texts were decidedly eclectic, containing information from scientific medicine, popular sources, materia medica, or jurisprudence, often in equal measure. This was definitely the case with the various treatments by Antaki and his students which we have already discussed (Chapter 4). In the *Memorial*, Antaki's eight potions were derived from materia medica, either directly or through the agency of medicine; his six suppositories derived from medicine; the five magical prescriptions from the *Mujarrabat*, the books devoted to magical means; the male ointments from both medicine and erotica (Antaki referred in the *Memorial* to both *The Rejuvenation of the Old Man* and the *Encyclopedia of Pleasure*).[53] Finally, the reasons he advanced for birth control showed a greater affinity with jurisprudence than with scientific medicine, although I am not suggesting that he learned his reasons from jurisprudence and not from life.

Another typical late text, Sanawbari's (fourteenth-century) *Kitab al-rahma fi al-tibb* was very similar in its composition. Sanawbari's chapter on contraception ("On Treating Multiparous Women, Thirty-Three Items on the Avoidance of Pregnancy") offered fourteen potions from materia medica or medicine; eight magical prescriptions from the occult and magical writings; six intra-vaginal suppositories from scientific medicine; and four male ointments from medicine and erotica.[54]

Ibn al-Khatib's *'Amal man tabba* (fourteenth century) contained two completely separate treatments of contraception. The first was pure medicine: fourteen prescriptions equally divided between potions and suppositories, mostly from the *Hawi*.[55] The second treatment was pure magic: eleven prescriptions from *Kitab al-khawass*.[56] The latter work was also cited by Antaki in his treatment of contraception in the *Nuzha*, and was the ultimate source of the magical prescriptions of Sanawbari (above) and Azraqi (below).

At long last we come across a "medical" text which begins its discussion of contraception with a reference to withdrawal and the legal regulations governing its practice – Ibrahim Ibn 'Abd al-Rahman al-Azraqi's *Tashil al-manafi' fi al-tibb* (fifteenth century):

> *(Chapter on Contraceptives)* The man may prefer the woman not to get pregnant. To this end he has available to him means including withdrawal, which he may practise with a concubine without her permission and with a free woman only with her consent. This is Ibn al-Jawzi's formulation, and he is a Hanbali, but we [Azraqi was a Shafi'i] believe that the man is allowed to practise withdrawal even without his wife's consent . . .

Azraqi then added two more male contraceptives from medicine and erotica, five suppositories from scientific medicine, two magical prescriptions from *Kitab al-khawass*, one potion from medicine, and two "miscellaneous" techniques.[57]

We concluded the last chapter by observing that it was not a story of "progress" in medical contraception, and it is important to say now that it was not a story of "decline" either. There has been a tendency, which we saw in Himes' *Medical History of Contraception*, to compare texts from the classical period, say Ibn Sina's *Canon*, with texts from the later Middle Ages, say Antaki's *Memorial,* and to find in the latter evidence of scientific and intellectual decline that touched the culture as a whole. But Antaki never replaced Ibn Sina in the sixteenth century or after, and the culture did not forget or reject the *Canon*. The *available* knowledge in society never "declined".

What about the later texts themselves? Are they not inferior in comparison with classical writings? When the later authors wrote about birth control techniques they included in the same discussion material from the various traditions. We can take their texts at face value and say that they diluted the scientific tradition by adding magical or other popular recipes, or by the same token say that they upgraded the popular and magical traditions by introducing material from scientific medicine.

Table 10. *Ibn Nasr al-Katib,* The Encyclopedia of Pleasure*: contraceptive and abortifacient methods*

A Means to be taken by the mouth	B Magical means	C Suppositories and tampons	D Techniques used by the man	E Miscellaneous techniques
	*1. arsenic in camel leather (9)‡ *2. arsenic in stag leather (10)	*1. scammony, after menstruation (5) *2. saltwort, fruit of cypress, camomile flowers, and narcissus pollen with water (6) *†3. sweet turfoil seeds, elephant dung, azarole seeds, red mustard with storax (8)	*1. withdrawal (2) anointing the penis with: *†2. ammonia, dill scammony, and rue in rose oil, before coitus (3) *3. soap root with honey (4) *4. scammony before coitus (5) *5. saltwort, fruit of cypress, flower of camomile, and narcissus pollen in water, before coitus (6) *6. corn poppy, *isqanqur* (?), gall bladder of *shabbut*, rue seeds, pearls, rough bindweed, and cinnamon, and camphor with honey (7)	*1. intercourse *min qu'ud* (A coital position) (1)

* Indicates a specifically contraceptive recipe.
† Indicates a contraceptive/abortifacient recipe.
‡ Numbers in brackets refer to the location of the recipe in Musallam, "Sex and Society in Islam" (Ph.D. dissertation, Harvard University, 1973).

Table 11. *Tifashi,* The Rejuvenation of the Old Man*: contraceptive and abortifacient methods*

A Means to be taken by the mouth	B Magical means	C Suppositories and tampons	D Techniques used by the man	E Miscellaneous techniques
*1. urine of mule with fire-bucket water (10)‡ *2. mule dung with honey (11) 3. ground dyers oak (12) *4. ginger in costive drink (14) *5. foam of sea waves (16)		*†1. seeds of sweet turfoil, elephant dung, red mustard, pepper seeds, azarole seeds, with liquid storax in wool (17)	*1. with-drawal (1) anointing the penis with: †2. rue and natron mixed with rue water, before coitus (3) (15) †3. galbanum with juice of rue and water of coriander, before coitus (4) †4. savin, rue leaves, scammony, and natron in rue water and fire-bucket water, before coitus (5 †5. tar, before coitus (6) *6. sweat and ear wax of mule, before coitus (7) †7. filings of mule hoof with mule fat, before coitus (8) *8. scammony and rue water, during coitus (9) *9. pellitory of Spain and ginger with honey, before coitus (13)	*1. no intercourse in days after menstruation (2)

* Indicates a specifically contraceptive recipe.
† Indicates a contraceptive/abortive recipe.
‡ Numbers in brackets refer to the location of the recipe in Musallam, "Sex and Society in Islam" (Ph.D. dissertation, Harvard University, 1973).

Table 12. *Nafzawi,* The Perfumed Garden*: contraceptive and abortifacient methods*

A Means to be taken by the mouth	B Magical means	C Suppositories and tampons	D Techniques used by the man	E Miscellaneous techniques
1. water of pie rhubarb with pepper (5)‡ 2. cinnamon and myrrh in conjunction with tampon of same (6)		†1. root of madder (1) 2. seeds of cabbage in a pipe, after fumigation (2) *3. alum, before coitus, also on penis (3) 4. cinnamon and myrrh in flock of wool (6)	anointing the penis with *1. alum, before penetration (3) †2. tar (4)	

* Indicates a specifically contraceptive recipe.
† Indicates a contraceptive/abortifacient recipe.
‡ Numbers in brackets refer to the location of the recipe in Musallam, "Sex and Society in Islam" (Ph.D. dissertation, Harvard University, 1973).

Table 13. *Ibn al-Jawzi,* Kitab iltiqat al-manafi'*: contraceptive and abortifacient methods*

A Means to be taken by the mouth	B Magical means	C Suppositories and tampons	D Techniques used by the man	E Miscellaneous techniques
*1. "foam" of camel in "rutting" season (1)†		1. tar (6)	*1. anointing penis with tar before coitus (2) *2. rue and natron in rue water, during coitus (3)	1. fumigation with hoof of horse, mule or donkey (5)

* An asterisk indicates a specifically contraceptive recipe.
† Numbers in brackets refer to the location of the recipe in Musallam, "Sex and Society in Islam" (Ph.D. dissertation, Harvard Unniversity, 1973).

Table 14. *Summary*

Author	Potions	Magic	Suppositories	Male	Misc.	Total
Al-Katib (Table 10)	0	2	3	6	1	12
Al-Tifashi (Table 11)	5	0	1	9	1	16
Al-Nafzawi (Table 12)	2	0	4	2	0	8
Ibn al-Jawzi (Table 13)	1	0	1	2	1	5
Al-Nuwairi	0	0	0	6	0	6
Total	8	2	9	25	3	47

Table 15. *Sha'rani,* Mukhtasar tadhkirat al-Suwaidi*: contraceptive methods*

A Means to be taken by the mouth	B Magical means	C Suppositories and tampons	D Techniques used by the man	E Miscellaneous techniques
1. rennet of foal (1)† 2. antimony (4) 3. leaves of willow, after purity (5) 4. liquid storax, after purity (11) 5. seeds of cabbage, after purity (11) 6. iron rust, after purity (14) 7. beans (16) 8. pepper (19) 9. leaves of cucumber (20) 10. asafetida (21) 11. leaves of willow (22) 12. blood of work horse (26) 13. urine of a ram (29)	1. smearing woman with parturition blood from first born (7) 2. seeds of wood-sorrel tied to upper left arm in cloth (17) 3. ankle of weasel as amulet (24) 4. skeleton of frog as amulet (27)	1. peppermint, before coitus (2) 2. blood from menses of another woman, before coitus (6) 3. juice of squirting cucumber (9) 4. seeds of cabbage, after coitus (10) 5. flowers of cabbage, after purity (12) 6. juice of cabbage (13) 7. iron rust, after purity (15) 8. elephant dung with pepper, after purity (18) 9. pepper in pessary, before or after coitus (19) 10. alum, before coitus (23) 11. stems of indigo in flock of cotton (25) 12. salt, before coitus (28)	1. tar, smeared on penis before coitus (3)	

† Numbers in brackets refer to the location of the recipe in Musallam, "Sex and Society in Islam" (Ph.D. dissertation, Harvard University, 1973).

CHAPTER 6

Population and Middle Eastern history

No one can argue that Catholics did not practise birth control simply because of the Church's condemnation; similarly, we cannot assume that birth control was practised in the pre-modern Middle East by virtue of the Islamic religious permission alone. For although the idea of birth control comfortably fits Islamic sexual morality, this does not mean that the actual practice of birth control was inevitable. I must now explain why I believe that the medieval evidence means that birth control was practised in the medieval Middle East.

It is perhaps best to start by looking at the modern West, the one example of limiting births by the use of contraception which is fully documented and generally known. Descriptions of the character of contraception in the modern West suit the material on medieval Middle Eastern contraception remarkably well:

> Contraception has, of course, been employed throughout human history. What is particularly striking about the present era are three factors related to the decision to conceive that were absent during earlier periods: the rationalization of techniques – that is, their employment in terms of a logical or even scientific cause – effect sequence rather than in terms of magic or folk beliefs; the widespread dissemination of scientific information; and the availability, or willingness, to use contraception – a willingness supported by moral, aesthetic, and related attitudes.[1]

In the medieval Middle East, the willingness to practise contraception was consistently supported by moral, aesthetic, and other attitudes; birth control information was widely disseminated; and contraceptive techniques were employed in terms of a rational cause–effect sequence.

It may be objected that information in the medieval Middle East could not possibly have been as "democratically" disseminated as in the modern West, and that mixed with the majority of rational contraceptive techniques there were some irrational recipes (especially in erotica and materia medica). Both points are correct but irrelevant, since for the purpose of limiting population numbers, the effect even of much more limited (and less effective) birth control than is practised in the modern West would have been very significant. This is so because mortality in medieval times was much higher than it is now, with births exceeding deaths by a very small margin – if at all. Consequently, some birth control practice, regardless of how much it was restricted, went a long way. In modern times, with a relatively low death rate, general and widespread practice of contraception is necessary to achieve similar results.

The extremely limited nature of birth control information for pre-modern times in general was a major problem that faced Norman E. Himes in his pioneering study, *The Medical History of Contraception* (1936).[2] As a result, his view of contraception in history (a view shared by the rest of the scholarly community) was that truly effective contraception had had to await modern times and the "democratization" of birth control information.[3] Himes concluded, for example, that although the methods he had found in Greek medicine were good, the knowledge of birth control techniques must have been limited to a select few:

> The scanty evidence available suggests that the contraceptive knowledge of antiquity was confined largely to the heads of medical encyclopaedists, to a few physicans and scholars.[4]

Although Himes was singularly impressed with the techniques in Arabic medicine, he reached a similar conclusion about the medieval Arabs because he assumed that the information he found in medical works was the totality of Arabic birth control information.

We now know that medicine was only one of many sources of birth control information in medieval Arabic, and that the other sources, such as jurisprudence and erotica, were more representative and popular, in form as well as in content. The remarkably wide range of medieval Arabic contraceptive information, from the most specialized to the most popular writings, suggests that this information was generally available. The validity of this suggestion is underlined by a closer look at the evidence. There is no reason why Arabic pharmacological lists should have contained birth control recipes alongside recipes for headaches, upset stomachs, and other health conditions, ailments, or diseases were these birth control remedies not in demand, and were they not being offered. As far as medieval Arabic civilization is concerned, it is difficult to argue that such knowledge was limited to a select few.

Among the contraceptive methods known to medieval men and women, withdrawal and pre-coital intra-vaginal insertions were clearly the most rational and effective. Withdrawal was the primary subject of the birth control discussions in jurisprudence; and withdrawal was readily available. Jurisprudence discussed in addition only intra-vaginal suppositories and tampons. To judge from the preponderance of these in the medical and pharmacological Arabic sources, they too were widely known.

More important still is the fact that there was simply no reference whatsoever in jurisprudence to any magical, indirect, or ineffective contraceptive techniques. To gain an immediate idea of the historical worth of birth control information in Islamic jurisprudence, one has only to consider the pre-eighteenth-century European references to contraception with their nearly exclusive emphasis on potions and magic.[5]

Only actual practice could have given rise to one of the important problems with which Muslim jurists had to deal – that of the disowning of children born despite regular coitus interruptus practice by their fathers. The reports about men who tried to deny their paternity on this basis demonstrate, in addition, the popular faith in the contraceptive effectiveness of withdrawal.[6]

No doubt the particular legal problems which coitus interruptus practice created – as an act dependent on male volition which conflicted with certain basic rights of women to unfettered sexual fulfilment and to progeny – had much to do with its dominance in the legal discussions. But the overwhelming stress in erotica on male contraceptives other than withdrawal can be explained only if we posit the existence of a common need to limit births. This need was the basis for the interest in contraceptives in the two popular literatures, jurisprudence and erotica.

But the weightiest argument in favour of the historical authenticity of the evidence is the total picture, the combination of these and other factors. The different categories of literature containing Arabic birth control evidence are the product of the same societies in the same geographical area at the same historical time. This material was written down by medieval persons who were quite unaware of the figure of the modern historian peering over their shoulder, "and therefore did not modify their words to impress him, or lie to deceive him".[7] In addition, the literatures were interconnected. For example, Ghazali, in one of the most influential books in historical Islam, *The Revival of the Religious Sciences*, appealed to medicine for authority on the biology of reproduction; some birth control chapters in erotica, itself half-popular half-medical, used the religious sanction from jurisprudence to introduce their collections of birth control recipes. Above all, the freedom and openness displayed in the birth control discussions in the secular literatures reflected the freedom with which the permissive religious attitude infused society as a whole.

The final stamp of authenticity on the evidence is bestowed by the very arguments that the medieval Muslims themselves advanced for birth control practice. These arguments expressed in simple and convincing ways the needs and desires of medieval men and women: birth control was practised to avoid the material hardship of a large number of dependants, to safeguard property, to guarantee the education of a child, to protect a woman from the dangers of childbirth (especially if she was young or sickly), or simply to preserve her health and beauty, to avoid fathering children who would be slaves, to protect a nursing infant from the ill-effects of a new pregnancy, etc. There was even a report that some medieval women practised contraception because they did not want to "bother" with pregnancy and breast-feeding.

In addition to the above, there were many stories, anecdotes, aphorisms and poems relating to birth control in medieval literature. Since literature has a different function from that of jurisprudence or medicine, one would have expected that material bearing on birth control in belles lettres would be less direct, more subtle and ambiguous. We have already seen that belles lettres, like the other literatures, had included the techniques of birth control as one of its subjects.

Belles lettres also give insight into some of the feelings and anxieties that may have led to birth control practice: the fear of unwanted pregnancy, and recoil at the responsibilities of family and children. Taken by itself this material may be open to more than one interpretation. Stories which have the fear of pregnancy as their subject can be used, perhaps, to show a lack of faith in the possibility of effective birth control. However, seen in light of the massive evidence on birth control in the legal, scientific, and popular sources (including belles lettres itself) already discussed, such an interpretation is by no means necessary.

There were, in medieval Arabic, stories that attempted to explain homosexuality as resulting from the fear of pregnancy,[8] and the same fear was an excuse given by women for hesitating to see their lovers.[9] In addition, there were other stories, all essentially the same, which distinguished between love play and sexual intercourse. In these, sexual intercourse was equated with reproduction and, for that reason, decried; the tone employed was disparaging – pregnancy was viewed as an infringement on love.[10]

Recoil at the responsibilities of family, concern for the well-being of children, and fear of bad times are anxieties which come across rather clearly in other stories. When Hasan al-Basri met friends coming to congratulate him on the birth of his first child, he was sad and distraught. Shocked, one of his friends reproached him for not properly appreciating God's gift. He answered: "I thank God for his gift . . . Still I do not welcome the child who will baffle me were I rich, and impoverish me when poor . . . For my child I fear poverty after I am dead . . ."[11] Another man, after divorcing his wife, was asked whether he planned remarriage. He responded: "Bearing abstinence is easier than meeting the responsibilities of a family (*al-'iyal*)."[12] Contraception figured also in the jokes of medieval people and even in their dreams.[13]

The evidence for birth control in the medieval Middle East can be found in all manner of books and in a variety of different forms. Birth control information was available, furthermore, in societies in which birth control was sanctioned by religion, attitudes toward sexuality were open, erotic books were written and published openly by estimable men, and birth control remedies were available. We cannot escape the conclusion that some medieval Middle Eastern people limited births by using contraception. This, I believe, is a cautious conclusion, supported by our comparative knowledge of birth control practice elsewhere. In this context, one basic fact of European historical demography should be recalled: that the modern secular decline in Western birth rates was first achieved by the use of traditional contraceptive techniques, primarily coitus interruptus, which preceded the development of modern contraceptives.

> The spread of family limitation in the West was based upon very crude techniques, requiring neither expenditure nor access to technical information.[14]

There was practically no contraceptive technique used by the Europeans in the second half of the nineteenth century which was not known in the medieval Middle East. In other words, there is no technological reason why birth control would not have mattered as a factor in the history of Middle Eastern populations as it did in that of the modern Europeans.

If the historian pursues, within a strictly religious–intellectual framework, the Islamic religious attitude toward contraception, and finds, as I have demonstrated earlier, that all Muslim interpretations of the religious law were unanimous in their permission of contraception, then his findings apply to all Muslims everywhere. Birth control *practice* and its demographic and historical significance require a different kind of treatment, for a discussion of practice necessarily leads to social and economic history, which is a different kind of terrain. A group of Muslims, in a certain place and time, and under particular conditions, may or may not have practised birth control. Here, although Islam's religious attitude matters, it matters as one of several factors.

Medieval Islam is not, by and large, a proper unit for the study of social, economic, or political history, for it makes little sense to treat the vast lands and different peoples between Morocco and China as a single and distinct unit. On the other hand, the Egypt and Syria of the Mamluk empire shared one political, economic, social, judicial, and military system. They formed one community of rule, land tenure, commerce, religion, and learning, and I therefore find it proper to treat them together.[15]

Most of the evidence used in this book is applicable to Egypt and Syria and includes extensive Egyptian and Syrian material. It has, however, a wider human and geographical range. For example, the literature of Islamic jurisprudence, written in Arabic, was the common heritage of the Arabic-speaking medieval Islamic civilization that included more than Egypt and Syria. The same is true of Arabic medicine.

Because Egypt and Syria were overwhelmingly Arabic-speaking Muslim societies, it is legitimate to use Islamic jurisprudence and Arabic medicine to interpret their history, even though these literatures have a wider scope. There were, however, conditions specific to the two lands, and it is essential to underline the reservation that the discussion below is limited to them and that the suggestions are not meant to apply to other Muslim communities. Moreover, what follows is a general essay, somewhat speculative, on questions suggested by the medieval evidence. I will discuss the question of population depression, the limits of quantitative research on the past of the Egyptian and Syrian populations, the significance of the demographic decline for explaining the general decline of Egypt and Syria, and the possibilities of interpreting the decline in terms of both a relatively high death rate and a relatively low birth rate.

One of the primary facts about Egyptian–Syrian history in late medieval times is that of a general depopulation. While there is reason to believe that, at least in Egypt, there was a steady decline from the Arab conquests on, there is no doubt that this process was accelerated in the fourteenth and fifteenth centuries, and then continued, with possible minor fluctuations, until the nineteenth. The populations of the two countries did not recover from this demographic depression until after 1800.

Late medieval historians and chroniclers recorded the wholesale abandonment of villages in the second half of the fourteenth and the beginning of the fifteenth centuries. In 1434 there were 2,170 villages in Egypt compared to 10,000 (!) in the tenth century. The historian Maqrizi described whole quarters of Cairo lying in ruin or abandonment at the beginning of the fifteenth century.[16] Medieval and modern scholars agree that "during the fourteenth and fifteenth centuries agricultural production progressively declined, and [. . .] the size of the crops and the extent of the cultivated land diminished".[17]

The long-term decline of the Egyptian and Syrian populations is a matter of general agreement, but the numbers are not. If we follow Hollingsworth's definition of historical demography, in which the object is to arrive at "accurate estimates" of past populations by the use of statistics,[18] then the historical demography of the pre-modern Middle East is an impossible task – we do not have, and are not likely to find, suitable data. Nevertheless there have been attempts to estimate the population of Egypt, and a consideration of two such attempts (by Hollingsworth and Russell) will give us some idea of the present limits of quantitative research. One observation can be offered immediately: it is difficult to realize by looking at the two sets of figures in Table 16 (p. 111) that the two scholars are discussing the same population. The differences between the two accounts are sometimes tenfold (Hollingsworth: 25 million Egyptians in A.D. 641; Russell: 2.6 million in A.D. 600), and sometimes more (Hollingsworth: 20+ million for the eleventh century A.D.; Russell: 1.7 million for the same period).

Table 16. *Comparison of Russell's and Hollingsworth's figures*

Russell		Hollingsworth	
Year	Millions	Millions	Year
30 B.C.	4.5	12–13	50 B.C.
4th–5th century A.D.	3	30	541 A.D.
600	2.6	25	641
8th–9th century	2.2–2.6	10	8th century
10th–11th century	1.7	20+	11th century
12th century	2.4	10	12th century
14th (pre-plague)	4.2	8+	14th (pre-plague)
1420	3.36–3.15	4	14th (post-plague)
1798	2.5	2.5	1798

Hollingsworth's method leaves much room for error: he accepts independent guesses by different medieval and modern scholars, who have used separate and unrelated bases for their assertions, to reconstruct the numbers of Egyptians from 664 B.C. to the present. It is too much to claim that his attempt "will lead us to an important general idea about population decline in the past".[19] The trend of population change that he describes (a decline from the Middle Ages until the nineteenth century) is reasonable and supported by the literary evidence, and his interpretation of it in terms of recurring epidemics is plausible. But one can double his estimates or divide them by two and still arrive at the same reasonable trend and use the same good explanation. The pursuit of numbers in this case, as in all other cases where there are no reliable statistics, defeats the purpose of historical demography (accurate estimates) as Hollingsworth defines it.

The second attempt to estimate the historical population of Egypt is by J. C. Russell who has contributed more than anyone else to medieval demography in recent decades. Russell is a daring scholar and his views have generated great controversy; however, few have had more experience in dealing with medieval numerical data. His use of scanty and limited material is often ingenious, yet in his study, "Late Ancient and Medieval Populations", he could do little with the data available to him on Egypt and Syria. About the area in general in the period A.D. 950–1348, he says that "the population of the east . . . was not increasing as fast as the west, if it was increasing at all", and he reaches this judgement not from any quantitative data but from "the direction of the crusade".[20] His guess for the population of Syria during this period is 2.7 million, and for that of Egypt, in the neighbourhood of 2 million.[21] Russell refrains from giving an estimate of Syria's population for the following period, 1348–1550 ("there seems to be very little information about Syrian population in the period"), but he estimates Egypt's population at 2.5 million and adds that "that was still the population at the beginning of the nineteenth century".[22]

The general impression that Russell gives in this study is one of a depressed and stagnant Egyptian and Syrian population from the tenth century to the nineteenth. This is an important conclusion, if for no other reason than that he arrives at it in the context of a comparative analysis of European and Mediterranean populations, from Roman times to the end of the Middle Ages, none of which seem to have experienced such a long-term trend.

Russell later applied himself to a study of the Egyptian population as such.[23] He employed poll and land tax returns and medieval Egyptian cadastres for his estimates which were also coloured throughout by general historical assumptions that he did not hesitate to make explicit. Russell's reconstruction of the numbers of Egyptians was much more modest than Hollingsworth's (as can be seen in the comparative Table 16), and its major merit, in comparison, was that it represented the calculations of one man who shared all his sources and assumptions with the reader. His figures were guesses, but they were not fanciful ones.

In this study Russell has revised his earlier notion of a stagnant and depressed Egyptian population into one which shows growth from the tenth to the fourteenth century, and decline from the fourteenth century on. He attributed the decline to epidemics and floods, and suggested that the curve of the Egyptian population may have followed that of Egypt's foreign trade.

Given the limited nature of the evidence, and the fact that no reliable or meaningful numbers exist, none of these estimates is very satisfactory, and we have to look elsewhere for breakthroughs in our understanding of the general history of Middle East populations.

The long-term decline of Egyptian and Syrian population, lasting several centuries, was a remarkable demographic phenomenon. It was especially so in the light of the fact that the population of Europe, despite setbacks due primarily to the mortality peaks of epidemics, was increasing, and that, in the Far East, the population of China rose sixfold between 1400 and 1800.[24] Yet, for the most part, historians of the Middle East have used the population depression merely as an aspect, or illustration, of the general economic, social, political, cultural, and intellectual "decline" of Middle Eastern societies. Not until very recently has anyone suggested that the demographic decline may lie at the root of the economic decline.

Charles Issawi has written more than once about the problem of Middle Eastern decline. Issawi sees a process of economic decline and social and cultural retrogression from the twelfth to the nineteenth century, and he lists several factors that "helped bring about this deterioration": (1) "from the twelfth century on Islamic society suffered from fatigue and rigidity in its intellectual and scientific life, and Islam as a religion became more dogmatic and intolerant"; (2) prolonged warfare; (3) the rise of the Mamluk regimes, "whose institutions were much less conducive to economic and social development"; (4) the breakdown of authority; (5) the emergence of petty dynasties; (6) growing bedouin depredations; (7) the unfavourable climate cycle. In addition, Issawi lists "three strictly economic factors": (1) the grave deficiencies of the Arab Middle East in forests, minerals, and rivers; (2) the lack of mechanical inventiveness of Islamic civilization; and (3) the growth of Europe's economic and commercial power and European domination of international trade.[25]

Although there is much food for thought here, it is difficult to see which of these factors are the more significant ones. In any case, although Issawi was aware of the population decline, and used it as an illustration of Middle Eastern retrogression, it was not one of the factors that he listed for the decline in general, and he made no mention of epidemics. In another list, Issawi did mention the plague as a factor, but he did not indicate its importance relative to wars, bedouins, etc.[26] Mortality from medieval wars, or even famines, never reached the high levels of mortality caused by medieval epidemics. Except for cases of mass migration, whose obvious movement ought always to have been noticed by the medieval chroniclers, all large changes of population in the short term must have resulted from the heavy mortality of epidemics.[27]

The neglect of demographic factors was also evident in other explanations. Ira Lapidus, in one of the most influential books on Mamluk Syrian and Egyptian society, dealt at length with Egyptian–Syrian decline in the fourteenth and fifteenth centuries.[28] Lapidus' is a masterly statement of the traditional interpretation of Middle Eastern decline shared by many scholars writing on the Middle East. According to this view, the source of the trouble is first to be seen in the destruction caused by invading armies, Mamluk civil wars, and nomad onslaught. These causes created the conditions for a decline which was then made complete by oppressive Mamluk policies:

> Economically disastrous was the destruction of productive agricultural areas. Bedouin unrest and fiscal exploitation had already precipitated rural decline. Now, in addition, marching and plundering armies, bedouins from whom all restraint had been removed by the diversions of the regime, and Turkomans infiltrating the empire did untold damage to agricultural production, the fundamental source of wealth. . . The Mamluks did no less to foster the ruin of the countryside. . . Oppression forced peasants to flee the villages. Greed meant neglect of irrigation and investments in agricultural production. The results cannot be immediately measured, but it seems that the enormous losses in revenue reported for the end of the fifteenth century and the beginning of the sixteenth originated in this time of troubles. . . Agricultural decline was the ultimate source of urban economic difficulties. . .[29]

It is not evident from Lapidus' account that the period he is describing is the aftermath of the Black Death (1348), when plagues recurred about every decade and in the life of every generation. The recurring plague was a killer far beyond the means of any medieval army or marauding bedouin.

This interpretation, because it neglects demographic factors leaves unanswered the important question of how Egypt and Syria continued to feed themselves despite their diminishing agricultural production. For if agricultural production diminished and the population did not, then the two countries should have suffered chronically from famine, or at least from continuous inflation of the price of agricultural products, and neither of these occurred. The explanation becomes apparent when we take the epidemics and their demographic consequences into account:

> We must conclude that demographic factors were at the root of Egypt's agricultural decline, and that smaller harvests were being produced by, and were feeding substantially fewer people.[30]

With the publication of Udovitch's article, from which the quotation above is taken, the importance of the catastrophic mortality rates of medieval epidemics to Middle Eastern life has finally been recognized. The grave population depression led to an absolute decline of both rural and urban economic activity. The causal relationship explaining the decline in the traditional interpretation has to be reversed: "it was not rapacious Mamluk policies which led to the decline, it was rather the decline that was responsible for these policies".[31]

Udovitch's significant correction reflected a historical insight which has a venerable and impeccable ancestry. Ibn Khaldun, medieval Islam's greatest historian, whose work should be understood primarily as a commentary on the conditions of his own time (the fourteenth century), viewed the plague of 1348, in which he lost his parents, as by far the most important event of his time. In describing a declining and depressed age, Ibn Khaldun had no doubts about the central importance of demographic decline ("Civilization decreased with the decrease of mankind"):

> In the middle of the eighth [fourteenth] century, civilization both in the East and in the West was visited by a destructive plague which devastated nations and caused populations to vanish. It swallowed up many of the good things of civilization and wiped them out . . . Civilization decreased with the decrease of mankind. Cities and buildings were laid waste, roads and way signs were obliterated, settlements and mansions became empty, dynasties and tribes grew weak. The entire inhabited world changed. . . It was as if the voice of existence in the world had called out for oblivion and restriction, and the world had responded to its call. . . When there is a general change of conditions, it is as if the entire creation has changed and the whole world been altered. . . Therefore, there is need at this time that someone should systematically set down the situation of the world among all regions and races, as well as the customs and sectarian beliefs that have changed for their adherents, doing for this age what al-Mas'udi did for his. This should be a model for future historians to follow.[32]

If we accept the notion that the population of Egypt and Syria decreased by an absolute loss of a third, or perhaps even half, of its numbers between

1000 and 1800, then we must explain this apparent demographic change. A population declines when deaths exceed births (there is no evidence of migrations out of Egypt and Syria during these centuries, and this factor can be discounted). This results either from an increase in the death rate, or a decrease in the birth rate, or some combination of both factors.

The decline of the Egyptian and Syrian population can be explained, in the first instance, by an increase in the death rate. The catastrophic mortality rates of epidemics are a satisfactory explanation for demographic decline, at least in the short term. In the case of Egypt and Syria the question remains, however, of why the birth rate did not rise after the epidemics and permit the population to regain its pre-plague numbers, as seems to have happened elsewhere.[33]

In a recent monograph on the plague in late medieval times, Michael W. Dols has discussed plague mortality.[34] He finds that the figures, fragmentary and contradictory as they are, are not useful for calculating either the mortality rates or the size of the population of Egypt and Syria. The figures simply add up to the observation that many people died, especially foreigners, women and children. The major contribution of Dols' work does not follow from his laborious effort in collecting numerical data, but is based on literary evidence par excellence: the medieval Arabic descriptions of the plague symptoms. The sources, according to him, indicate that pneumonic plague, a more infectious and deadlier form than the bubonic, was present in recurrences of the plague in Syria and Egypt.[35] In Europe, the pneumonic form was virtually absent after A.D.1348.[36] This is a potent discovery with far-reaching implications. Without reference to exact figures (which we do not have anyway) we can surmise that mortality from the plague recurrences was higher in Egypt and Syria than in Europe.

Using this evidence, Dols[37] and Udovitch[38] have suggested an explanation for the long-term Egyptian and Syrian demographic decline: even if there was a rise in birth rates, the death rates, because of the plague recurrences, remained consistently higher and did not allow the population to heal its demographic wounds. Try as they might, the Egyptians and Syrians were not able to reproduce enough children to compensate for the dead.

The Arabic birth control evidence suggests another possible explanation: the birth rates were lower than is commonly assumed, or they did not rise after the epidemics, or they even declined. A relatively low fertility *together* with a relatively high mortality may have been the two factors behind demographic depression in Egypt and Syria.

There are, of course, many factors affecting fertility beside birth control: age at marriage, percentage of persons married, relative fecundity, sterility, pregnancy wastage, etc. We have negligible information about these factors for the pre-modern Middle East. Marriages may have been postponed in years of disaster, a larger proportion than usual of the population may have remained unmarried as a result of economic difficulties, or malnutrition and disease may have adversely affected fecundity, the biological capacity to conceive and bear children.

Although it is plausible that any or all of these things may have happened, we are on surer ground so far as birth control is concerned. The Arabic birth control evidence establishes that contraception was a factor in pre-modern Middle Eastern populations. Contraception was present: it was sanctioned by Islamic religious law from the first Islamic century; the sanction was general and widely known; rationalizations of contraceptive practice, linked openly and favourably to a reduction of family size, were put in terms of economic necessity and future expectations from the tenth century on; and there was general knowledge, discussion, and dissemination of effective birth control techniques through such media as jurisprudence, medicine, sexual manuals, and lists of drugs from the beginning of Islamic civilization in the Middle East and throughout the centuries under discussion.

The evidence, however, is purely qualitative. It says nothing about the extent of birth control practice. I have argued above that, given the high mortality rates of pre-modern times, some birth control practice would have been a significant factor. (For example, if we assume that the population of Egypt was ten million in 1000 and that it declined to only two million in 1800, a difference of merely two per thousand annually between the death rate and the birth rate – in favour of the former – can account for such a hypothetical decline. Birth control by itself does not have to account for all of this difference, because there were other factors which could have depressed fertility – in addition to the increase in the death rate due to recurring epidemics.)

The evidence of this book makes it equally possible to argue that contraception was practised in the twelfth century, the fourteenth, or the sixteenth, and to the same limit or extent. The personal reasons which were usually mentioned for the practice (the burdens of a large family, the fear for the mother's life, etc.) were as meaningful for all these times as they are for our own time. Such reasons must have always been behind contraceptive practice. The question remains of whether, in a particular period and under certain conditions, contraception became a relatively more widespread practice resorted to by a relatively larger proportion of the population.

The last part of this chapter will suggest that birth control may have been practised more in the later Middle Ages than before. This hypothesis cannot be more than educated speculation at this time: with the development of a serious gap between the aspirations of the medieval Egyptian and Syrian urban communities on the one hand, and their deteriorating conditions of existence on the other, the option of birth control, available all along, was taken to limit the number of dependants, and thereby preserve a measure of civilized existence. The argument for this hypothesis is based on the course of Egyptian and Syrian history, the Arabic birth control evidence, certain assumptions about the nature of urban society in Egypt and Syria, and historical birth control experience elsewhere.

In the first three centuries of Islam, the Arab conquests led to the rise of a new and vigorous empire within whose borders commerce, learning, and a new civilized community developed. During this time, the urban, learned, and successful classes of the Islamic cities realized an ideal of civilized existence. This is the source of the claim by later scholars that Islam is an urban religion, requiring cities and city life for its full flowering.

In their times of trouble, beginning in the tenth century with the disintegration of the empire (a manifold process involving the breakdown of authority, the arrival of foreign invading armies in the heartlands of Islam, civil wars, the rise of petty dynasties, bedouin assaults, the disruption of economic activity, etc.) the basis of their vision of the good life began to break down. Their seeming control of their existence was slowly but surely eroded. With the rise of the Mamluk regimes this process became complete.

The Mamluk system had originated under the Abbassid Caliphs, but by the eleventh and twelfth centuries it had become general in the Arab Middle East. The Mamluks, slave soldiers from Central Asia, moved into the positions of rule earlier occupied by the old Arab elites. Egypt and Syria especially, from the thirteenth century on, were always ruled by foreigners alien to the native Arabic-speaking populations in race, origin, language, habits and view of life. The urban communities of Egypt and Syria had clearly lost all effective control over their political life, military defence, land, and economy. With the further development of the Mamluk regime even foreign trade became a monopoly of the sultans.

With the Black Death of 1348, ushering in the "golden age of bacteria" and its ominous mortality rates, it must have seemed that even the biological basis of the community's existence was threatened. The plague was medieval man's major traumatic experience and represented a much higher order of misery than that which normally afflicted him.

It is the combined conditions above that civilized men in the Islamic urban communities of Egypt and Syria experienced and called "bad times" (*fasad al-zaman*, *su' al-zaman*). Their reaction to their manifold trials, embodied in their interpretations of the Islamic law, their attitudes and temperament, was a sustained attempt to preserve as much as possible of civilized Islamic existence amid the desolation that surrounded them. Their major impulse was simply to stave off the worst, and much of the relationship of these elites ('ulama, notables, etc.) with Mamluks, invading Mongols, Ottomans, and others can be understood in the light of this. It is this impulse that was behind "that preference for social peace at almost any price which was the principle of later Islamic society"[39] in Egypt and Syria.

The desire to ward off the worst can also be extended to cover their reaction to their other trials, like the plague and economic deterioration. If too many dependants would threaten a man's chance to lead a civilized life, then birth control was a desirable, available, and proper course of action: "Some of the reasons which lead to the practice of coitus interruptus are the attempt to escape having too many dependants, or to escape having any dependants at all."[40] The following are the voices of Ibn al-Humam, al-Tahtawi, Ibn Nujaim, and Ibn 'Abidin for the unconditional sanction of contraception under these conditions:

Coitus interruptus is permitted without a free woman's consent because the times are bad.[41]

Coitus interruptus is lawful without permission because the times are bad.[42]

In our age it is permitted because the times are bad.[43]

Yes, a consideration of how bad the times are indicates that [contraception] is permitted to both [men and women].[44]

The fear of "bad times" was more complex than the simple fear of famine. Even in the worst of times the urban population was never pressed against the limits of existence for very long. The concept "bad times" was used by old and urbane communities with a clear idea of what a civilized level of existence was. This was apparent in Ghazali's argument in support of birth control practised for economic motives. Ghazali did not say that a person may want to avoid a large family because he will not be able to feed more mouths; he simply said that a large number of dependants will increase a man's financial burdens and may involve him in unnecessary toil; that is, a smaller family was more conducive to a better quality of life: "Financial well-being (*qillat al-haraj*, the literal sense is, "avoidance of hardship" or "the minimizing of difficulties") is an aid (*mu'in*) to Religion (or, proper Islamic life, *al-din*)."[45]

The medieval urban societies of Egypt and Syria viewed contraception, abortion, and infanticide together as agents of population reduction – more specifically, as agents for a smaller family size. Their religious law tolerated abortion, and condemned infanticide not because of its motive, but because it entailed murder. To be sure, the jurists pointed out that infanticide had the same motive (escape from dependants) as contraception – and contraception was universally permitted.

It is true that the sanction of contraception was already present in the earliest Islamic reasoning on the matter, the *hadith* of the Prophet. But it should be noted that there was basically one idea in these *hadith*: God is all-powerful and has already willed everything. The economic, personal, social, and medical reasons for birth control appeared in the later reasoning of the classical schools of law from the tenth century on. Since the early *hadith* did not reflect these reasons, and the later arguments did, it is reasonable to take them as a reflection of the attitudes of their own time.

As an aid to analysis it is useful to distinguish between two separate things, the vicissitudes themselves (epidemics, invasions, economic deterioration, bedouin assaults, etc.), and society's *reaction* to them, the interpretation people made of what was happening around them and to them, their expectations for the future, and the way they behaved.

The high mortality rate can be seen as belonging completely to the first category, and explanations in terms of a high death rate alone are inherent in all other explanations of the demographic decline of Egyptian and Syrian populations, whether the agent is the plague, wars, bedouins, famines, malnutrition, or the like. Inherent in such interpretations is the view of Egyptian and Syrian populations as passive. All they had to do was be there, and death came with plagues and Mongols; death, except for suicide, is not a personal decision.

Contraception, like suicide, is exactly the opposite: it is one of man's most personal and private actions. When I argue that Egyptian and Syrian populations, or certain of their members, practised contraception largely in response to "bad times", I am positing societies that were capable of affecting their own destinies. It is only when we shift our attention to the second category above, society's reaction, that the significance of a decline in fertility emerges. The reduction of the population size is then seen not simply as a biological event, the sum total and result of plague mortality heaped upon medieval man's normally high death rates, but also as a conscious reaction of society to its environment.

Birth control is one reaction of man to his conditions of life which, once a significant number of individuals resort to it, has a profound effect on society as a whole. It is not an inevitable reaction, but it fits well the medieval Islamic view of the universe and parallels other developments in late medieval Islamic society. It is commonplace to point out the emphasis in Islamic law on the individual: "The emphasis was on the freedom of the individual to seek the goods of this world and the next in his own way, and to dispose freely of them."[46] The reasons for birth control advanced by the medieval Muslims lend convincing support to this emphasis, for they mostly stem from individual need and interest (Chapter 1).

The tendency to depend on the ultimate resources of self rather than community, and to turn inwards, is apparent in the medieval Egyptian and Syrian reaction to the plague. In Europe, the distraught populations, told that the plague was the direct consequence of their sins, transformed their guilt and anguish into communal form in the Flagellant movement and the murderous persecution of minorities, especially the Jews.[47] In the stricken cities of Egypt and Syria, on the other hand, there was no escape into mass hysteria, and the plague was viewed as another disaster, more overwhelming than, but akin to, invasion, famine, and oppression: "What could the plague do in a country where every day its tyranny is a plague?" asked Ibn al-Wardi in Aleppo in 1348, just before he himself succumbed to the Black Death.[48]

This emphasis on the individual, according to Sauvaget, determined even the physical shape of the Islamic city. In Hourani's succinct summary of Sauvaget's views:

> A certain lack of grandeur in the Islamic conception of the city, and the emphasis of Islamic law on the individual, led to the gradual encroachment of shops and dwellings on the broad avenues [of the earlier, classical city], and when the period of insecurity succeeded that of the early caliphate, the insecurity of life caused the population to withdraw into the city quarters, small units where the ties of neighbourhood were reinforced by those of common religious allegiance and ethnic origin.[49]

The Islamic emphasis on the individual, together with the family as the irreducible unit of social life, led, in the period of insecurity, to a "clear separation between public and private life" in which "private life turned inwards, towards the courtyard and not towards the street".[50]

Jurisprudence said explicitly that birth control was a proper reaction to the insecurity of life, and I therefore do not regard the medieval Islamic practice of birth control as surprising. Under certain conditions, Islamic jurisprudence even legally required birth control. The late medieval Hanbalis, strictest of jurists, insisted that birth control was mandatory for a Muslim family under enemy control: *yu'zalu wujubann bi dar harb* ("Coitus interruptus is mandatory in enemy territory").[51] Under conditions of extreme insecurity, the appeal was not to any public source of protection (such as an army), but to a highly personal means of defence, birth control.

Although there is no doubt it was birth control within marriage that caused the modern fertility decline in the West, explanations for the growing use of birth control have been, in most instances, merely catalogues of the various characteristics of modern society: economic development, industrialization, urbanization, the rise of the middle classes, feminism and the emancipation of women, the availability of modern contraceptive techniques, the spread of literacy, the weakening of the hold of the Church and religious ideas on Western man, and the like. Such explanations do not tell us how change occurred.[52]

There is one interpretation, however, that offers insight into the process of change. The idea was first formulated by J. A. Banks in *Prosperity and Parenthood*.[53] Banks suggested that the late Victorian English middle classes resorted to birth control in response to the growing conflict between their aspirations and their levels of living. The demographers had established that the middle classes had embarked upon family limitation by the use of contraception. Banks argued that the middle classes had, at the same time, become conscious of a gap between their aspirations and their levels of living. He supported his argument by specific case studies, and showed that the important factor was the middle classes' *perception* of a decline in their standards of life (regardless of whether there was, in reality, a decline).

Banks went a step further and suggested that the middle classes, having achieved an idea of the good life, sought to preserve their newly acquired living standard – when the increasing cost of children seemed to threaten its basis – by the use of contraception. Surveys done in the twentieth century confirm Banks' insight, as married individuals practising birth control invariably mentioned economic motivation and the cost of children as their most important motive.[54]

The medieval Arabic birth control evidence lends heavy support to this hypothesis and, in one important respect, is better than nineteenth-century British evidence, for the medieval Middle Easterners themselves made explicit the connection between family limitation and bad times.

Notes

Introduction

1. The issue has revolved around which came first, and the point of contention, demographically, was whether it was a rising birth rate (in response to industrialization) or a declining death rate (independent of industrialization) which was behind the expansion in population. Some economic historians argue that it was the birth rate, rising in response to the opportunities presented by industrialization, which was responsible for the expansion in British population in the eighteenth century. Habakkuk also argues that a rise in the birth rate preceded the Industrial Revolution and was perhaps one of its contributory causes. The more likely explanation for the rise in population numbers is, however, a decline in the death rate, and this is the view preferred by historical demographers, although the exact reasons for the decline are not matters of general agreement (it is not clear whether it was medical advances or simply the more general "rise in the standard of living" which were responsible, though the latter explanation seems more plausible). The best short critical reviews of the arguments are by Phyllis Deane, *The First Industrial Revolution* (Cambridge University Press, Cambridge, 1965), pp. 20–35, and Thomas McKeown, "Medicine and World Population" in M. C. Sheps and J. C. Ridley, eds., *Public Health and Population Change* (University of Pittsburgh Press, 1965), pp. 25–40. For the problem in France, a critical discussion is in C. P. Kindelberger, *Economic Growth in France and Britain, 1851–1950* (Harvard University Press, Cambridge, Mass., 1964), pp. 67–87. Some of the most important articles on the subject (by T. H. Marshall, H. J. Habakkuk, D. V. Glass, J. D. Chambers, and T. McKeown and R. J. Brown) are collected in David Glass and D. E. C. Eversley, eds., *Population in History* (Chicago, 1965). See also Thomas McKeown, *The Modern Rise of Population* (New York, 1967) and the review in *Population Studies*, vol. 31, no. 1, March 1977, pp. 179–81.
2. For England, the late nineteenth and early twentieth centuries.
3. T. H. Hollingsworth, *Historical Demography* (Cornell University Press, Ithaca, 1969), p. 14.
4. Historical demography "is the study of the ebb and flow of the numbers of mankind in time and space by a combination of geography and history using statistics, and the main concern is to achieve accurate estimates of human numbers". *Ibid.*, p. 37.
5. "Demographic history must clearly be history, a sister of political history and constitutional history. It must seek to describe past events in a coherent way, using population as its yardstick, and population changes as the events of main interest that other factors must explain." *Ibid.*, p. 39. The division into demography, historical demography and demographic history is from Hollingsworth. His book is specifically concerned with the second, historical demography. Demographic history, which is

concerned with the implications and meanings of statistical research into the past of human populations, is dealt with only in the last chapter of the book (chapter 10, "Implications") and then very briefly. Hollingsworth's division of the field is not very exact, as he readily admits (p. 39), but is helpful nevertheless because it differentiates between the search for and proper interpretation of statistical data on historical populations (historical demography) and historical writings which attempt to order, explain, narrate, and interpret population change and movement (demographic history).

6. Modern historical demography begins with the work of French demographers in the early 1950s. The most useful account of its early genesis is by Louis Henry, "Historical Demography", in David Glass and Roger Revelle, eds., *Population and Social Change* (London, 1972), pp. 43–54.
7. "In traditional societies, fertility and mortality are high. In modern societies, fertility and mortality are low. In between there is demographic transition. These propositions connecting basic demographic phenomena with the degree of modernity are neither subtle nor precise . . . Yet, with all their ambiguities, *these three sentences unquestionably describe the central preoccupation of modern demography*" (italics mine). Paul Demeny, "Early Fertility Decline in Austria-Hungary: A Lesson in Demographic Transition", in Glass and Revelle, eds., *Population and Social Change*, p. 153.
8. The best discussion is by A. J. Coale, "The Demographic Transition Re-considered", *International Population Conference* (Liège, 1973), pp. 53–72. A comprehensive and lucid discussion of the problem which integrates the most recent work is by Etienne van de Walle and John Knodel, "Europe's Fertility Transition: New Evidence and Lessons for Today's Developing World", *Population Bulletin*, vol. 34, no. 6 (Population Reference Bureau, Inc., Washington D.C., 1980). See also W. D. Borrie, *The Growth and Control of World Population* (Weidenfeld and Nicolson, London, 1970), chapter 1, especially pp. 13ff. An earlier account is by George J. Stolnitz, "The Demographic Transition: From High to Low Birth Rates and Death Rates", in Ronald Freedman, ed., *Population, The Vital Revolution* (Anchor Books, Doubleday, New York, 1964), pp. 30–46. In the same anthology of essays, Philip M. Hauser's article, "The Population of the World: Recent Trends and Prospects", pp. 15–29, is a more direct and blunt statement of the theory.
9. Frank W. Notestein, "Economic Problems of Population Change", in *Proceedings of the Eighth International Conference of Agricultural Economists* (Oxford University Press, London, 1953).
10. D. V. Glass, "Introduction", in Glass and Eversley, eds., *Population in History*, p. 4.
11. D. V. Glass, "Population Growth and Population Policy", in Sheps and Ridley, eds., *Public Health and Population Change*, pp. 3–24.
12. Glass' major point is to question whether in the transition theory one has to start with the decline in mortality; for, as the example of France shows, fertility decline may have started earlier. Thus the decline in fertility is seen as independent of the decline in mortality as such: "If . . . we abandon the fall in mortality as the necessary starting point for analysis, we may look at the problem in somewhat different terms. We may assume – as an aid to analysis – that the deliberate and persistent control of reproductive behavior . . . involves a conflict between levels of living and aspirations . . ." (*ibid.*, p. 18). This hypothesis (linking birth control to a conflict between levels of living and aspirations) has been tested by the available evidence for late nineteenth-century England (by J. A. Banks in *Prosperity and Parenthood* (Routledge and Kegan Paul, London, 1954)). In another one of his works, Glass adopts Banks' hypothesis as an explanation for English fertility decline in the nineteenth century: "For middle-class families in the late 1870s saw a new *malaise*, the emergence of a serious gap between aspirations and levels of living . . . the middle class began to limit the number of their

children, and established a pattern which the rest of the community soon came to emulate" (David Glass and E. Grebenik, "World Population 1800–1950", *Cambridge Economic History of Europe*, vol. 6, part 1, p. 116). Here Glass applies the hypothesis to the eighteenth century: the conflict between levels of living and aspirations "may take place at various levels of living" (Glass, "Population Growth and Population Policy", p. 18). This may very well be one of the major, and most useful, insights into population history, for it separates the spread of birth control from the mechanistic interpretations which simply link it to various elements of "modernity". Tension and conflict between levels of living and aspirations is theoretically possible in the medieval Middle East or China as well as in eighteenth–nineteenth century England.

13. Two quotations from *bona fide* historical demographers will suffice, though they could be multiplied. The following is from David Glass:

    There is no doubt that the major concern among demographers today is with specific policies for a particular situation. Discussion has become focused primarily upon policies to reduce fertility in developing societies. . . . How far can we, as demographers or more generally as social scientists, offer pertinent suggestions about the kinds of actions which may help to produce the desired changes in the rate of population growth? ("Population Growth and Population Policy", pp. 3–4).

    The second quotation is from Demeny:

    It would, of course, be naive to assume that a theory specific enough to serve as a guide for policy can result from historical investigation alone. . . . Nevertheless, history could provide some highly useful insights into the hierarchy of forces presently at work in shaping the levels of fertility . . ." ("Early Fertility Decline", pp. 154–5).

14. Perhaps the most significant difference between West European populations and the rest of humanity in the crucial period from the sixteenth to the nineteenth centuries is the so-called "West European marriage pattern", the unique combination of two factors: (1) a substantial proportion of persons never marry; and (2) those who marry do so relatively late. John Hajnal, "European Marriage Studies in Perspective", in Glass and Eversley, eds., *Population in History*.
15. "Save in the case of Ireland, it is through the spread of birth control and of the more persistent use of birth control, that family size has been brought down in the West . . ." Glass and Grebenik, "World Population 1800–1950", p. 113. "It is clear that the decline [of fertility in Western populations] is closely related to the spread of birth control during the nineteenth and twentieth centuries." Massimo Livi-Bacci, "Fertility and Population Growth in Spain in the Eighteenth and Nineteenth Centuries", in Glass and Revelle, *Population and Social Change*, pp. 173ff.
16. Louis Henry, "Some Data on Natural Fertility", *Eugenics Quarterly*, vol. 8, no. 2 (1961) p. 81.
17. Coale, "The Demographic Transition Re-considered", p. 59.
18. Susan B. Hanley, "Fertility, Mortality, and Life Expectancy in Pre-Modern Japan", in *Population Studies*, vol. 28, no. 1 (March 1974), p. 136.
19. *Ibid.*, p. 134.
20. *Ibid.*, p. 134.
21. Henry, "Some Data on Natural Fertility", pp. 81–91; Coale, "The Demographic Transition Re-considered", especially p. 56; and D. E. C. Eversley, "Population, Economy and Society", in Glass and Eversley, eds., *Population in History*, p. 46.
22. Henry, "Some Data on Natural Fertility", especially pp. 90–1.
23. Etienne van de Walle, "Marriage and Marital Fertility", in Glass and Revelle, eds., *Population and Social Change*, p. 140. Van de Walle has also written the best study of the French material, "Motivations and Technology in the Decline of French Fertility",

in Robert Wheaton and Tamara Hareven, eds. *Family and Sexuality in French History* (University of Pennsylvania Press, Philadelphia, 1980), pp. 135–78.

24. David Glass, "Introduction", p. 4; and Henry himself: "I am not a historian, and I came to historical demography because I needed information on natural fertility [fertility unlimited by birth control]." Henry, "Historical Demography", p. 48.
25. "Should the reader find the postulate of pre-decline birth control an easy one to accept, let him be reminded that it is in sharp conflict with much of received theorizing on demographic transition." Demeny, "Early Fertility Decline", p. 162. See also Livi-Bacci, "Fertility and Population Growth", pp. 173–84; and Pierre Goubert, "Legitimate Fecundity and Infant Mortality in France During the Eighteenth Century: A Comparison", in Glass and Revelle, eds., *Population and Social Change*, pp. 321–30. There is also an earlier and important article by E. A. Wrigley, "Family Limitation in Pre-Industrial England", *Economic History Review*, Second Series, vol. 19, no. 1 (1966), pp. 82–109. These scholars have based their conclusions solely on data which show marked differences in fertility, and they have posited birth control as explanations even though they have had no direct evidence of either the means of control or the motivations. The condition of pre-modern Middle Eastern evidence is the exact opposite: we have much direct evidence of both techniques and motivations, but no statistical data.
26. The first clear statement of the alternatives is by Gosta Carlsson, "The Decline of Fertility: Innovation or Adjustment Process", *Population Studies*, vol. 20, no. 2 (November 1966), pp. 149–74.
27. Van de Walle, "Marriage and Marital Fertility", p. 139; and note 23 above.
28. Hollingsworth, *Historical Demography*, p. 327. However, Van de Walle and Knodel, in their most recent review of the problem, defend an essentially un-reformed "natural fertility" argument based on Henry: "Several reasons account for these differences [in levels of premodern fertility], but it is important to recall that deliberate attempts to limit family size are not among them." "Europe's Fertility Transition", p. 12.
29. In the first half of the twentieth century, early birth control clinic personnel, eager to push their own appliances (usually diaphragms or cervical caps), alleged high failure rates for coitus interruptus. "Yet the evidence contradicts this view . . . Requiring neither prior preparation nor medical supervision and costing nothing, coitus interruptus is widely practised without apparent harm and with considerable success." John Peel and Malcolm Potts, *Textbook of Contraceptive Practice* (Cambridge University Press, Cambridge, 1969, pp. 50–1). The fact that coitus interruptus is a highly effective technique for the prevention of conception was demonstrated first in the important study by R. K. Stiks and F. W. Notestein, *Controlled Fertility, An Evaluation of Clinical Service* (The Williams and Wilkins Company, Baltimore, 1940). I have called coitus interruptus a "medieval" method as a concession to the American preoccupation with mechanical and chemical intervention. In a French context, on the other hand, one would not hesitate to regard coitus interruptus as *the* modern method of birth control: "Coitus interruptus, or onanism, the chief means of contraception in the modern period . . ." Jean-Louis Flandrin, in *Annales E.S.C.* (Nov.–Dec. 1969), pp. 1370–90.

1 Why Islam permitted contraception

1. John T. Noonan, Jr, "Intellectual and Demographic History", in Glass and Revelle, eds., *Population and Social Change*, (London, 1972).
2. On the relationship between Christianity and Islam in medieval times, with an emphasis on Christian perceptions of Islam, see Norman Daniel, *Islam and the West, The Making of an Image* (Edinburgh University Press, Edinburgh, 1960).

3. R. W. Southern, *Western Views of Islam in the Middle Ages* (Harvard University Press, Cambridge, Mass., 1962), p. 58.
4. Daniel, *Islam and the West*, p. 135.
5. Ibn 'Abidin, *Radd*, p. 622.
6. See note 62, p. 129.
7. Daniel, *Islam and the West*, pp. 142, 147.
8. John T. Noonan, Jr, *Contraception, A History of Its Treatment by the Catholic Theologians and Canonists* (Harvard University Press, Cambridge, Mass., 1966).
9. Noonan, *Contraception*, p. 2, and chapter 7, especially pp. 200–5, 212–13.
10. *Ibid.*, pp. 200–1.
11. D. M. Feldman, *Birth Control in Jewish Law* (New York University Press, New York, 1968).
12. On pre-modern European medicine and contraception, see N. Himes, *The Medical History of Contraception* (Baltimore, 1936; reprinted New York, 1963), pp. 160ff., and Noonan, *Contraception*, pp. 222–7, 346–51.
13. A significant number of Arabic-speaking physicians were Jews and Christians: see Chapter 4, pp. 65–6.
14. In studying the Christian attitude toward contraception, scholars face the problem of the position of the "Church", which can be seen as above and separate from the opinions of individual Christians, regardless of how prevalent, rooted in tradition, and continuous in history these opinions may be. All Christian theologians and thinkers could have been wrong or heretical: "Only the Church is free from errors." Noonan asks about his sources:

   > Are these writers and legislative enactments to be equated with the Church? There is a tendency among some historians to make the identification, to say that the Catholic Church taught this or did that, when all that one can be certain of is that particular men, baptized Christians, occupying a particular role in the ecclesiastical system, did this or taught that . . . no great original theologian, not even an Augustine or a Thomas, has been able to write extensively on theology without writing what later has been determined to be heresy. Only the Church is free from error.
   >
   > (Noonan, *Contraception*, pp. 4–5.)

15. > The ulama were not a distinct class, but a category of persons overlapping other classes and social divisions, permeating the whole of society. So diverse were their contacts that they played a crucial role in the processes by which social communication was carried on and thus in the integration of the society into a working whole . . . By this interpenetration with all levels of society, the ulama . . . provided the framework of a common social and normative order.
   >
   > (Ira Lapidus, *Muslim Cities in the Later Middle Ages* (Harvard University Press, Cambridge, Mass., 1967), pp. 108–11.)

   The relationship between the 'ulama and the merchant class has been convincingly worked out, especially by Lapidus. In a sample of 600 merchants, 225 were found to be 'ulama, "not merely educated in the traditions, but practising teachers, sheiks, members of law schools, prayer leaders, and preachers ... judges, market inspectors, professional witnesses, and administrators of waqfs." (*Ibid.*, p. 109.) (For the complete lists and references see Lapidus, "The Muslim City in Mamluk Times", Ph.D. dissertation, Harvard University (1964), Appendices D, E, and F.) As a result of this study Lapidus contends that "instead of two classes, one broad 'ulama merchant body was formed". On the connection between the 'ulama and the "bourgeois families", see also A. H. Hourani, "Introduction: The Islamic City in the Light of Recent Research", in Hourani and Stern, eds., *The Islamic City* (Bruno Cassirer, Oxford, 1970), pp. 17–18, 22.

16. H. A. R. Gibb, "Islamic Biographical Literature", in B. Lewis and P. M. Holt, eds., *Historians of the Middle East* (Oxford University Press, London, 1962), pp. 54–58. One of the biographers of the fifteenth century defined his own sense of history as follows:

    History as a technical term means the communication of time, whereby the circumstances are accurately registered of the birth of *transmitters* and *imams*, and their death, health, intelligence, bodily state, journeys, pilgrimages, powers of memory, accuracy, and reputation of trustworthiness or otherwise . . . (Ibid., p. 55)

    The record of important events is subsidiary to this. See also F. Rosenthal, *A History of Muslim Historiography* (2nd edn, Leiden, 1968), p. 273.
17. Joseph Schacht, *An Introduction to Islamic Law* (Oxford University Press, Oxford, 1964), p. 34.
18. The *hadith* of the Prophet were collected in six principal "Collections of Traditions" in the second half of the third Islamic century. These "six books", the collections of Bukhari, Muslim, Ibn Maja, Abu Dawud, Tirmidhi, and Nasa'i, are particularly authoritative in Orthodox Islam (especially the first two, Bukhari and Muslim, usually referred to as the "two *sahihs*", or "correct ones").
19. For an index of these references see "'Azl allowed", and "'Azl disapproved of" in A. J. Wensinck, *Handbook of Early Muhammadan Tradition* (E. J. Brill, Leiden, 1960), p. 112.
20. *Ghila* is the act of sexual intercourse with a woman in lactation.
21. Schacht, *Islamic Law*; and N. J. Coulson, *A History of Islamic Law* (Edinburgh University Press, Edinburgh, 1964).
22. Ghazali, *Ihya'*, vol. 2, pp. 41–2.
23. Ghazali continues that a living being has gradations. The first state is the union of the male and female semens in the womb "in preparation for receiving life". To kill this would be a crime. When the embryo becomes a *mudgha*, the crime is worse; and when the body is formed and the foetus is ensouled, the crime is worse still. The height of the criminal offence is to kill the child after birth. The Islamic view of the stages of foetal development and regulations in Islamic law on abortion are discussed in Chapter 3.
24. Schacht, *Islamic Law*, pp. 63–4.
25. Ibn Hazm, *Muhalla*, vol. 10, pp. 70–1.
26. It was the opinion of the man more than his school of law that caught the attention of later jurists. Later writers refer to the opinion of "the school of Ibn Hazm". For example, Shawkani, *Nail al-awtar*, vol. 6, p. 348.
27. Ibn Qayyim, *Zad*, vol. 4, pp. 16–18. Ibn Qayyim's discussion here is perhaps the best survey of *hadith* and juridical opinion concerning birth control.
28. Shawkani, *Nail al-awtar*, vol. 4, p. 349.
29. The relevant *hadith* are discussed by Ibn Qayyim and Shawkani in the works cited above. They are of course available in the standard collections of *hadith*, such as those of Muslim and Bukhari. In this study, a *hadith* is considered relevant when it is used in argument by the Muslim jurists.
30. Ibn Qayyim, *Miftah*, vol. 2, p. 271.
31. Ibn Nujaim, *Bahr*, vol. 3, p. 214; Ibn al-Humam, *Sharh*, vol. 2, p. 295; Ibn 'Abidin, *Minhat*, vol. 3, p. 214; and elsewhere.
32. This was the opinion of Hanbali jurist, Ibn Qudama, *Mughni*, vol. 8, p. 134. Maliki opinion was as follows: "With the practice of coitus interruptus the child follows the husband anyway" (Ibn Juzaiy, *Qawanin*, p. 212). Ibn Qayyim's answer is similar: "If the man practised coitus interruptus the child is his anyway. Children are possible with the practice of withdrawal. There is a saying that 'All my children resulted from coitus interruptus'" (*Zad*, vol. 4, p. 18). The implication of the jurists' opinions is apparent –

the thing to correct was over-confidence in the reliability of the method, hence the insistence that "*children* are possible with the practice of withdrawal".

33. Ibn Nujaim, *Bahr*, vol. 3, p. 214. It is clear that the conditions for repudiation which the Hanafis listed were so strict as to make the possibility only theoretical. Nevertheless, it is in such discussions that the medieval knowledge of the most effective practice of coitus interruptus is elaborated. Some jurists tried to add sleeping and walking to urinating as another indication for the permission of repudiation, a suggestion that was perhaps based on the lapse of time between one coital act and the other. But the majority rejected this suggestion: "Urine washes it [the semen] out completely while sleeping and walking do not. Some semen is left on the glans and causes pregnancy" (Tahtawi, *Hashiyat*, vol. 2, p. 77). Urinating, by itself, was not enough: "Washing the penis should be required in addition to urinating to discount any possibility that some semen had remained on the glans. Washing removes such a remnant" (Ibn 'Abidin, *Radd*, p. 293; and *Minhat*, vol. 3, p. 214). There were even more elaborate instructions on this point, such as the following by Abu Hanifa, founder of the school: "When a man washes his penis before urinating, and then urinates causing a remnant of the semen to emerge, he should repeat washing his penis" (quoted by Ibn Nujaim, *Bahr*, vol. 3, p. 214, and Ibn al-Humam, *Sharh*, vol. 2, p. 295). Hanafi jurists could not have been more careful.
34. It must have been impossible to establish the facts about such consistent birth control practice as the jurists had demanded. Repudiation was possible, then, on social rather than technical grounds. This is clear in the classical case from the *Fatawa of Qadikhan* on disownership. The case concerned a man and his concubine who came in and out of his house at will. The jurists ruled that the master had a legal right for repudiating the child, but only because the woman was not a *muhsana (muhsana* means sheltered, of unblemished reputation): "If he had practised withdrawal and did not repeat intercourse, and had reason to suspect that the child was not his, then he is probably right provided she is not a *muhsana*." In contrast, "had she been a *muhsana*, the master could not have repudiated the child, because even though he practised withdrawal some of the semen may have dropped on the outer vulva and then entered her. Coitus interruptus could not be depended on [absolutely]" (Ibn Nujaim, *Bahr*, vol. 3, p. 215. Also Ibn al-Humam, *Sharh*, vol. 2, p. 295, Tahtawi, *Hashiyat*, vol. 2, p. 77).
35. Hilli, *Mukhtasar*, vol. 1, p. 193.
36. Related by Ibn Hanbal: Bahuti, *Kashshaf*, vol. 5, pp. 189–90.
37. Sha'rani, *Mizan*, vol. 2, p. 117.
38. Kasani, *Bada'i' al-sana'i'*, vol. 2, p. 334.
39. Shawkani, *Nail al-awtar*, vol. 6, pp. 346–350, for this and all other relevant *hadith*.
40. The *hadith* in question is the one after Abu Sa'id, where the Jews were reported to say that coitus interruptus "is minor infanticide".
41. Ibn Qayyim, *Zad*, vol. 4, p. 17.
42. Ibn Taimiya, *'Ilm al-suluk*, pp. 26–7.
43. Ghazali, *Ihya'*, vol. 2, pp. 41–2.
44. Feldman, *Birth Control in Jewish Law*, pp. 152–3.
45. *Ibid.*, p. 109.
46. *Ibid.*, p. 114.
47. This includes coitus interruptus, the condom, pre-coital intra-vaginal suppositories and tampons (including diaphragms and cervical caps, etc.): *Ibid.*, pp. 144, 152, 298.
48. *Ibid.*, pp. 302–3. Two examples from rabbinical *responsa* follow: (1) "But for those who would do so [that is, practise birth control] without reason, just because it is better for them without children, or because they lack faith, or have worries of support, Heaven forbid that they should be permitted." (2) "Where there is no fear of physical danger, just to avoid poverty, all would agree that it is forbidden."

49. Noonan, *Contraception*, p. 138.
50. *Ibid.*, p. 240.
51. *Ibid.*, pp. 257, 238–46.
52. *Ibid.*, p. 177.
53. *Ibid.*, p. 370.
54. Shawkani, *Nail al-awtar*, vol. 6, p. 350.
55. Himes, *Medical History of Contraception*, pp. 141, 149.
56. Ibn Qudama, *Mughni*, vol. 8, p. 133.
57. Ghazali, Ibn 'Abidin, Shawkani, in their works cited in notes 22, 33, 39 above, and San'ani, *Subul*, vol. 2, p. 193.
59. R. G. Potter, M. L. New, J. B. Wyon, and J. E. Gordon, "Lactation and Its Effects Upon Birth Intervals in Eleven Punjab Villages, India", *Journal of Chronic Diseases*, vol. 18, pp. 1125–40. The quotation is from p. 1131.
59. Ibn Hajar, *Fath al-bari*, vol. 11, pp. 219–20.
60. Bujairimi, *Iqna'*, vol. 3, p. 40.
61. Shawkani, San'ani, Ibn Qayyim, Ibn Qudama, cited notes 39, 58, 43, 32 above. Maqdisi, *Sharh*, vol. 8, p. 133, and Shirazi, *Muhadhdhab*, vol. 2, p. 66.
62. Ibn al-Najjar, *Muntaha*, vol. 2, p. 227; Ibn Abi Bakr, *Ghayat*, vol. 3, p. 91; Bahuti, *Kashshaf*, vol. 5, p. 189; Mardawi, *Tanqih*, p. 230; Ruhaibani, *Matalib*, vol. 5, p. 263; and Ibn Qudama, *Mughni*, vol. 8, p. 134.
63. *Revised Standard Version.*
64. Noonan, *Contraception*, chapter 14, pp. 438ff.
65. *Ibid.*, pp. 445–6; and Pius XII, "To members of the Congress of the Italian Association of Catholic Midwives: Castel Gandolfo, Monday, 29 October 1951", *Catholic Documents* 6 (1952), pp. 1–16.
66. Feldman, *Birth Control in Jewish Law*, chapter 13, "An Oral Contraceptive", pp. 235ff.

2 Contraception and the rights of women

1. Joseph Schacht, *An Introduction to Islamic Law* (Oxford University Press, Oxford, 1964). *The Origins of Muhammadan Jurisprudence* (Oxford University Press, Oxford, 1950), also by Schacht, is an earlier and more specialized treatise. N. J. Coulson, *A History of Islamic Law* (Edinburgh University Press, Edinburgh, 1964) is particularly useful as a corrective to some of the excesses of Schacht's theory on the origins of the Traditions (*Hadith*). For quick reference, the articles in the *Encyclopedia of Islam* (*EI*), New Edition; and the *Shorter EI*, are often adequate (many of these were written by Schacht). A short but perceptive introduction to Islamic law is by H. A. R. Gibb, *Mohammedanism* (Oxford University Press Galaxy Books, New York, 1962, 2nd edition; first published 1953), chapter 6, "The Shari'a", pp. 88–106.
2. Schacht, *Islamic Law*, p. 67.
3. Schacht, *Islamic Law*, pp. 120–3, 200–2; Schacht, *Origins*, pp. 283–7; Schacht, "Ahkam", *EI*, new edn; R. Brunschvig, "Perspectives", in G. E. von Grunebaum, ed., *Unity and Variety in Muslim Civilization* (Chicago, 1955), pp. 52ff.
4. Schacht, *Islamic Law*, pp. 120–3, 200–2.
5. Shafi'i, *Umm*, vol. 7, p. 173; Ghazali, *Ihya'*, vol. 2, p. 141; Ghazali, *Wajiz*, vol. 2, p. 21; Sha'rani, *Mizan*, vol. 2, p. 117; Dimashqi, *Ikhtilaf*, p. 106; Minhaji, *Jawahir*, vol. 2, p. 51. Ghazali mentions opposite opinions, and Sha'rani, Dimashqi, and Minhaji report the different Hanafi, Maliki, and Hanbali opinions. Perhaps the best general discussion of Shafi'i attitudes is by Zabidi, *Ithaf*, vol. 5, p. 379 – his great commentary on Ghazali's *Ihya'*, where he also surveys the opinions of the other schools of law.
6. The discussion by Ibn Hajar, *Fath al-bari*, vol. 11, pp. 216ff, is a rich and lucid survey

of Shafi'i and other opinions, especially pp. 220–2. See also Qastallani, *Irshad al-sari*, vol. 8, p. 104; Nawawi, *Sharh*, vol. 6, p. 192; 'Aini, *'Umdat al-qari*, vol. 20, p. 195; and 'Iraqi, *Tarh al-tathrib*, vol. 7, p. 60.

7. Shirazi, *Muhadhdhab*, vol. 2, p. 66.
8. "Those who permit it without condition say that the woman has a right to orgasm (*dhawq al-'usaila*), not to ejaculation" (Ibn Qayyim, *Zad*, vol. 4, p. 16). See the discussion of *dhawq al-'usaila* by 'Iraqi, *Tarh al-tathrib*, vol. 7, pp. 97–9, and the very important analysis by Ibn al-'Arabi, *Ahkam al-qur'an*, vol. 1, p. 407.
9. Sijistani, *Masa'il*, p. 168; Ibn Qudama, *Muqanni'*, vol. 3, p. 103; Ibn 'Ubaidan, *Zawa'id*, p. 205; Hajawi, *Rawd*, part 2, p. 286; Manqur, *Masa'il*, vol. 2, p. 119; Mardawi, *Insaf*, vol. 8, p. 348; Mardawi, *Tanqih*, p. 230; Ibn al-Najjar, *Muntaha*, part 2, p. 227; Bahuti, *Kashshaf*, vol. 5, p. 189; Ibn Abi Bakr, *Ghayat*, vol. 3, p. 91; Ruhaibani, *Matalib*, vol. 5, p. 261; Ibn Duyan, *Manar*, vol. 2, p. 217; Najdi, *Hidayat*, pp. 472–3.
10. Ibn Qudama, *Mughni*, vol. 8, p. 134; Al-Husain, *Zawa'id*, p. 679.
11. Ibn Duyan, *Manar*, vol. 2, p. 217; Ibn Qudama, *Mughni*, vol. 8, p. 133; Al-Husain, *Zawa'id*, p. 679.
12. Mardawi (Muhammad), *'Iqd*, vol. 2, p. 119; Mardawi ('Ali) *Insaf*, vol. 8, p. 348; Ibn 'Ubaidan, *Zawa'id*, p. 205; Maqdisi, *Sharh*, vol. 8, p. 133, mentions Shafi'i by name; Ibn Qayyim, *Zad*, vol. 4, pp. 16–18.
13. Maqdisi, *Sharh*, vol. 8, p. 132.
14. Maqdisi, *Sharh*, vol. 8, p. 133; Ibn Qudama, *Mughni*, vol. 8, p. 133; Mardawi, *Tanqih*, p. 230; Bahuti, *Kashshaf*, vol. 5, p. 189; Ibn Abi Bakr, *Ghayat*, vol. 3, p. 91; Ruhaibani, *Matalib*, vol. 5, p. 261.
15. Tahawi, *Mukhtasar*, p. 190; Sarakhsi, *Sharh al-siyar*, vol. 1, p. 165; Khuwarizmi, *Jami'*, vol. 2, p. 118; Razi, *Ahkam al-qur'an*, vol. 1, pp. 416–17; Quduri, *Jawhara*, vol. 2, p. 26; Kasani, *Bada'i' al-sana'i'* , vol. 2, p. 334; Marghinani, *Hidaya*, vol. 1, p. 157; Ibn Nujaim, *Bahr*, vol. 3, p. 214; Ibn al-Humam, *Sharh*, vol. 2, pp. 494–5; Babarti, *Sharh*, vol. 2, pp. 494–5; Ibn 'Abidin, *Radd*, p. 622; *Fatawa al-'Alamgiriyya*, vol. 1, p. 355; Ibn 'Abidin ('Ala'), *Hadiyya*, p. 246; 'Abd al-Ghaffar, *Ahkam*, p. 45.
16. Ibn Nujaim, *Bahr*, vol. 3, p. 214; Ibn al-Humam, *Sharh*, vol. 2, p. 494; Sindi, *Matana*, p. 437; Ibn 'Abidin, *Minhat*, vol. 3, p. 214; Ibn 'Abidin, *Radd*, p. 622; 'Abd al-Ghaffar, *Ahkam*, pp. 45–6.
17. Ibn 'Abidin, *Radd*, p. 622.
18. Malik, *Muwatta'*, vol. 2, p. 596; Ibn Juzaiy, *Qawanin*, p. 212; Wazzani, *Mi'yar*, vol. 3, p. 226; Ibn Yamun, *Adab al-nikah*, no regular pagination; Dardir, *Sharh*, vol. 2, p. 266; Dasuqi, *Hashiyat*, vol. 2, p. 266; 'Ulaish, *Fath*, vol. 1, p. 398; Kasadawi, *Badr*, pp. 262–3.
19. Hattab, *Mawahib*, vol. 3, pp. 476–7; Ibn Yamun, *Adab al-nikah*, no pagination – in his discussion of *'azl*; Dardir, *Sharh*, vol. 2, p. 266; 'Ulaish, *Fath*, vol. 1, p. 398.
20. 'Ulaish, *Fath*, vol. 1, p. 398; Kasadawi, *Badr*, pp. 262–3.
21. Tusi, *Mabsut*, vol. 4, p. 267; Hilli, *Mukhtasar*, vol. 1, p. 172; Hilli, *Shara'i'*, vol. 2, p. 270; Hilli (Ibn Mutahhar), *Sharh*, vol. 2, p. 109; *idem, Tadhkirat*, vol. 2, no pagination, under "ahkam al-khalwa"; 'Amili, *Masalik*, no pagination, under *'azl*; Kashani, *Tahdhib*, vol. 3, p. 114.
22. Hilli, *Shara'i'*, vol. 2, p. 270; 'Amili, *Rawda*, vol. 5, p. 102; 'Amili, *Masalik*, under *'azl*; Hilli (Ibn Mutahhar), *Tadhkirat*, under "ahkam al-khalwa"; Yazdi, *'Urwa*, vol. 2, p. 628; 'Amili (al-Hurr), *Wasa'il*, vol. 7, p. 106.
23. Tusi, *Mabsut*, vol. 4, p. 267 (Tusi uses the term *kaffara*, religious expiation, instead of *diya*, blood money, which is used by the authorities below); Hilli, *Mukhtasar*, vol. 1, p. 172; Hilli, *Shara'i'*, vol. 2, p. 270; 'Amili, *Rawda*, vol. 5, p. 103; Yazdi, *'Urwa*, vol. 2, p. 628; 'Ajali, *Sara'ir*, no pagination, under *bab ma yustahabb fi'luh*.
24. Tusi, *Mabsut*, vol. 4, p. 267.

25. "'Ala al-istihbab": Hilli, *Shara'i'*, vol. 2, p. 270; 'Amili, *Rawda*, vol. 5, p. 103; 'Ajali, *Sara'ir*, under *bab ma yustahabb fi'luh*.
26. Tusi, *Nihaya*, p. 492, says, "The man is permitted to practise withdrawal, even without a precondition [in the marriage contract]." See also 'Amili, *Masalik*, under *'azl*; 'Amili (al-Hurr), *Wasa'il*, vol. 7, pp. 105–6. The chapter on coitus interruptus in an early (fourth Islamic century) Shi'i book consists simply of four traditions to the effect that "withdrawal is the man's right", and that "it is proper to practise withdrawal with a free woman if the man so wishes, even when she protests, for it is none of her business". Razi (Muhammad Ibn Ya'qub), *Kafi*, vol. 5, p. 504. Ibn al-Muttahar al-Hilli in the *Tadhkirat*, vol. 2, under "ahkam al-khalwa", explained these traditions by adding that the woman "has a right to intercourse, but not to ejaculation", a view similar to that of the Shafi'i and other Sunni jurists who sanctioned coitus interruptus without the free woman's consent.
27. Al-Qadi al-Nu'man, *Da'a'im*, vol. 2, p. 210.
28. Atfiyash, *Sharh al-nil*, vol. 3, p. 298.
29. Murtada, *Al-Bahr al-zakhkhar*, vol. 3, pp. 80–1. The Zaidis, like the Hanafis and Hanbalis, also argued that coitus interruptus is absolutely licit when serious "harm" was foreseen in case of a pregnancy.
30. Ibn Qayyim, *Rawdat*, pp. 119–20, 134, and *Bada'i'*, vol. 4, pp. 96–8. See also Ibn Rajab, *Qawa'id*, pp. 265–6.
31. Ibn Qayyim, *Bada'i'*, vol. 4, p. 96.
32. "In the case of a woman without a husband, and who suffers from sexual deprivation, some [Hanbali jurists] have said (*wa qala ba'du ashabina*) that she is permitted to use a dildo (*kir-ranj*), which is something in the shape of a penis made of leather. The woman introduces it, or something like it such as tiny cucumbers or squash" (Ibn Qayyim, *Bada'i'*, vol. 4, pp. 96–7). See also Ibn Qayyim, *Rawdat*, p. 120.
33. "When men abstain from sexual intercourse, the semen accumulates, turns cold, and acquires poisonous [qualities]. The semen sends to the heart and brain harmful and poisonous fumes . . . You should know that the retention of semen is extremely harmful, and may cause one of the testicles to recede" (Ibn Sina, *Qanun*, vol. 2, p. 535).
34. Ibn Qayyim, *Rawdat*, pp. 119, 134, and *Badai'*, vol. 4, pp. 97–8.
35. Nawawi, *Rawdat al-talibin*, vol. 7, p. 206. The Malikis as well took the same position – see Ibn al-Madani, *Jawahir*, no pagination. An excellent survey of the subject is by Zabidi, *Ithaf*, vol. 5, pp. 306–7 and 377. See also Qurtubi, *Jami'*, vol. 12, pp. 105–6; Khazin, *Lubab al-ta'wil*, vol. 5, p. 32; Baghawi, *Ma'alim al-tanzil*, vol. 5, p. 32; Jamal, *Futuhat*, vol. 3, p. 184; Sha'rani, *Kashf al-ghimma*, vol. 2, pp. 113fff.
36. "Abu Hanifa and Ahmad [Ibn Hanbal] permit masturbation when a man fears sin (*al-fitna*); masturbation by the hand of his wife or concubine is also permitted, but Qadi Husain adds that it is permitted with *karaha* (that is, the rank of "blameworthy"), because it is similar to coitus interruptus" (Brusawi, *Ruh al-bayan*, vol. 6, p. 69).
37. "The slave has rights as a person; in particular, he or she can get married. The male slave may marry up to two female slaves; the female slave may also marry a free man who is not her owner" (Schacht, *Islamic Law*, p. 127; see also R. Brunschvig, "'Abd", *EI*, new edn, vol. 1, pp. 24–40).
38. Ghazali, *Wajiz*, vol. 2, p. 21; Nawawi, *Sharh*, vol. 6, p. 192; 'Aini, *'Umdat al-qari*, vol. 20, p. 195; 'Iraqi, *Tarh al-tathrib*, vol. 7, p. 60; Sha'rani, *Mizan*, vol. 2, p. 117; Dimashqi, *Ikhtilaf*, p. 214; Minhaji, *Jawahir*, vol. 2, p. 51; Shirazi, *Muhadhdhab*, vol. 2, p. 66; Matba'i, *Majmu'*, vol. 15, p. 577.
39. Ibn Qudama, *Muqanni'*, vol. 3, p. 103; Hajawi, *Rawd*, part 2, p. 286; Mardawi, *Khilaf*, vol. 8, pp. 348–9; Mardawi, *Tanqih*, p. 230; Mardawi, *'Iqd*, vol. 2, p. 119; Ibn al-Najjar, *Muntaha*, vol. 2, p. 227; Bahuti, *Kashshaf*, vol. 5, p. 189; Ibn Abi Bakr,

Ghayat, vol. 3, p. 91; Ruhaibani, *Matalib*, vol. 5, p. 261; Najdi, *Hidayat*, p. 473; Al-Husain, *Zawa'id*, p. 679.

40. Mardawi, *Insaf*, vol. 8, pp. 348–9; Ruhaibani, *Matalib*, vol. 5, p. 261.
41. Maqdisi, *Sharh*, vol. 8, p. 134. Maqdisi adds that in the *hadith* ("The Prophet forbade the practice of coitus interruptus with a free woman except with her permission") there is no mention of slave masters. The consent, he says, "is specific to the free wife".
42. Ibn Qudama, *Mughni*, vol. 8, p. 134; Mardawi, *Insaf*, vol. 8, pp. 348–9.
43. Ibn Abi Bakr, *Ghayat*, vol. 3, p. 91; Ruhaibani, *Matalib*, vol. 5, p. 261.
44. Maqdisi, *Sharh*, vol. 8, p. 134.
45. Shaibàni, *Muwatta'*, vol. 1, p. 185.
46. For insistence on the master's permission, see Khuwarizmi, *Jami'*, vol. 2, p. 119; Ibn Nujaim, *Bahr*, vol. 3, p. 214; Ibn 'Abidin, *Radd*, p. 622. Ibn Nujaim and Ibn 'Abidin report and reject the opposite view. The following do not mention opposing views: Mawla Khusraw, *Durar*, vol. 1, p. 351; Ibn al-Humam, *Sharh*, vol. 2, pp. 494–5; *Fatawa al-'Alamgiriyya*, vol. 1, p. 355. For insistence on the slave wife's permission, see Tahawi, *Mukhtasar*, p. 190. Kasani thought that either the permission of the master or that of the slave-wife is needed, "and God knows best" (*Bada'i'*, vol. 2, p. 334).
47. Tahawi, *Mukhtasar*, p. 190; Quduri, *Jawhara*, vol. 2, p. 26; 'Aini, *Ramz*, vol. 1, p. 161; Kasani, *Bada'i'*, vol. 2, p. 334; Marghinani, *Hidaya*, vol. 1, p. 157; Halabi, *Multaqa*, p. 97; Ibn Nujaim, *Bahr*, vol. 3, p. 214; Ibn 'Abidin, *Radd*, p. 622; Babarti, *Sharh*, vol. 2, pp. 494–5; Afghani, *Kashf*, vol. 1, p. 181.
48. Malik, *Muwatta'*, vol. 2, p. 596; Ibn Juzaiy, *Qawanin*, p. 212; Wazzani, *Mi'yar*, vol. 3, p. 226; Ibn Yamun, *Adab al-nikah*; Ibn al-Madani, *Jawahir*.
49. Zurqani, *Sharh*, vol. 4, pp. 155–6; Dardir, *Sharh*, vol. 2, p. 226; 'Ulaish, *Fath*, vol. 1, p. 398.
50. Dasuqi, *Hashiyat*, vol. 2, p. 266.
51. Neither the slave-wife's nor her master's permission was needed. Razi (Muhammad Ibn Ya'qub), *Kafi*, vol. 5, p. 504; Tusi, *Mabsut*, vol. 4, pp. 266–7; Hilli, *Mukhtasar*, vol. 1, p. 172; 'Amili, *Rawda*, vol. 5, pp. 102–3; 'Amili, *Masalik*, no pagination, under *'azl*; Kashani, *Tahdhib*, vol. 3, p. 114.
52. Zaidi jurisprudence cited the whole range of opinion: the need for the master's permission, the need for the slave-wife's permission, and unconditional sanction are mentioned. The last view was preferred because of the possible slavery of children, even when their liberty was a condition in the marriage contract, "in fear of deceit" (Murtada, *Al-Bahr al-zakhkhar*, vol. 3, pp. 80–1).
53. "Because her children belong to the master" (Al-Qadi al-Nu'man, *Da'a'im*, vol. 2, p. 210).
54. Atfiyash, *Sharh al-nil*, vol. 3, p. 298.
55. See the article on "Mut'a", H. A. R. Gibb and J. H. Kramers, eds., *Shorter Encyclopedia of Islam* (Leiden, 1961), pp. 418–20.
56. Faid al-Kashi, *Tahdhib*, vol. 3, p. 114.
57. 'Amili (Al-Hurr), *Wasa'il*, vol. 7, pp. 488–9.
58. *Ibid.*
59. According to Ghazali, *Ihya'*, vol. 2, p. 41: "Some women refuse to bear children because of a dislike of pregnancy, a fetish for absolute cleanliness, or an extreme precaution regarding the bother of childbirth, post-partum, and nursing."
60. Chapter 4, Table 9, p. 88.
61. Ibn Taimiya, *Fatawa*, vol. 1, p. 71, no. 36.
62. Ibn Nujaim, *Bahr*, vol. 3, p. 215, followed by Ibn 'Abidin, *Hadiyya*, p. 246.
63. He probably meant that with coitus interruptus the woman's permission was required by the jurists because withdrawal impinged on two of her basic rights (children and

sexual fulfilment), and it was practised by the *man*. The practice became proper when she gave her permission. Apparently the same problem did not exist when she herself practised a form of birth control. What about the man's right to children? Ibn 'Abidin, *Radd*, p. 622, and *Minhat*, vol. 3, p. 215, followed by 'Abd al-Ghaffar, *Ahkam*, p. 45.

64. 'Ulaish, *Fath*, vol. 1, p. 398.
65. *"Al-akhbar khaliya 'anhu"*, 'Amili, *Rawda*, vol. 5, p. 103.
66. E. Tyan, "Fatwa", *EI*, new edn, vol. 2, pp. 886–7.
67. Ibn Nujaim, *Bahr*, vol. 3, p. 215.
68. Ibn 'Abidin, *Radd*, p. 622.

3 Conception theory in Muslim thought

1. The work of Manfred Ullmann, in *Die Medizin im Islam* (E. J. Brill, Leiden, 1970), and *Die Natur- und Geheimwissenschaften im Islam* (E. J. Brill, Leiden, 1972), pp. 5–61 is the basic guide to the rich biological sources in Arabic.
2. A very useful introduction to these ideas, with copious quotations from the original writings is by Howard B. Adelmann, *Marcello Malpighi and the Evolution of Embryology*, 5 vols. (Cornell University Press, Ithaca, 1966), vol. 2, ch. 22, "The Ancients", pp. 729–48.
3. In addition to the discussion and references below, consult: Ikhwan al-Safa', *Rasa'il*, vol. 2, *risala* 25, pp. 417–55; Ibn Malka, *Mu'tabar*, vol. 2, pp. 236–71; Razi (Fakhr al-Din), *Mabahith*, vol. 2, pp. 226–9, 258–79; Qazwini, *Hikmat al-'ain*, pp. 640–56; Mulla Sadra, *Asfar*, vol. 8, pp. 108–29, 143–8; *idem*, *Mabda'*, p. 210; Karmani, *Rahat*, pp. 430–1; Qazwini, *'Aja'ib*, vol. 1, pp. 322ff.; Mas'udi, *Muruj*, vol. 2, pp. 354ff.; Balkhi, *Bad'*, vol. 2, pp. 74–83; Tabari, *Ta'rikh*, vol. 1, part 1, pp. 81, 86–91, 132–7; Ibn al-Jawzi, *Wafa*, vol. 1, pp. 340–3; Zabidi, *Ithaf*, vol. 5, p. 381; Saffuri, *Nuzhat*, vol. 2, pp. 28–32. In particular, the following treatments are similar in method to that of Ibn Qayyim: Mas'udi, *Muruj*; Qazwini, *'Aja'ib*; Saffuri, *Nuzhat*; Mulla Sadra, *Mabda'*; and Zabidi, *Ithaf*.

   One of Ibn Qayyim's books, *Miftah dar al-sa'ada*, his most ambitious natural theology (which also treated generation, vol. 1, pp. 258ff., and *passim*), has had an interesting history. The *Miftah* was abbreviated three separate times, apparently by different hands, between the fourteenth and eighteenth centuries. These abbreviations were then attributed to three other authors, all towering figures in the medieval culture. Ghazali was the putative author of the abbreviation which dropped the references to scientific authorities and kept the references to the Quran and *hadith* (Anonymous, *Al-Hikma fi makhluqat Allah*). To Jahiz was attributed the version which dropped the religious references and kept and augmented the references to scientific authorities (Anonymous, *Al-Dala'il wa al-i'tibar 'ala al-khalq wa al-tadbir*). The Shi'i version *Kitab tawhid al-Mufaddal*, was attributed to no less than the Imam Ja'far al-Sadiq (Majlisi, *Bihar al-anwar*, vol. 2, pp. 19–47, and vol. 14, *passim*).
4. Jacques Roger, *Les sciences de la vie dans la pensée francaise du XVIII*[e] *siecle* (2nd edn, Paris, 1971) is the best work. See also F. J. Cole, *Early Theories of Sexual Generation* (Oxford University Press, Oxford, 1930); Joseph Needham, *A History of Embryology* (Cambridge, University Press, Cambridge, 1934); Elizabeth Gasking, *Investigations into Generation 1651–1828* (London, 1967); Adelmann, *Marcello Malpighi*; Frederick B. Churchill, "The History of Embryology as Intellectual History", *Journal of the History of Biology*, vol. 3, no. 1, (1970), pp. 65–86.
5. The standard modern work is by Erna Lesky, *Die Zeugungs- und Vererbungslehren der Antike und ihr Nachwirken* (Abhandlungen der Geistes- und Sozial-wissenschaftlichen Klasse, Akademie der Wissenschaften und der Literatur in Mainz, no. 19, 1950). The *Journal of the History of Biology* has published important work in the last dozen years.

The following three articles are especially relevant: Anthony Preus, "Science and Philosophy in Aristotle's *Generation of Animals*" vol. 3, no. 2 (1970), pp. 1–52, and "Galen's Criticism of Aristotle's Conception Theory", vol. 10, no. 1 (1977), pp. 65–86, and Maryanne Cline Horowitz, "Aristotle and Women", vol. 9, no. 2. (1976), pp. 183–214.

6. Consider the pitiful chapter, "From Galen to the Renaissance", pp. 749–51 in vol. 2 of Adelmann's *Marcello Malpighi.*
7. But here a word of caution is necessary: technological advances in the history of biology have not always led to progress in theory. Consider the curious history of the idea of preformation in the seventeenth and eighteenth centuries. The first microscopes allowed the early modern scientists to see what the naked eye before them could not see. But some of these scientists, observing semen under a primitive microscope, found it to be swimming with tiny creatures complete with heads and limbs. And other, better scientists, who could not themselves see this so-called "homunculus" or "little man", nevertheless believed in its existence. All the ancient and medieval scientists, on the other hand, had dismissed, when they considered at all, the idea that the semen contained a tiny, completely formed animal. See Roger, *Les sciences*, Cole, *Sexual Generation*, and Gasking, *Investigations.*
8. Hippocrates, *The Seed*, translated by I. M. Lonie in *Hippocratic Writings*, ed. G. E. R. Lloyd (Penguin, London, 1978), p. 322.
9. Thus, in the second half of the nineteenth century, shortly before all such speculation was to be ended by the development of modern genetics, Hippocrates' theory was still vital as one alternative in a two-thousand-year-old debate: "I assume that [the various tissues and substances of the body] throw off minute granules which are dispersed throughout the whole system . . . These granules may be called gemmules. They are collected from all parts of the system to constitute the sexual elements, and their development in the next generation forms a new being . . . Hence, it is not the reproductive organs or buds which generate new organisms, but the units of which each individual is composed. These assumptions constitute the provisional hypothesis which I have called Pangenesis" (Charles Darwin, *The Variation of Animals and Plants under Cultivation*, 2 vols. (2nd edn, New York, 1897), pp. 369–70). In a note to his passage above, Darwin writes, "More than two thousand years ago Aristotle combated a view of this kind, which, as I hear from Dr. W. Ogle, was held by Hippocrates and others" (*ibid.*, p. 370) (this was the second authorized edition of the book).

   The Hippocratic arguments in support of pangenesis, Aristotle's objections to them, and a medieval rebuttal of Aristotle from a Hippocratic point of view (all from a medieval Arabic source) are given below in notes 47, 48, and 50, pp. 137–9.
10. Aristotle, *Generation of Animals*, English translation by A. L. Peck (Loeb Classical Library, Harvard University Press, Cambridge, Mass., 1942), 726b. Unless otherwise indicated, all references to the *Generation of Animals* (*GA*) are to this edition.
11. *GA*, 766b, lines 7–12.
12. *GA*, 728a.
13. *GA*, 726b, line 31 to 727a, line 4.
14. In the final analysis, it is nearly incidental that some male animals have semen – the material substance is really superfluous to the male principle in generation. According to Aristotle, some male creatures do not have semen and can "form" the foetus without it. Where the male semen does exist, it soon dissolves and disappears after entering the uterus because, constituted as it is of *pneuma* (spirit) and water, the visible element – water – is inactive. *GA*, 730b.
15. *GA*, 738b.
16. Preus, "Science and Philosophy", especially pp. 1–4.

17. Aristotle's primary concern with this grand theme of embryology largely accounts for the praise he has received in histories of the subject.
18. This was Ibn Sina's elegant way of putting the question, *Hayawan*, IX, 2 (Tehran edn, p. 430).
19. *GA*, 736b–7a: the crucial passage is on pp. 170–3 of Peck.
20. William Harvey, a great student of Aristotle in the seventeenth century, registered this exasperated but penetrating complaint concerning Aristotle's solution: "[The most excellent philosopher] is driven to acknowledge something incorporeal, and coming from foreign sources, which he supposes (like art or the mind) to form the foetus with intelligence and foresight, and to institute and ordain all the parts for its welfare. He takes refuge, I say, in a thing which is not recognizable by us; namely, in a spirit contained in the seed, and in a frothy body, and in the nature of that spirit, corresponding in proportion to the elements of the stars. But what this is he has nowhere informed us." ("On Animal Generation", in *The Works of William Harvey*, translated by R. Willis, (London, 1847), pp. 349–50, quoted by Gasking, *Investigations*, p. 34).

    It was but an easy step for Aristotelian monotheist theologians like Fakhr al-Din Razi (*Tafsir*, vol. 19, pp. 224–5) and Thomas Aquinas (*Summa Theologiae*, vol. 15, Questions 118 and 119, pp. 145ff.) to replace *pneuma* by the direct action of God or his angels as their own explanation of foetal development.
21. Horowitz, "Aristotle and Women", discusses some of these considerations. The response by Johannes Morsnick, "Was Aristotle's Biology Sexist?", *Journal of the History of Biology*, vol. 12, no. 1 (1979), pp. 83–112, is not really convincing.
22. *GA*, Book IV, especially 767a to 769a.
23. *GA*, 717a (Peck pp. 19–21): "Now it is evident that this part is not *necessary* for generation ... This then is the object for which the testes have been contrived: they make the movement of the seminal residue more steady ... In man they do this by maintaining in position the doubling back of the passages ..., since the testes are no integral part of the passages: they are merely attached thereto, just like the stone weights which women hang on their looms when they are weaving . . . A bull immediately after castration has been known to mount a cow and effect impregnation . . ." Jahiz had great fun with Aristotle and his bull in the *Hayawan* (Beirut edn, vol. 5, pp. 264–5).
24. Galen, *De semine*, II, 1 (Kuhn IV), pp. 593–4; Ibn Sina, *Hayawan*, IX, 2 (Tehran edn, pp. 428–9).
25. Galen, *De semine*, I, 5 (Kuhn IV), pp. 527ff.
26. Aristotle's mechanism for semen formation had the virtue of associating spermatic production with the central physiological system of the body, that of digestion and nourishment. Here semen was seen as natural residue of the body. Semen – a giver of life – was derived from the purest nourishment, blood that begins as food – the source of life. In contrast, the Hippocratic mechanism, in as much as it described semen as a kind of "melting" or "secretion" from the organs, was associated with waste products, such as sweat or urine.
27. Owsei Temkin, *Galenism: Rise and Decline of a Medical Philosophy* (Cornell University Press, Ithaca, 1973) is essential reading on Galenism. Unfortunately, it does not deal much with the problem of generation.
28. This was one of Ibn Sina's important achievements. The early medieval Arabic translation of Aristotle's *Generation of Animals* was especially poor. Ibn Sina's summary was the essential guide to understanding it, and also proved to be a potent substitute for it. The original Arabic translation, commonly ascribed to Yahya Ibn al-Batriq, has been edited, with Introduction and Glossary, by J. Brugman and H. J. Drossart Lulofs, *Aristotle's Generation of Animals, the Arabic Translation* (E. J. Brill,

Leiden, 1971). Fakhr al-Din Razi in his *Mabahith*, vol. 2, cleared up the remaining problems with Ibn Sina's presentation of Aristotle's argument. (We can draw a line to show the introduction of Aristotle's biology into medieval thought. In the Middle East it was from Aristotle to Ibn Sina to Razi; in Europe, from Aristotle to Ibn Sina to Albertus Magnus.)

29. Ibn Sina, *Hayawan*, IX, 1 (Tehran edn, p. 427).
30. Ibn Sina's opening statement makes clear the extent to which Galenism had come to define the basic issues of generation. He begins defensively by saying that Aristotle *does not* deny (1) that the female contribution to generation is "something like semen", and (2) that the male semen "mixes" with the female contribution to form the foetus. This assertion, at first reading, appears to depart substantially from Aristotle, but Ibn Sina's interpretation ultimately strengthens the original position of Aristotle in the *Generation of Animals* (Hayawan, IX, 1 (Tehran edn, pp. 427–8)). Ibn Sina's description of the ovaries is in XV, 1 (Tehran edn, p. 509).
31. *Hayawan*, IX, 3 (Tehran edn, p. 433). Ibn Sina is careful not to say that "female semen" and "menses" are one and the same thing; on the contrary, he admits that the female semen is a specific and independent substance which has undergone further concoction than simple menstrual blood (IX, 1 (Tehran edn, p. 428)). However, loyalty to Aristotle drives him to use language suggesting that Aristotle was *justified* in calling the female contribution "menses": "there is no reason not to call every humidity that is a product of blood in the womb 'menses'" (*ibid*).
32. The passage in question is *GA*, 728a, lines 26–31. Ibn Sina quotes the crucial sentence verbatim from the Arabic translation of *GA*, *Hayawan*, XV, 3 (Tehran edn, p. 512).
33. *Hayawan*, XV, 3 (Tehran edn, pp. 512–13). Also IX, 3 (Tehran edn, pp. 433–4a) and XV, 1 (Tehran edn, p. 507) for Ibn Sina's reaffirmation of Aristotle's original ideas.
34. Galen was able to accept Aristotle's idea that semen is formed of blood in the final state of nourishment, and still hold the Hippocratic view that both male and female produce semen. Ibn Sina was able to accept the Hippocratic–Galenic view that females contribute semen, and then give it the role which Aristotle had assigned to the menses.
35. In his dissection of the ovaries, Galen had described the ovarian ducts and reported finding in them a fluid which he identified as the "female semen". Someone who still wanted to defend Aristotle could argue, as Ibn Rushd did, that this fluid (observable at intercourse?) is merely lubrication, and has nothing directly to do with generation. Ibn Rushd continues: "As to the 'testicles' which Galen claims women have, it is possible that they play no role in generation – if the 'semen' they produce has no role in generation. This is not strange when you consider that breasts in the female are organs of generation, but do not have such a function in the male. Both observation and reason show that the female semen does not have a role in generation. As far as evidence from observation is concerned, Aristotle has argued that a woman can become pregnant without ever experiencing emission. I too have pursued this matter by observation and found the experience true . . . Also I have asked women about it, and they tell me the same. That is, they often become pregnant without experiencing pleasure. The argument [from theory] is that if the female semen could do what the male can, a female should be able to generate by herself, and there would be no need for the male" (*Kulliyat*, p. 30).
36. Luke Demaitre and Anthony A. Travill, "Human Embryology and Development in the Works of Albertus Magnus", pp. 405–40, and Nancy G. Siraisi, "The Medical Learning of Albertus Magnus", pp. 379–404, in James A. Weisheipl, ed., *Albertus Magnus and the Sciences* (Pontifical Institute of Medieval Studies, Toronto, 1980).
37. George Sarton, *Introduction to the History of Science* (Baltimore, 1927–48), vol. 2, part 1, p. 63.
38. Ibn Sina, *Qanun*, vol. 2, pp. 533–4.

39. Ibn Rushd, *Kulliyat*, p. 31. Also Kazaruni, *Mughni*, p. 695.
40. Ibn Sina, *Hayawan*, IX, (Tehran edn, p. 428), and all of IX, 2: "On Galen's Criticism of Aristotle, and the Refutation of That Criticism, and the Establishment of Its Fatuousness" (Tehran edn, pp. 428–32).
41. Ibn Sina, *Qanun*, vol. 2, p. 534.
42. Ibn Sina's principle of "following the physicians" in his medical (as distinct from his philosophical) writings was noted in medieval times by Bukhari *Sharh al-'ain*, p. 653. Ibn Sina himself explicitly stated this principle in the opening pages of the *Qanun*.
43. Tabari, *Firdaws*, pp. 30–40; Razi, *Hawi*, part 9, pp. 75–127; Ibn 'Abbas, *Kamil*, vol. 1, pp. 117–21; 'Arib Ibn Sa'id, *Khalq al-janin*, pp. 8–40 and *passim*; Ibn al-Quff, *'Umda*, vol. 1, pp. 123–30, etc.
44. Ibn Malka, *Mu'tabar*, vol. 2, pp. 236–71; Razi, *Mabahith*, vol. 2, pp. 226–9, 258–79; Qazwini, *Hikmat al-'ain*, pp. 640–56; Mulla Sadra, *Asfar*, vol. 8, pp. 108–29, 143–8; Karmani, *Rahat* (the Isma'ili propagandist was Aristotelian in regard to generation, see especially pp. 430–1).
45. Razi was a great theologian as well as a philosopher. In his philosophical work, the *Mabahith*, he followed Ibn Sina and Aristotle faithfully and presented their arguments with great intelligence and clarity. In his huge Quranic exegesis *Al-Tafsir al-kabir*, he introduced a great amount of scientific information, including the theories of generation. Unfortunately for him, the *hadith* statements were explicitly contrary to Aristotle's ideas. A short note cannot possibly do credit to Razi's dilemma, and an adequate analysis will ultimately concentrate on the following three elements which characterize his treatment of the subject in the *Tafsir*: (1) He repeatedly insinuates the Aristotelian theory of (male) semen and (female) menses, nearly always seemingly approving of it, but without explicitly saying so (vol. 23, pp. 6ff, pp. 83ff.; vol. 24, p. 144; vol. 27, p. 85; vol. 30, p. 236). (2) Sometimes he attacks the "naturalists" as "unbelievers", but most explicitly when he is expounding Hippocratic–Galenic views (the best example is vol. 31, pp. 130–1). Finally (3) he forcefully presents the argument that whether semen is homogeneous (Aristotle) or heterogeneous (Hippocrates), generation still requires the intervention of God – for nothing else can explain organization and differentiation of the foetus (the emphasis is on differentiation in the first case, and organization in the second) (vol. 19, pp. 224–5). The affinity of this notion to the role which Aristotle had assigned to the *pneuma* is striking. Ibn Qayyim, who knew the scientific arguments well, considered Razi's argument in the *Tafsir* Aristotelian and responded to it as such (*Tibyan*, pp. 330–1). A different treatment of Razi and generation is by S. Belgueds, "La Collection Hippocratique et l'embryologie Coranique", in *La Collection Hippocratique et son role dans l'histoire de la medicine* (E. J. Brill, Leiden, 1975), pp. 321–33.
46. *Tibyan*, pp. 327–8.
47. (1) Sexual pleasure at orgasm envelops the whole body. (2) The organs of the child resemble those of the parents; the total similarity indicates that every organ contributes its own share. (3) If the semen were a homogeneous substance, it would be impossible for the various organs with their different forms to be generated, since a single form acts in matter only to produce its own likeness. (4) The general weakness of the body after ejaculation indicates that the semen is formed from the whole body.

These are essentially the arguments for pangenesis as Aristotle stated them (*GA*, 721b) *with one significant difference*: Ibn Qayyim omits the argument that "mutilated parents produce mutilated offspring": "It is alleged that because the parent is deficient in some one part no semen comes from that part, and that the part from which no semen comes does not get formed in the offspring" (*GA*, 721b; Peck, p. 51). Aristotle was not always fair to his opponents, and this extreme formulation of the argument from resemblance is a case in point. The Hippocratic sources which Ibn Qayyim knew intimately, *The Seed* and the *Nature of the Child*, were more subtle on this issue than Aristotle's account of pangenesis would lead one to believe: "The children of deformed parents are usually sound. This is because although an animal may be deformed, it still has exactly the same *components* as what is sound. But when there is some disease involved, and the four innate species of the fluid [that is, blood, bile, water, and phlegm] from which the seed is derived form sperm which is not complete, but deficient in the deformed part, it is not in my opinion anomalous that the child should be deformed similarly to its parent" (*The Seed*, p. 323); *Tibyan*, pp. 328–9.

48. *Tibyan*, pp. 329–31: (1) Since sexual pleasure at orgasm results from the passage of semen through the organs, then orgasm ought to be experienced for a long time before ejaculation if semen starts its passage from the head and other extremities (*GA*, 723b–4a). (2) If pangenesis were true, then the semen of the father and the semen of the mother should always produce two embryos in the womb, one a male after the father, one a female after the mother [because each semen includes a complete set of representative substance from all the organs of the parents] (*GA*, 722b). (3) As to the argument based on total similarity, general resemblance also involves the nails and hair which [by mutual agreement] do not excrete anything (*GA*, 722a). (4) The child may look like a distant ancestor, rather than its parents (*GA*, 722a); and there is a *hadith* which supports this. A man complained that his wife gave birth to a black child. The Prophet asked him: "Do you have camels?" and the man said yes:
—"What is their colour?"
—"Black."
—"Did they ever beget a grey camel?"
—"Yes."
—"How was that possible?"
—"Perhaps it is a tendency in the heredity."
—"Then the [child] also resulted from a tendency in the heredity."
(5) If the semen included parts from all the organs, then these parts either occupy their proper place in relation to each other, or do not. If they do, the implication is that the semen is a tiny animal in its own right. If you reject the implication, then there is no ultimate resemblance (*GA*, 722b). Yet such an organism is impossible, because semen is a liquid, and even though it is thick, it cannot preserve the right place of the different organs and their proper arrangement (Razi, *Tafsir*, vol. 19, p. 225).

These are the original Aristotelian arguments against pangenesis, illustrated by one apt *hadith*, except for the very last notion, which is by Fakhr al-Din Razi. These arguments against pangenesis, meant to destroy the theory that the semen is representative of the whole body, immediately posed the problem of differentiation: if the semen did not include their origin, how are the different organs and parts generated? Razi argued that the principle of differentiation and organization cannot be located in the semen anyway. Formation and development depend on the Creator (*Tafsir*, vol. 19, pp. 224–5). The *hadith* says: "God has assigned to each foetus an angel . . ." Ibn Qayyim, eager to support pangenesis, responded to Razi's Aristotelian appeal for God's intervention as follows: "The fact that the semen is extracted from all parts of the body does not contradict God's ability, will, or wisdom, but supports them even more" (*Tibyan*, p. 331).

49. That is, the arguments as they were presented by Ibn Sina in the *Hayawan* and *Razi* in the *Mabahith*. Ibn Qayyim was responding to the argument as it was current in the medieval culture, even though he knew the original Aristotle. He tells us elsewhere, and proudly, that he owned "a corrected, well-cared-for copy of Aristotle's *Book on Animals*". His direct quotations from this book (*Miftah*, vol. 2, pp. 155–6) show that it contained the *Generation of Animals*, and that it was the same translation which Brugman and Drossaart Lulofs published in 1971. Brugman, in his introduction,

"Aristotle's *De Generatione Animalium* in the Orient", pp. 38–53, did not look in all the right places and thus missed the true importance of the *Generation of Animals* for Arabic science and thought.

50. *Tibyan*, pp. 331–4: (1) The argument against sexual pleasure enveloping the whole body represents mere stubbornness. During orgasm you feel as if something has been extracted from your whole body, from your hearing and eyesight and power, and deposited in the womb. You feel as if you had been clothed and suddenly went naked. (2) The argument that pangenesis implies the formation always of two embryos, one male and one female, is best answered by the *hadith*: "When the male semen dominates the female semen, it will be a male; when the female semen dominates the male semen, it will be a female." (3) The nails and hair are subordinate to other organs: when the organs themselves look alike, their subordinates naturally follow. (4) Resemblance to distant ancestors is, on the contrary, one of the strongest arguments for pangenesis, for this distant resemblance persists in the seminal material from generation to generation to reach the child and determine his resemblance to his ancestors. (5) As to the implication that the semen is a tiny animal, the answer is as follows: if it is meant that the different parts are present in the semen *actually* (*bi al-fi'l*), then this is not the case; but if it is meant that the parts are present *potentially* (*bi al-quwwah*), then yes. What possible objection can there be to the idea that semen is potentially a tiny, or even a large, animal? (6) Equally well, this last also answers the objection that the semen is a liquid which is incapable of preserving the proper arrangement of the parts.

    So far as I know, Ibn Qayyim's rebuttal of Aristotle's arguments against pangenesis is quite original. Alone among medieval writers, he bypassed Galen to argue against Aristotle from the perspective of the original Hippocratic theory which centred around observations regarding resemblance and heredity. He based himself directly on Hippocrates because his knowledge of the original Hippocratic writings convinced him that Hippocrates was right. Had he wished merely to support the *hadith* theory of equal male and female seminal contributions, Galen's formulation could have served his purpose equally well.

51. *Tibyan*, pp. 334–5. Parallel discussions in Ibn Qayyim's *Tuhfat*, pp. 274–5, 277; and *Turuq*, pp. 198–9.
52. *Tibyan*, p. 335. Ibn Qayyim adds that it should not be said that menstrual blood is the cause of resemblance to the mother. Menstrual blood does not combine with the male semen. God has established the principle that generation happens only when two like elements meet – it is only then that a third is generated.
53. *Ibid.* Compare to Razi, *Tafsir*, vol. 30, p. 236.
54. *Tibyan*, p. 352.
55. *Ibid.* Ibn Qayyim adds that even while agreeing on the contribution of male and female to the foetus, Islamic religious opinion differed about detail. Some turn Aristotle's idea upside down and claim that it is the male semen that contributes material for the organs and parts of the child, and the female semen its form!
56. *Tibyan*, pp. 344–5. Also in Ibn Qayyim, *Tuhfat*, p. 277; Razi, *Tafsir*, vol. 30, p. 236. See Tabari, *Firdaws*, p. 32, for a Hippocratic parallel in Arabic medicine.
57. *Tibyan*, pp. 352–3. *Quran* 49:13.
58. *Tibyan*, p. 353. The most complete discussion is in Ibn Qayyim, *Zad*, vol. 4, pp. 121ff.
59. Qurtubi, *Jami'*, vol. 12, p. 8.
60. Ibn Sina, *Hayawan*, IX, 1 (Tehran edn, p. 428).
61. The hold that these two ideas had on Muslim religious thinkers guaranteed that preformationist notions remained tightly circumscribed. When these notions existed, their interpretation remained strictly limited by the Quran's explicit view that the foetus is a new creation which undergoes many transformations. A necessary corollary

of preformation is the notion that God created all future individuals, including every human soul, at the beginning. Generation is the process of unfolding these pre-existing souls in a series; it involves growth, but not differentiation. The Islamic belief in the creation of every individual soul for the first time as a foetus in the womb would have precluded, by itself, serious consideration of preformation. But the Islamic view that both parents contributed equally to generation provided another obstacle to preformation. Since preformation imagined the future individual as a tiny, fully formed creature that only needs the environment of the womb for growth, only one of the parents can be the source. The future individual could exist either in the father or in the mother.

The *hadith* which described how God took out all future men from Adam's back so that they could recognize by oath His sovereignty (the "primal oath": see Roy P. Mottahedeh, *Loyalty and Leadership in an Early Islamic Society* (Princeton, 1980), p. 62), was interpreted mostly in light of the two dominant Islamic ideas on generation described above (see Ibn Qutaiba, *Ta'wil*, pp. 104–7; and Ibn Qayyim, *Ruh*, pp. 177, 182, 192ff. (especially 198–9), 208, 213–14, 215–16. Quranic exegesis, in discussing generation, mostly neglected this *hadith* (see note 64 below). A few late Shi'i Quranic commentators, however, suddenly (?) introduce it in the seventeenth century (Faid al-Kashi, *Safi*, vol. 2, part 1, pp. 111–12; and Bahrani, *Burhan*, vol. 3, p. 78).

62. To be sure, there was violent argument between the followers of Aristotle (the camp of the philosophers) and the followers of Galen (the camp of the physicians) about the order of development of the major organs, the heart, brain, and liver. This argument sometimes obscures the basic scientific consensus regarding epigenesis.
63. I have modified the translation by Sale and Arberry in the light of historical Arabic Quran exegesis. See note 64 below.
64. Tabari, *Jami'*, vol. 18, p. 7; Tusi, *Tibyan*, vol. 7, p. 291; Baghawi, *Ma'alim*, vol. 5, p. 4; Tabarsi, *Majma' al-bayan*, vol. 7, p. 71; Ibn al-Jawzi, *Zad al-masir*, vol. 5, pp. 462, 406; Razi, *Tafsir*, vol. 25, pp. 109, 173; Baidawi, *Tafsir*, vol. 6, p. 282 (Abu al-Sa'ud, *Irshad*, vol. 4, pp. 6ff. and 48ff., follows Baidawi); Khazin, *Lubab*, vol. 5, p. 4; Ibn Juzaiy, *Tashil*, vol. 3, p. 35; Ibn Kathir, *Tafsir*, vol. 3, p. 206.
65. The two most explicit statements are by Tusi and Baidawi, note 64 above.
66. Tabari, *Jami'*, vol. 18, pp. 11, 117; Tusi, *Tibyan*, vol. 7, p. 354; Tabarsi, *Majma' al-bayan*, vol. 7, p. 101; Zamakhshari, *Kashshaf*, vol. 3, p. 178; Razi, *Tafsir*, vol. 30, p. 234; Baidawi, *Tafsir*, vol. 6, p. 323; Ibn al-Jawzi, *Zad al-masir*, vol. 5, p. 406; Ibn Juzai, *Tashil*, vol. 3, p. 49; Khazin, *Lubab*, vol. 5, p. 33. All Quranic commentators emphasize epigenesis. Compare with esoteric Isma'ili interpretations of the quotation from the chapter of *The Believers*, in Karmani, *Rahat*, pp. 481–2; and Shihab al-Din, *Idah*, pp. 28ff.
67. Galen, *De Semine*, pp. 512ff. (Kuhn, IV).
68. Ibn Sina, *Qanun*, vol. 2, p. 558; Ibn 'Abbas, *Kamil*, vol. 1, pp. 119–20; Qazwini, *'Aja'ib*, vol. 1, pp. 322–3; Kazaruni, *Mughni*, p. 35; Ikhwan al-Safa', *Rasa'il*, vol. 2, pp. 421–4 (the four basic stages, but with an astrological treatment).
69. Tabari, *Firdaws*, p. 32; Ibn Sina, *Qanun*, vol. 2, p. 558; 'Arib Ibn Sa'id, *Khalq al-janin*, p. 29; Qazwini, *'Aja'ib*, vol. 1, pp. 322–3; Ibn Malka, *Mu'tabar*, vol. 2, p. 269; Razi, *Tafsir*, vol. 28, pp. 15–16; Ibn Rajab, *Jami'*, vol. 1, p. 109; Ibn Hajar, *Fath al-bari*, vol. 14, p. 281 (where he quotes Ibn Qayyim); Saffuri, *Nuzhat*, vol. 2, p. 28.
70. Ibn Qayyim, *Tibyan*, pp. 336–7.
71. *Ibid.*, pp. 337–8.
72. Ibn Qayyim, *Tuhfat*, pp. 254–91.
73. *Tuhfat*, pp. 248–52. What is the relationship between statements in revelation and statements in science about the same subject? Ibn Qayyim answers the question with firmness: "The statements of the Prophet confirm one another, and agree with what really exists. They do not contradict reality (*al-wujud*). Instead, they inform us of those

things that observation and reason cannot discover merely by themselves, not of what contradicts reason and observation" (*Tibyan*, p. 349).

He asserts elsewhere, but in the context of the same discussion, that the relation of the statements of revelation to reason is of three types, and three types only: (1) statements which reason and common sense acknowledge as true; (2) statements which they acknowledge in general, but not in detail; and (3) statements which reason is incapable of judging. Those matters which clear reason (*al-'aql al-sarih*) rejects, and proves false, are nowhere to be found in Prophetic teaching: "it is of no consequence that some pretenders to knowledge claim that some Prophetic teaching is of this type, for their claims are based on ignorance of revelation, or ignorance of science or both". Furthermore, "even if you lived as long as Noah, you will never find one case where the philosophers have disagreed with revelation, and yet were able to agree among themselves. The Prophets never taught anything that contradicts clear reason. Instead, they teach those things which are beyond the reach of reason" (*Tuhfat*, p. 264).

Ibn Qayyim invites those who wish to dispute these assertions to consider the limitations of the biological sciences of his own and earlier times. The Hippocratic treatise *On Nutriment* contained an arithmetic table to calculate the time of birth as follows:

> If the foetus is formed in a certain span of time, say 30 days, add an equal number of days, and the result will give you the time of quickening: 60 days. Double this number and add the result to the preceding. The total is 180 days. In this case the child will be born in six months. Similarly, if the foetus is formed in 35 days, it will quicken in 70, and the child will be born in seven months. If in 40 days, quickens in 80, will be born in eight months. If in 45 days, quickens in 90, will be born in 9 months, and so on.

In the medieval culture this table had great currency, and it is clear that few objected to it in so far as it gave a rough estimate of development and birth. However, its detail contradicted the *hadith* which has the foetus ensouled (that is, quickened) after 120 days. In his attempt to show that the physicians and philosophers did not know any better than the Prophet so far as this question is concerned, Ibn Qayyim gives a remarkable assessment of the nature and limitations of premodern biology.

Firstly, he argues that all those who mention this table are simply imitating Hippocrates, and do not have independent evidence for their assertions based on continual, uninterrupted experience (*tajriba muttarida*). It is true, he adds, that they have used dissection, but in dissection they find the foetus at a certain stage, the nature of which they have to guess. Have they ever taken a virgin, and established the moment at which she had fruitful intercourse, and then counted the days until the foetus reached a certain stage, and then dissected her to discover whether they were right about their guesses? Of course they have not, nor have they presented such claims.

Instead, "all they have are generalities and analogies, and statements to the effect that it ought to happen this or that way, that the "natural order" requires this or that". What method they have consists in taking the time of birth and then arguing back – that it must have been a *nutfa* for so many days, then a *'alaqa* for so many days, etc.; then they double the figures, and make that the timing for foetal movement. This method cannot be taken too seriously, for it is based neither on the best methods of science, nor on the independent source of revelation. It is true, Ibn Qayyim adds, that the best tools that the scientists have are dissection and closely argued induction, and no one denies their value, but these have not produced any evidence to contradict relevation (*Tuhfat*, pp. 261–3).

Generally, Ibn Qayyim thought that the investigation both of nature and of revelation increase man's understanding of God and His ways. He says that it is this which has moved him to discuss these biological and natural subjects in such detail:

"Most often this discussion is conducted only in one of two ways. The first is that of the physician who rejects revelation and imitates Hippocrates, and his group [normally] disregards the prophets and their teaching . . . The second way is that of those who deny all that [i.e., the scientific tradition] and assume that it contradicts the religious law, and in so doing they deny the wisdom and excellence of God in His creation. Both of these approaches are to be condemned, and both lead nowhere. Mostly what has led people astray is that they see only the unbelieving naturalist, who disregards the religious laws, or the [religious] person who is lazy and ignorant of the ways of God's wisdom and will in His creation, and so he denies the natural faculties, elements, causes . . ." (*Tibyan*, pp. 374–5).

74. Ibn Qayyim, *Tibyan*, p. 337.
75. What he means by this is not that religion and science are necessarily segregated in terms of their subject matter. Religion and science can be two ways of looking at the same thing. Or so it seems in the light of one of the last questions he discusses in his treatment of generation: why does the child cry immediately upon birth? He says that there is a hidden reason (*sabab batin*) which the scientists are ignorant of and only the Prophet teaches: God in his wisdom has assigned a demon to every human being. This demon awaits the moment of separation to stab the child in the waist, and thus greets it with the old animosity that has existed between their fathers [whatever meaning this notion has, it is ethical, religious, social]. The Prophet says nothing about the other, apparent reason (*sabab zahir*), because it is common knowledge, and people can learn about it from each other: the child leaves his familiar habitat to a strange environment, he moves from a warm body to cold air and an unknown place (*Tibyan*, pp. 359–62; and *Tuhfat*, pp. 287–8, 291).
76. In any case, Ibn Qayyim rejected the explanations advanced by the natural philosophers. These explanations included arguments from the theory of humours, and notions such as this: that a balanced temperament produces males, and a corrupt temperament produces females (Ibn Sina, *Qanun*, vol. 2, p. 560, offers nearly all the possible options). In Ibn Qayyim's opinion, all such explanations are pure nonsense (*Tibyan*, p. 340. Razi also thought so: *Tafsir*, vol. 20, pp. 80–1). His consistency on this subject is impressive, for after all there existed *hadith* which contained a natural explanation of sex differentiation: "When the male semen overpowers the female semen, it will be a male; when the female semen overpowers the male semen, it will be a female." He deals squarely with this *hadith*, and openly casts doubt as to its authenticity. He argues that only one of the standard collections of *hadith*, that of Muslim, includes this particular version; that many experts have cast doubt as to its authenticity; that most other similar *hadith* merely discuss resemblance; that these latter are the only ones which are universally considered authentic; and that no doubt some transmitters corrupted what must originally have been an authentic statement about resemblance into one about sex differentiation (this perhaps was an easy mistake to make, he suggests, "because complete resemblance would include resemblance as to sex") (*Tibyan*, pp. 340–1; and *Tuhfat*, p. 281).

Some light is thrown on the source of Ibn Qayyim's unease with natural explanations of sex differentiation by his commentary on the following verse of the Quran (49:50):

The kingdom of the heavens and earth belongs to God. He creates what He pleases, for some He grants females, for some He grants males, for some He grants males and females, and some He makes childless. He is Wise and Capable.

Why did God mention females first in this list? Ibn Qayyim likes the suggestion that since parents most of the time desire to have males, God begins by mentioning the sex that He wants, not the sex that they want. His own interpretation is that God gave females precedence in opposition to the pre-Islamic attitude of contempt, sometimes to the point of infanticide, towards female infants: "God is saying that the ones you have considered least, He considers first" (*Tuhfat*, pp. 20–1).

77. Muhammad Salam Madkur, *Al-Janin wa al-ahkam al-muta'alliqa bihi fi al-fiqh al-Islami* (Cairo, 1969).
78. Ibn Nujaim, *Bahr*, vol. 3, p. 214; Ibn 'Abidin, *Minhat*, vol. 3, p. 215; Ibn 'Abidin, *Hadiyya*, p. 246.
79. Ibn 'Abidin, *Minhat*, vol. 3, p. 215, and *Radd*, p. 622; and Ibn 'Abidin, *Hadiyya*, p. 246.
80. 'Ulaish, *Fath*, vol. 1, p. 398; Dardir, *Sharh*, vol. 2, p. 267; Kasadawi, *Badr*, pp. 263–4; Ibn Juzaiy, *Qawanin*, p. 212.
81. Dasuqi, *Hashiyat*, vol. 2, p. 267, says that it is only a *makruh* before forty days. They do not explain directly how they arrived at this figure of forty days, but it is obviously related to the medieval understanding of the first stage of foetal development, at the end of which an embryo begins to look human (above, pp. 53–5).
82. Hanafi: Ibn Nujaim, *Bahr*, vol. 3, p. 214; Ibn 'Abidin, *Minhat*, vol. 3, p. 215; *idem*, *Radd*, p. 622; Ibn al-Humam, *Sharh*, vol. 2, p. 495; *Fatawa al-'Alamgiriyya*, vol. 1, p. 335; Ibn 'Abidin, *Hadiyya*, p. 246. Hanbali: "It is permitted to induce abortion . . ., but Ibn al-Jawzi said in *Ahkam al-nisa'* that abortion is prohibited . . . [However] Ibn 'Aqil said . . . it is permitted before ensoulment" (Mardawi, *Insaf*, vol. 1, p. 386). Shafi'i: Ghazali, in discussing contraception (see Chapter 1 above), prohibited abortion, but in another context found room for permission before ensoulment. Some Shafi'is maintained that it was licit to abort the *nutfa* and *'alaqa* (the first two stages, eighty days or younger). See the article on *"Ijhad", Mawsu'at Jamal 'Abd al-Nasir fi al-fiqh al-Islami* (Cairo, A.H. 1388), vol. 3, pp. 158–71.
83. For example, Ghazali, *Ihya'*, vol. 2, p. 41.
84. Ibn 'Abidin, *Minhat*, vol. 3, p. 215.
85. Noonan, *Contraception*, p. 90.
86. Murtada, *Al-Bahr al-zakhkhar*, vol. 3, p. 81.

4 Arabic medicine and birth control

1. Norman E. Himes, *The Medical History of Contraception* (Baltimore, 1936), has not really been surpassed as a record of man's contraceptive experience, but it is also important as a general statement on birth control technology and experience as they were in the 1930s.
2. *Ibid.*, p. 135.
3. Edward G. Browne, *Arabian Medicine* (Cambridge, University Press, 1921), pp. 44, 48ff. See also George Sarton, *Introduction to the History of Science* (The Williams and Wilkins Company, for the Carnegie Institution, Baltimore 1927–48; reprinted 1950), vol. 1, p. 609.
4. Bayard Dodge, ed., *The Fihrist of al-Nadim* (Columbia University Press, New York, 1970), vol. 2, pp. 701–9.
5. Razi, *Hawi*.
6. *Hawi*, part IX, pp. 127ff. I have edited and translated Razi's birth control notes. This edited text, together with the writings on birth control of the later physicians who are discussed below, are available in an appendix to my Harvard dissertation, "Sex and Society in Islam" (1973) and in "Contraceptive Medicine in the Medieval Middle East", forthcoming.
7. Out of a total number of 176 prescriptions in the text, 35 are from Galen, 28 from Dioscorides, and 12 from Ibn Masawayh.
8. There are 39 prescriptions which Razi identifies as his own.

9. Himes, *Medical History of Contraception*, pp. 147–9, and *passim*.
10. Table 1, column C, nos. 11, 12, 17, 18, 22, 26, 33, 34, 39, 40, 41, 42, 43, 44, 47, 48, 49, 52, 53, 58, 67, 72, 73, 74, 75, 76, 78, 79, 80, 82, and 83.
11. Table 1, column A, nos, 17, 32, 36, 37, 38, 39, 40, and 45.
12. Table 1, column B, no. 3.
13. Table 1, column D, nos. 2, 3, and 4.
14. Table 1, column E, nos. 6, 11, 20, 21, 23, 24, and 25.
15. Table 1, supplement, no. 8.
16. Table 1, column C, nos. 11, 12, 17, 18, and 22.
17. Table 1, column E, no. 6.
18. Himes, *Medical History of Contraception*, p. 80, n. 4, and p. 152, n. 44.
19. Thabit Ibn Qurra *Dhakhira*, p. 186.
20. Ibn al-Khatib, (1374) *'Amal man tabba*.
21. Ibn 'Abbas, *Kamil*, vol. 1, p. 5.

    Shortly before his death, Razi published an edited version of the first four books of the *Hawi*. A manuscript of this work is at the Wellcome Historical Medical Library (London). A. Z. Iskandar, *Arabic Manuscripts on Medicine and Science*, in the Wellcome Historical Medical Library (London, 1967), pp. 1–2.
22. Razi, *Mansuri*, f. 122. The full text is given, edited and translated, in Musallam, "Sex and Society", Appendix Texts (II), and "Contraceptive Medicine in the Medieval Middle East", forthcoming. The number in brackets after each prescription in Table 2 refers to the location of the recipe in this edited text.
23. Ibn Rushd, *Kulliyat*, p. 30.
24. Hippocrates, *The Nature of the Child*, in *Hippocratic Writings*, ed. G. E. R. Lloyd (Penguin, London, 1978). The translation is by I. M. Lonie.
25. Razi, *Hawi*, part IX, pp. 128, 129, 152.
26. Ibn 'Abbas, *Kamil*, vol. 1, p. 5.
27. The Haly (or Ali) Abbas of medieval Europe.
28. For example, Ibn Abi 'Usaibi'a, *Tabaqat*, vol. 1, pp. 236–7. Brockelman, however, mentions a medical manuscript at Gotha, which he attributes to 'Ali Ibn 'Abbas (Carl Brockelman, *Geschichte der Arabischen Litteratur* (Weimar, 1898), vol. 1, p. 237).
29. Sarton, *Introduction*, p. 677. See also Browne, *Arabian Medicine*, pp. 53–7., and Manfred Ullmann, *Islamic Medicine* (Edinburgh, University Press, 1978), *passim*.
30. Ibn 'Abbas, *Kamil*, vol. 2, pp. 439–40. The full text is given, translated into English, in Musallam, "Sex and Society", Appendix, and the forthcoming "Contraceptive Medicine". There is a translation of the same text available in Himes, *Medical History of Contraception*, pp. 139–41. The latter translation suffers from one error. The phrase,

    الأدوية التي تنفع من احتباس الطمث

    is translated: "remedies calculated to suppress the menses". The meaning, however, is exactly the opposite, and the phrase should be translated: "medicines which cause the menses to flow".
31. C1 refers to column C, recipe 1; D2 to column D, recipe 2, etc. When followed by an R, it indicates that the subject is an ingredient in a more complex recipe. An asterisk (*) indicates a specifically contraceptive (rather than abortifacient) recipe:

Table 3 (Kamil)		*Table 1 (Hawi)*
1. *C1	=	C21, C32
2. *C2	=	*C34, *C41R, *C43, *C48R, *C49R, *C78R, *C82, *C83.
3. *C3 (rennet of rabbit)	=	(none)

Table 3 (Kamil)	*Table 1 (Hawi)*
4. *C4	= *C40R (and A5, *A17, *A26, *A40R)
5. *C5	= *C40R (and *A39, *A40R)
6. *D1	= C21 (different application)
7. *D2	= *D3

32. Ibn Jumai', *Irshad*. The substance of the three manuscripts of this text is essentially the same, except for directions that a couple of the recipes (Table 7, C1, C2, and A1) be used before coitus. The directions exist in the Bodleian manuscripts, but not in the Cairo manuscript (which is a later copy, probably from the nineteenth century). The edited text is given in Musallam "Sex and Society", Appendix, and in "Contraceptive Medicine", forthcoming. Its substance is in Table 7 (contraceptives) and Table 8 (abortifacients).

33.

Table 7 (Irshad)	*Table 1 (Hawi)*
1. *A1	= *A32
2. *C1	= *C17, *C58
3. *C2	= *C18, C36, *C48R
4. *C3 (seeds of leek)	= (none)
5. *C4	= C69R
6. *D1	= *D1
7. *D2 (oil of any kind)	= *D4

34. Ibn Jumai', *Irshad*, "Al-Maqala al-Thaniya fi al-'Adwiya al Mufrada wa al-'Agdhiya", ("Book Two on simple medicines and foods"), Bodleian MS. Hunt. 19, f. 30. In addition, neither Ibn Sina in the *Canon* nor Ibn al-Baitar in the *Treatise* attribute any contraceptive qualities to beans.
35. Bodleian MS. Marsh 106, f. 158; Bodleian MS. Hunt. 19, f. 95. The substance of the text is in Table 8.

36.

Table 8 (Irshad)	*Table 1 (Hawi)*
1. A1	= A8
2. A2	= A1, A6
3. A3	= A12, A13R, A22R, A41, A42
4. A4	= A4, A21, A31
5. B1	= B1, B2
6. C1	= C10, *C73, *C79, *C80
7. C2	= C19
8. C3	= C1R, C4, C20, C61
9. C4	= Supp. 1
10. C5	= C35
11. C6	= C25
12. E1	= E1, E15

37. Ibn Maimun *Al-Tibb al-qadim*. The book begins this way: "The physician Musa Ibn 'Ubaid Allah al-Isra'ili al-Qurtubi said the following: I have received a letter from our master the Sultan al-Malik al-Afdal, the son of our master the Sultan Salah al-Din al-Ayyubi, may God's mercy be upon him, in which he complains of constipation all the time without relief, [and that] sometimes he suffers depression (*ka'aba wa fikra wa istihash*) and expectations of death, and that his digestion is weak. So I prepared the regimen in four chapters" (p. 3). The contraceptives are from p. 94.
38. Browne, *Arabian Medicine*, pp. 124–5; Sarton, *Introduction*, p. 772.
39. 'Abu al-Hasan al-Tabib, *Khalq al-'insan*, ff. 29–30. The abortifacient prescriptions contained in Table 6 are from ff. 28–9. The edited text is given in Musallam, "Sex and Society", Appendix, and in "Contraceptive Medicine", forthcoming.

40.

Table 5 (The Creation of Man)	*Table 1 (Hawi)*
1. *A1	= A5, *A17, *A26, *A40
2. *A2	= *A32
3. *A3	= *A37
4. *A4	= *A38
5. *A5	= *A45
6. *A6	= A43
7. *A7	= A12
8. *A8	= A8, A22R, A41
9. *C1	= *C41R, C51
10. *C2	= *C53
11. *C3	= *C40
12. *C4	= *C17, *C58
13. *C5	= *C34, *C43, *C83R
14. *C6	= *C48
15. *C7	= *C39R, *C49R, C60
16. *C8	= *C49R
17. *C9 (recipe lost)	= ?
18. *C10	=*C11, *C82
19. *C11	= *C22 and *C76
20. *C12	= C51
21. *D1	= (none) (after Ibn Sina, Table 4, *D1)
22. *D2 (juice of watermint on penis)	= (none)
23. *D3	= *D3
24. *D4	= *D4
25. *D5	= *D1
26. *E1 (avoiding form (time ?) of coitus favouring conception)	= (none) (after Ibn Sina, Table 4, *E1)
27. *E2 (avoiding simultaneous orgasms)	= (*Mansuri*, Table 2, *D2 and Ibn Sina, Table 4, *E2)
28. *E3	= *E11
29. *E4	= *E20

41. Although there are twenty-nine recipes in the text, one of them, C9 in Table 5, is incomplete and considered lost.
42. D2 in Table 5.
43. Ibn Sina, *Qanun*.
44. Ibn Abi Usaibi'a, *Tabaqat*, vol. 2, pp. 2–20; Sarton, *Introduction*, pp. 709–13; Browne, *Arabian Medicine*, pp. 57–64.
45. Ibn Sina, *Qanun*, vol. 1, pp. 343–470.
    1. common melilot (*Melilotus officinalis*, اكليل الملك), p. 243
    2. savin (*Juniperus sabina*, ابهل), p. 249
    3. rennets, all (انفحة), p. 250
    4. gools (*Calendula arvensis*, اذريون), p. 251
    5. dorema (*Dorema ammoniacum*, اشق), p. 252
    6. barberry (*Berberis vulgaris*, انبرباريس), p. 253
    7. saltwort (*Salsola kali*, اشنان), p. 254
    8. iris (*Iris florentina*, ايرسا), p. 256
    9. rennet of wild rabbit (انفحة ارنب بري), p. 259
    10. blood of menses (دم الحيض), pp. 261, 295
    11. camomile (*Anthemis nobilis*, بابونج), p. 265
    12. balsam (*Commiphora opabalsamum*, بلسان), p. 266

13. mugwort (*Anthemis vulgaris*, برنجاسف), p. 267
14. opopanax (*Opopanax chironium* جاوشير), p. 282
15. yellow gentian (*Gentiana lutea*, جنطيانا), p. 283
16. cinnamon (*Cinnamomum zeilanicum*, دار صيني), p. 289
17. spiny broom (*Calycoton spinosa*, دارشيشعان), p. 290
18. elephant dung (زبل الفيل), p. 309
19. aristoloch (*Aristolochia longa*, and *rotunda*, زراوند), p. 312
20. watercress (*Nasturtium officinale*, حرف), p. 314
21. colocynth (*Citrullus colocynthis*, حنظل), p. 317
22. chickpeas (*Cicer arietinum*, حمص), p. 317
23. white popular (*Populus alba*, حور), p. 323
24. common germander (*Teucrium chamaedrys*, كمادريوس), p. 339
25. soap root (*Gypsophilla struthium*, كندس), p. 339
26. Macedonian parsley (*Athamentha macedonica*, كماشير), p. 342
27. celery (*Apium graveolens*, كرفس), p. 345
28. cabbage (*Brassica olẹracea*, كرنب), p. 347
29. luffa (*Luffa cylindrica*, لوف), p. 352
30. false myrrh gagal (*Commiphora mukul*, مقل اليهود), p. 363
31. dittany of Crete (*Origanum dictamnus*, مشكطراشير), p. 365
32. myrrh (*Commiphora myrrha*, مر), p. 368
33. narcissus (*Narcissus poeticus*, نرجس), p. 374
34. peppermint (*Mentha piperita*, نعناع), p. 375
35. male fern (*Dryoptaris filix mas*, سرخس), p. 379
36. scammony (*Convolvulus scammonia*, سقمونيا), pp. 385–6
37. *Ferula scowitziana* (قنّة), p. 386
38. cinnamon (*Cinamomum cassia*, سليخة), p. 392
39. sesame (*Sesamum indicum*, سمسم), p. 392
40. cyclamen (*Cyclamen europaeum*, عرطنيثا), p. 396
41. madder (*Rubia tinctorum*, فوة الصباغين), p. 406
42. pepper (*Piper nigrum*, فلفل), p. 407
43. white bryony (*Bryonia alba*, فاشرا), p. 407
44. pennyroyal (*Mentha pulegium*, فودنج), p. 409
45. cyclamen (*Cyclamen Europaeum*, فقلامينوس = بخور مريم), p. 413
46. lesser cardamum (*Elettaria cardamomum*, قردمانا), p. 417
47. centaury (*Erythraea centaurium*, قنطوريون), p. 419
48. wood tar (قطران), p. 420
49. Arabian costus (*Costus speciosus*, قسط), p. 420
50. galbanum plant (*Ferula galbaniflua*, قنة), p. 421
51. ivy (*Hedera helix*, قسوس), p. 423
52. southernwood (*Artemisia abrotanum*, قيصوم), p. 424
53. squirting cucumber (*Ecbalium elaterium*, قثاء الحمار), p. 426
54. vervain (*Verbena officinalis*, رعى الحمام), p. 428
55. bonduc (*Caesalpinia bonducella*, رتة), p. 429
56. cedar of Lebanon (*Cedrus Libani*, شربين), p. 440
57. lupine (*Lupinus termis*, ترمس), p. 444
58. alkanet (*Alkanna tinctoria*, خس الحمار), p. 459
59. iron dross (خبث الحديد), p. 463
60. laurel (*Laurus nobilis*, غار), p. 468

Also the dung of the Egyptian vulture, *Neophron percnopterus*; zool (زبل الرخمة), p. 432; and سقولوقندريون (?), p. 386; and اثيمديون (?), p. 264. The exceptions, which do not exist in Razi, are numbers 1, 6, 10, 22, 25, 51, 52, 54, 55 and 58 above.

46. Ibn Sina, *Qanun*, vol. 2, p. 597. The edited text is in Musallam "Sex and Society", Appendix, and in "Contraceptive Medicine", forthcoming.
47. R following an entry indicates that the subject is an ingredient in a more complex recipe. An asterisk (*) indicates a specifically contraceptive (rather than abortifacient) recipe.

Table 4 (Qanun)	*Table 1 (Hawi)*
1. *A1	= *A37
2. *C1	= *C39R, *C41R, *C49R, C54, *C72R, *C78R
3. *C2	= *C76 (without alum)
4. *C3	= C34, *C41R, *C43, *C48R, *C49R, *C82, *C83
5. *C4	= *C48 (without flowers; plus watercress)
6. *C5	= *C40R
7. *C6	=*C40
8. *C7	= *C39 (complete except sulphur)
9. *C8	= *C12, *C42
10. *C9	= *C44, *C67
11. *C10 (leaves of bindweed)	= (none)
12. *D1	= (none)
13. *D2	= *D3
14. *D3	= *D4, *C73, *C74
15. *D4 (sesame oil)	= *D4 (balm oil)
16. *E1 (avoiding form of coitus favouring conception)	= (none)
17. *E2	= (*Mansuri*, Table 2, D2)
18. *E3	= *E11
19. *E4	= *E20
20. *E5 (fumigation with elephant dung)	= *C44, *C67 (different application)

48. Table 4, C10 and E1.
49. Himes, *Medical History of Contraception*, p. 142, note 12.
50. Noonan, *Contraception*, chapter 7, "Contraceptive Techniques: Means and Dissemination in the High Middle Ages", pp. 200–30, is the indispensable guide to medieval European material.
51. *Ibid.*, pp. 205–6.
52. Noonan, *Contraception*, p. 104.
53. George Devereux, *A Study of Abortion in Primitive Societies* (revised edn, International Universities Press, New York, 1976).
54. Ibn Sina, *Qanun*, vol. 2, p. 575.
55. *Ibid.*, vol. 2, p. 579.
56. Abu al-Hasan al-Tabib, *Khalq al-insan*, f. 28.
57. Ibn 'Abbas, *Kamil*, vol. 2, pp. 439–40.
58. Ibn Hubal, *Mukhtarat*, vol. 4, p. 60.
59. Ibn 'Abbas, *Kamil*, vol. 1, p. 8.
60. Razi, *Hawi*, part IX, p. 139.
61. Ibn Jumai', *Irshad*, Bodleian MS. Marsh 106, f. 158; and MS. Hunt. 19, f. 95.
62. Al-Katib, *Jawami'*, f. 170.
63. See note 45 above, p. 146.
64. See note 34 above, p. 145.

65. See the article on "al-'Attar", *EI*, new edn, vol. 1, pp. 751–2.
66. Al-Kuhin al-'Attar, *Minhaj al-dukkan*. This text is especially interesting because it has no reference whatsoever to birth control, reflecting no doubt the Jewish religious prohibition. Other Arab Christian and Jewish physicians and druggists, however, exhibit no such reticence with regard to birth control remedies, apparently following the standard of the dominant Muslim culture. The Jewish physicians Ibn Jumai' and Maimonides who were discussed above are cases in point.
67. Cyril Elgood, *A Medical History of Persia and the Eastern Caliphate* (Cambridge University Press, Cambridge, 1951), p. 254.
68. *Ibid.*, pp. 272–5.
69. Browne, *Arabian Medicine*, pp. 103–9. Browne describes the contents of ten of the letters.
70. *Ibid.*, p. 104.
71. *Ibid.*, p. 107.
72. A rich impression of the activity and range of medieval Middle Eastern merchants can be gathered from the studies of the *Karimi* merchants of the thirteenth to fifteenth centuries. On the *Karimi* merchants, see Eli Ashtor, "The Karimi Merchants", *Journal of the Royal Asiatic Society*, vol. 00 (London, 1956), pp. 45–56; Walter J. Fischel, "The Spice Trade in Mamluk Egypt", *Journal of the Economic and Social History of the Orient* (Leiden, vol. 1, 1958), pp. 502–14; S. D. Goitein, "From the Mediterranean to India", *Speculum*, vol. 39 (1954), pp. 181–97; 4. Gaston Wiet, "Les Marchands d'épices sous les Sultans Mamlouks", *Cahiers d'Histoire Egyptienne*, vol. 7, (Cairo, 1955), pp. 81–147. Also useful are D. S. Richards (ed.), *Islam and the Trade of Asia* (Bruno Cassirer, Oxford, 1970); and M. A. Cook (ed.), *Studies in the Economic History of the Middle East, from the Rise of Islam to the Present Day* (Oxford University Press, London, 1970), Part 1, "The Middle Ages", pp. 3–155.
73. S. D. Goitein, *A Mediterranean Society*, vol. 1 (Economic Foundations, University of California Press, 1967), p. 153. An average case is that of a merchant resident in Alexandria (eleventh to twelfth centuries) who dealt in the following: (1) saffron, imported from Tunisia; and brazilwood exported from the Indies to North Africa; (2) medical and culinary herbs – scammony imported from Syria and cubeb from Sucatra; (3) glass; (4) silk; (5) other textiles; (6) corals – imported from Europe and North Africa; (7) perfumes (ambergris and musk); (8) wax – from Tunisia; (9) millstones – from Syria; (10) various cloths and household goods. A few years earlier, another Egyptian merchant was engaged in an even greater variety of commercial fields and on a larger scale. He was active in the following fields, arranged according to the volume of business in each: (1) flax – to Tunisia and Sicily; (2) silk – from Spain and Sicily; other fabrics, Syrian and European cotton, North African felt; (3) olive oil, soap and wax from Tunisia, Syria, and Palestine; (4) spices from the Orient (pepper, cinnamon, and clove) sent to the West; (5) brazilwood, lacquer, and indigo – from East to West, sumac and gallnuts – from Syria, and saffron – from Tunisia to the East; (6) metals (copper, iron, lead, mercury, tin, and silver) – from West to East; (7) books; (8) aromatics, perfumes, and gums (also, ambergris, camphor, frankincense, gum Arabic, mastic gum, musk and betel leaves); (9) jewelry and semi-precious stones; (10) materials used for ornaments and trinkets; (11) chemicals (alkali, alum, antimony, arsenic, bamboo crystals, borax, naphta, sulphur, starch, and vitriol); (12) foodstuffs – sugar exported from Egypt, and dried fruits – imported from Syria; (13) leather and leather products – from Tunisia and Sicily; (14) Pitch, etc. This is not an exhaustive list (Goitein, *Mediterranean Society*, pp. 153–4).
74. *Ibid.*, p. 155.
75. Sarton, *Introduction*, vol. 2, p. 663; and vol. 2, part 1, pp. 51–2.
76. Ibn Abi Usaibi'a, *Tabaqat*, vol. 2, p. 133; *EI*, new edn, vol. 3, p. 737.

77. Ibn al-Baitar, *Mufradat*, 4 vols., Arabic text, printed in Cairo, Bulaq (1874–5). A good French translation is by Lucien Leclerc, *Traité des Simples*, in *Notices et Extraits de la Bibliothèque Nationale et autres Bibliothèques*, vol. 23 (1877), vol. 25 (1881), and vol. 26 (1883), Paris.
78. Sarton, *Introduction*, p. 664.
79. Himes, *Medical History of Contraception*, pp. 149–55. I found it more profitable to use the text of Ibn al-Baitar's *Treatise* in a different way. The majority of medicines mentioned in the medical and erotic texts we have studied were checked one by one in the four volumes of the *Treatise*. The object was to find whether the birth control use of these medicines was preserved in Ibn al-Baitar. Of eighty-six such simple drugs, the *Treatise* preserved memory of sixty-four (or 74.4 per cent). There were twenty-two drugs mentioned in medicine and erotica as relevant to birth control which had no such mention in Ibn al-Baitar: henbane, sweet basil, mustard, poppy, spiny broom, pulp of pomegranates, iron rust, azarole seeds, dill, *shabbut*, poison hemlock, aloe, pennyroyal, pellitory of Spain, mulberry, camphor, coriander, bindweed, pearls, rock salt, narcissus, and natron. (Eleven of these twenty-two simples are from erotica.) There are only ten specifically contraceptive recipes among the sixty-four from the *Treatise*: four are suppositories (alum, black pepper, cauliflower seeds, and peppermint), vol. 3, pp. 53, 166, 170, and vol. 4, pp. 58, 60; one is a potion (weeping willow), vol. 3, p. 154; two are magical (root of woodbine and cyclamen), vol. 1, pp. 58, 84; and three are listed without indicating the method of application (iron dross, rue, and male fern), vol. 2, p. 48, vol. 3, p. 6, and vol. 3, p. 7. Wood-tar (*qitran*) is the only medicine which is recommended as a male contraceptive, vol. 3, pp. 60–1.
80. Himes, *Medical History of Contraception*, p. 155.
81. Ibn al-Baitar, *Mufradat*: references to Dioscorides in the context of birth control occur as follows (the first number indicates the volume, and the second the page): 1, 108; 2, 160; 3, 166; 4, 58; 1, 73–4; 2, 55; 4, 34–5; 2, 84; 2, 36; 4, 81; 1, 84; 3, 74; 1, 35; 4, 162; 3, 23; 3, 12; 4, 37; 4, 33–4; 2, 2; 2, 54; 3, 159; 3, 145; 4, 7; 4, 144; 1, 134; 3, 169; 3, 7; 1, 85; 4, 145; 1, 96; 1, 155; 3, 170; 4, 181; 1, 7; 4, 50; 2, 82; 1, 174; 2, 16; 3, 154; 1, 162; 1, 170.
82. Antaki, *Tadhkirat*.
83. *Ibid.*, vol. 1, p. 146.
84. *Ibid.*, vol. 3, pp. 129–30, margin.
85. *Ibid.*, vol. 3, p. 189.
86. *Ibid.*, vol. 3, pp. 147ff.

5 Birth control in the popular tradition

1. Arabic erotica have received very little scholarly attention. G. H. Bousquet, *L'ethique sexuelle de l'Islam* (Paris, 1966) does not deal with them at all. There is a very general introduction to erotica in Arabic, Salah al-Din al-Munajjid's *Al-Hayat al-jinsiyya 'ind al-'arab* (Beirut, 1958), which does a service by providing the tables of content of seven medieval erotic works in an appendix, pp. 99–128. Since most of these books exist in manuscript form only, and none has been critically edited, Munajjid's appendix is a valuable service indeed. Abdelwahab Bouhdiba, *La sexualité en Islam* (Paris, 1975) deals with erotica with heavy reliance on Munajjid. Bouhdiba's work is valuable as a comprehensive discussion of sexuality in Islam. The short essay by Franz Rosenthal, "Fiction and Reality: Sources for the Role of Sex in Medieval Muslim Society", in A. L. al-Sayyid-Marsot, ed., *Society and the Sexes in Medieval Islam* (Undena Publications, Malibu, California, 1979), pp. 3–22, is a thoughtful introduction to the field in general, with valuable remarks on the problems of method and approach. Rosenthal makes good use of al-Katib's *Jawami' al-ladhdha*, the best medieval erotic

treatise. The best available guide to the manuscript literature, with a brief discussion, is Manfred Ullman's *Die Medizin im Islam* (E. J. Brill, Leiden, 1970), pp. 193–8.

2. On Indian and Chinese erotica see Sushil Kumar De, *Ancient Indian Erotics and Erotic Literature* (Calcutta, 1959), especially pp. 85–106; Johann Jakob Meyer, *Sexual Life in Ancient India* (2 vols., London, 1930); Khazan Chand, *Indian Sexology* (New Delhi, 1972); Agehananda Bharati, *The Tantric Tradition* (London, 1965); Devangana Desai, *Erotic Sculpture of India* (New Delhi, 1976); Sheng Wu-shan, *Erotologie de la Chine* (Paris, 1963); M. Beurdeley, ed., *The Clouds and the Rain: The Art of Love in China* (London, 1969); and Robert H. Van Gulik, *Sexual Life in Ancient China* (E. J. Brill, Leiden, 1961).
3. Himes, in a chapter on "China, India, and Japan", searched Indian erotica from the eighth to the sixteenth centuries for contraceptive recipes. He came up with a total of 26. Among these, "quasi rational or rational recipes are mentioned only three times". Himes, *Medical History of Contraception*, pp. 114–22, and 131–2.
4. *Ibid.*, p. 178.
5. George Sarton, *Introduction to the History of Science* (Baltimore, 1927–48), vol. 2, part 1, p. 79.
6. For example: *Al-wishah fi fawa'id al-nikah*; *Nawasir al-'aik fi nawadir al-naik*; *Rashf al-zalal min al-sihr al-halal*; and *Al-yawaqit al-thamina fi sifat al-samina*. All in manuscript form.
7. Ibn al-Nadim, *Fihrist*, chapter 8, section 3, pp. 735–6.
8. "Chapter on the avoidance of pregnancy", in al-Katib, *Jawami'* (*Encyclopedia of Pleasure*) (tenth century); "Chapter on conception . . . and abortifacients", in *Nuzhat al-ashab fi mu'asharat al-ahbab*, by al-Samaw'al al-Isra'ili (twelfth century A.D.); "On the knowledge of medicines which are contraceptive in many instances . . .", in Tifashi, *Ruju'* (*The Rejuvenation of the Old Man*) (thirteenth century); "On medicines which, inserted intra-vaginally by the woman, will prevent her from conceiving as long as she continues using them . . .", in *Kitab al-bahiyya wa al-tarakib al-sultaniyyah*, by Tusi (thirteenth century); "On medicines which expel the semen from the uterus", in Nafzawi, *Rawd* (*Perfumed Garden*) (sixteenth century). See Munajjid, *Al-Hayat al-jinsiyya*, pp. 99–128.
9. "An ointment, known as 'cinnamon ointment' which, if used by the man, will void his semen. This medicine has three advantages. First, it prevents conception; second, it increases the woman's love for the man; and third, it aids the man in coitus and strengthens the penis . . ." (al-Katib, *Jawami'* f. 174); and "prescription for an ointment on the penis which prevents pregnancy: pellitory of Spain (*Anacyctus pyrethrum*) and ginger (*Zinigiber officinale*) are mixed with ... The woman will never conceive. Furthermore, it increases the desire for coitus, enlarges the penis, and makes the woman experience great pleasure" (Tifashi, *Ruju'*, pp. 58–9).
10. Table 10, C3.
11. Table 11, C1, D2, D3, D4, D5, D7.
12. Table 12, C3, D1.
13. Table 12, A1, A2, C2, C4.
14. Table 12, C1, D2.
15. Table 13, A1, D1, D2, contraceptive; C1, E1, abortifacient.
16. Al-Katib died in 986/7 according to Ibn Taghri-Birdi, *Nujum*, vol. 4, p. 149. A different date for the death of 'Ali Ibn Nasr (1001) is given by Abu Shuja' and Al-Sabi, *Kitab Tajarib al-'umara', The Eclipse of the Abbasid Caliphate*, ed. D. S. Margoliouth and H. F. Amedroz (Oxford, Blackwell, 1920–1), vol. 6, p. 434.
17. Ibn al-Nadim, *Fihrist*, vol. 1, pp. 287–8; vol. 2, Index, p. 1070. The *Fihrist* lists only two of his books, one on the "Training of the Sultan".

18. *Encyclopedia of Islam*, vol. 4 (E. J. Brill, Leiden, 1934), p. 751; Sarton, *Introduction*, vol. 2, part 1, p. 80.
19. At least three erotic books by Tifashi are known: (1) *Ruju' al-shaykh ila sibah*; (2) *Fi ma yahtaju ilaihi al-rijal wa al-nisa' fi isti'mal al-bah mimma yadurr wa yanfa'* (Brockleman, *Geschichte der Arabischen Litteratur* (Weimar, 1898), vol. 1, p. 652); and (3) *Nuzhat al-ahbab fi ma la yujad fi kitab*, Munajjid, *Al-Hayat al-jinsiyya*, pp. 114–15.
20. Sir Richard Burton, *The Perfumed Garden of the Sheykh Nefzawi* (Castle Books, New York, 1964).
21. Al-Katib, *Jawami'*: the "Chapter on Contraception" is on ff. 170–4 of the manuscript. A large part of the chapter (starting on f. 171 and continuing to f. 173) is devoted to a story illustrating the trials and sufferings of unwanted pregnancy. The edited text is available in Musallam, "Sex and Society", and "Contraceptive Medicine", forthcoming.
22. Table 10, C1/D4 and C2/D6.
23. Tifashi, *Ruju'*, part 1, chapter 27, pp. 58–9. In this edition the book is attributed, wrongly, to Ahmad Ibn Sulaiman (Ibn Kamal Pasha). There are enough early manuscripts of the book attributed to al-Tifashi to establish him, nevertheless, as the true author: (1) Gotha 2055; (2) Franck 558; (3) Alex Tibb 41; and (4) Cairo VI, 16, all ascribed to Tifashi. Brockleman, *Geschichte*, vol. 1, p. 652. The translation of the chapter is given in Musallam, "Sex and Society", and "Contraceptive Medicine", forthcoming.
24. The count is actually seventeen, but one recipe is given twice (Table 11, D2).
25. Tifashi balances this somewhat by mentioning, a little later, a recipe whereby the woman "will experience great pleasure" in intercourse.
26. Table 11, C1 = Table 10, C3. The recipe is the same except for the addition of one ingredient (pepper seeds) in the *Rejuvenation*.
27. Nafzawi, *Rawd*. The following discussion, however, is based on the printed Arabic text of the book, *Al-Rawd al-'atir fi nuzhat al-khatir* (Maktabat al-Manar Tunis, n.d.). The birth control chapter is ch. 16 in this text, while it is ch. 15 in Burton's translation. There are gaps in Burton's text (which used a variant manuscript). The Burton translation misses two recipes completely and has a different reading for part of a third recipe (laurel instead of pie rhubarb as in the Arabic text). These are important differences in a short text limited to six recipes. My translation is given in "Sex and Society", and in "Contraceptive Medicine", forthcoming.
28. Table 12, C3 and D1.
29. C1 refers to column C, recipe 1; D2 to column D, recipe 2, etc. For more explanation see Chapter 4, note 31 above.

Perfumed Garden (Table 12)	*Medical Texts*
1. A1 (pie rhubarb)	= (none)
2. A2 (cinnamon and myrrh)	= Table 1, A4
3. C1 (madder root)	= Table 1, C35 and Supp. No. 15R
4. C2 (cabbage seeds)	= Table 1, *C34, *C43, *C83R
5. C3 (alum)	= Table 4, *C2R
6. C4 (cinnamon and myrrh)	= Table 1, C9
7. D1 (alum)	= Table 4, *C2 (different application)
8. D2 (tar)	= Table 1, D3; Table 2, D1; Table 3, D2; Table 4, D2; Table 5, D3.

30. Al-Katib, *Jawami'*, f. 170.
31. Tifashi, *Ruju'*, p. 58.

32. Isfahani, *Muhadarat*, vol. 3, p. 266. Another version is given by Antaki, *Tazyin*, vol. 2, p. 526.
33. Jahiz, *Hayawan*, vol. 1, pp. 69, 118; vol. 2, p. 277.
34. *Ibid.*, vol. 4, p. 614.
35. Ibn Qutaiba, *'Uyun*, vol. 3, p. 286.
36. *Ibid.*, p. 290.
37. Isfahani, *Muhadarat*, vol. 3, p. 237.
38. Henry Laoust, 'Ibn al-Djawzi", *EI*, new edn, vol. 3, p. 451.
39. Ibn al-Jawzi, *Iltiqat*, Hunt. Donat. 31, ff. 178–207; the birth control discussion is on f. 180.
40. Ibn Rajab, *Dhail*, vol. 1, pp. 399–434.
41. Ibn al-Jawzi (Table 13)

Ibn al-Jawzi (Table 13)	*Medical and erotic texts*
1. A1 (foam of camel in rutting season)	= (none)
2. C1	= Table 1, C39R, C41R, C49R, C54, C72R, etc.
3. D1	= Table 1, D3, Table 4 D2, etc.
4. D2	= Table 11, D2
5. E1 (hoof of horse, mule, or donkey)	= Table 1, E25 (hoof of donkey only)

42. Ibn al-Khatib, *'Amal man tabba*, p. 248.
43. Sanawbari, *Rahma*, chapter 153, p. 162.
44. M. W. Hilton-Simpson, *Arab Medicine and Surgery* (Oxford University Press, London, 1922), p. 90.
45. Nuwairi, *Nihayat al-'arab*, vol. 12, p. 210.
46. Sarton, *Introduction*, vol. 2, part 2, pp. 661–2.
47. "Al-Sha'rani", *EI*, vol. 4, pp. 318–19.
48. Sha'rani, *Tadhkirat*, vol. 2, pp. 60–4. The substance of the recipes is in Table 15.
49. Sha'rani (Table 15)

Sha'rani (Table 15)	Other texts
1. A1 (rennet of foal)	= (none)
2. A2 (antimony)	= (none)
3. A3	= Table 1, A5, *A17, *A26
4. A4	= Table 10, *C3R (d.a.); Table 11, *C1R
5. A5	= Table 1, *C34, *C43, *C83R (d.a.)
6. A6	= Table 1, *A27
7. A7	= Table 1, *A32
8. A8	= Table 1, *C11, *C42 (d.a.)
9. A9	= (none)
10. A10	= Table 1G, Supp. no. 1
11. A11	= Table 1, A5, *A17, A26
12. A12 (blood of menses)	= (none)
13. A13 (urine of ram)	= (none) but compare Table 11, *A1
14. B1 (parturition blood)	= (none)
15. B2 (seeds of wood sorrel)	= (none)
16. B3 (ankle of weasel)	= (none)
17. B4 (skeleton of frog)	= (none)
18. C1	= Table 1, *C17, *C58
19. C2	= (none)
20. C3	= Table 1, C6, C37, C62, C70R (d.a.)

21. C4	= Table 1, *C54, *C43, *C83R
22. C5	= Table 1, *C11, *C82
23. C6 (juice of cabbage)	= (none)
24. C7	= Table 1, A27 (d.a.)
25. C8	= Table 1, *C44, *C67
26. C9	= Table 1, *C11, *C42
27. C10	= Table 4, *C2R
28. C11 (stems of indigo)	= (none)
29. C12	= Table 1, C21, C32
30. D1	= Table 1, *C39R, *C41R, *C49R, *C54, *C72R, *C78R

50. On Al-Tabari see Edward G. Browne, *Arabian Medicine* (Cambridge, University Press, 1921), pp. 37–40.
51. Tabari, *Firdaws*; the reference to tar is on p. 405. For other references to contraceptives, see pp. 380, 421, 430, and 436. References to abortifacients are on pp. 39, 380, 402, 421, 423, 424, 525, and 535.
52. Ullmann, *Islamic Medicine*, pp. 107ff.
53. Antaki, *Tadhkirat*, vol. 1, pp. 72, 74.
54. Sanawbari, *Rahma*, chapter 153, pp. 160–2.
55. Ibn al-Khatib, *'Amal man habba*, p. 247.
56. *Ibid.*, p. 248.
57. Azraqi, *Tashil*, p. 223.

6 Population and Middle Eastern history

1. J. A. Banks, "Historical Sociology and the Study of Population", *Daedalus* (1968), pp. 409–10.
2. Norman E. Himes, *The Medical History of Contraception* (Baltimore, 1936; reprinted New York, 1963).
3. *Ibid.*, chapter 13, "The Result: Democratized Birth Control".
4. *Ibid.*, p. 100.
5. On pre-eighteenth-century European contraceptive medicine see Himes, *Medical History of Contraception*, pp. 160–9, and John T. Noonan Jr., *Contraception, A History of its Treatment by the Catholic Theologians and Canonists* (Harvard University Press, Cambridge, Mass., 1966), pp. 222–7, 346–51.
6. Chapter 1, pp. 19–20 above.
7. G. K. Clark, *The Critical Historian* (London, 1967), p. 57.
8. A story is told about a famous whore of Medina who, upon hearing that many women were turning to lesbianism "to be able to do without men", questioned one of the lesbians about the matter. The woman defended her sexual preference by saying that "it is better than pregnancy, wherein lies scandal" (al-Katib, *Jawami'*, f. 88). Another woman was heard to recite a poem in which she said that she chose lesbianism "because of the fear of pregnancy" (*ibid.*, f. 85). See also Isfahani, *Muhadarat*, vol. 3, pp. 243, 273. According to Ibn Qayyim, some male homosexuals defended their preference by arguing that "it was safer than pregnancy, childbirth, the burdens of marriage, etc." (*Ighathat*, vol. 2, pp. 138–40).
9. A young woman was asked why she did not wish to see her lover. She answered: "In fear of becoming pregnant" (al-Katib, *Jawami'*, f. 85). An account similar to this has a man writing to his beloved and begging her to visit him. She writes back saying that she loves him too much to abstain if she sees him, but she is also afraid of pregnancy, and this fear keeps her away from him (*ibid.*).

   For stories of women asking men to practise withdrawal, see Isfahani, *Muhadarat*, vol. 3, p. 267. Jahiz speculated on the appeal of eunuchs to women, and thought that women were attracted to them for two reasons, because they were forbidden, and because there was no risk of pregnancy: "a woman can be with [a eunuch] and be safe from the greatest shame, something which will heighten her pleasure and passion" (*Hayawan*, Beirut edn, vol. 1, pp. 102–3). Others used the argument of absence of risk of pregnancy to recommend marriage to women over forty (Isfahani, *Muhadarat*, vol. 3, p. 204).

10. At the gates of the city of Basrah a bedouin was heard reciting the following line: "Love is kissing and the touching of hands/Going beyond that is asking for a child" (Ibn al-Jawzi, *Akhbar al-nisa*, p. 51). In another story the following dialogue occurs:

    Man: What do you do when you are alone with your beloved?
    Bedouin: We touch, kiss and the like. What do you do?
    Man: I throw her on her back and penetrate between the thighs.
    Bedouin: You are no lover! You are the seeker of a child!

    (*Ibid.*, pp. 46, 50).
    For more of the same, see Ibn Qutaiba, *'Uyun*, vol. 4, p. 92; Isfahani, *Muhadarat*, vol. 3, p. 229; and Tijani, *Tuhfat*, pp. 163–4.
11. Qali, *Amali*, vol. 2, p. 29; Tha'alibi, *Tamthil*, p. 260, for similar sentiments.
12. Ibn al-Jawzi, *Akhbar al-nisa'*, p. 80. For similar evidence consult Ibn Qutaiba, *'Uyun*, vol. 4, p. 81; Isfahani, *Muhadarat*, vol. 3, p. 201; Tha'alibi, *Tamthil*, p. 197; and 'Amili, *Mukhlat*, pp. 96–7.
13. Nabulsi, *Ta'bir*, vol. 2, p. 89, interpreted the practice of withdrawal in dreams to mean a waste of money and denial of family. We have already come across medieval jokes involving contraception (Chapter 5, p. 92). Here is another one (the same Arabic term *'azl* means both withdrawal (i.e., coitus interruptus) and removal (from office)): The Umayyad governor Yusuf Ibn 'Umar had a favourite concubine who was always in his company. One day he received a letter and his face changed suddenly. She asked: *'azl*? He said: How did you know? She answered: Because your face changed without notice. Yet you have practised *'azl* with me every day, and this is your first taste of it! (Isfahani, *Muhadarat*, vol. 3, p. 266; another version is in vol. 1, p. 178).
14. D. V. Glass and E. Grebenik, "World Population 1800–1950", *Cambridge Economic History of Europe* (Cambridge University Press, Cambridge, 1965), vol. 6, part 1, p. 128.
15. Two treatments of the history of Egypt–Syria in Mamluk times are by Ira Lapidus, *Muslim Cities in the Later Middle Ages*, (Harvard University Press, Cambridge, Mass., 1967) – historical sociology; and Bernard Lewis, "Egypt and Syria", in P. M. Holt, Ann Lambton, and B. Lewis, eds., *The Cambridge History of Islam* (Cambridge, University Press, 1970), part 2, chapter 2, pp. 175–230 – political history.
16. Eliyahu Ashtor, *Histoire des prix et des salaires dans l'Orient mediéval* (Paris, 1969), pp. 272–3 for evidence, and pp. 539–53 for a general discussion of the problem of decline.
17. Abraham Udovitch, in Robert Lopez, Harry Miskimin, and A. Udovitch, "England to Egypt: Long-Term Trends and Long-Distance Trade", in Michael A. Cook, ed., *Studies in the Economic History of the Middle East* (Oxford University Press, London, 1970), p. 116.
18. Historical demography "is the study of the ebb and flow of the numbers of mankind in time and space by a combination of geography and history using statistics, and the main concern is to achieve accurate estimates of human numbers" (T. H. Hollingsworth, *Historical Demography* (Cornell University Press, Ithaca, 1969), p. 37).
19. *Ibid.*, pp. 307–10.
20. J. C. Russell, "Late Ancient and Medieval Populations", *Transactions of the American Philosophical Society*, new series, 48 (3) (1958), p. 99.

21. *Ibid.*, p. 101.
22. *Ibid.*, pp. 130–1.
23. J. C. Russell, "The Population of Medieval Egypt", *Journal of the American Research Center in Egypt*, 5 (1966), pp. 69–82.
24. Dwight H. Perkins, *Agricultural Development in China 1386–1968* (Aldine Publishing Company, Chicago, 1969), p. 24.
25. Charles Issawi, *The Economic History of the Middle East 1800–1914* (The University Press, Chicago, 1966), pp. 3–5.
26. Charles Issawi, "The Decline of Middle Eastern Trade, 1100–1850", in D. S. Richards, ed., *Islam and the Trade of Asia* (Bruno Cassirer, Oxford, 1970), p. 247.
27. Hollingsworth, *Historical Demography*, p. 355.
28. Lapidus, *Muslim Cities*, chapter 1, "A History of Cities in the Mamluk Empire", pp. 9–43, especially pp. 25ff.
29. *Ibid.*, pp. 28–30.
30. Udovitch, "England to Egypt", p. 118.
31. *Ibid.*, p. 120.
32. Ibn Khaldun, *Muqaddimah*, vol. 1, pp. 64–5.
33. J. M. W. Bean, "Plague, Population, and Economic Decline in England in the Later Middle Ages", *The Economic History Review*, 2nd series, vol. 15 (1962–3), pp. 431–2.
34. Michael Walters Dols, *The Black Death in the Middle East* (Princeton, 1977), pp. 143–235.
35. "The pneumonic form of the plague is very deadly indeed, recovery being rare. Pneumonic plague is, in fact, about the most fatal infectious disease that is known" (Hollingsworth, *Historical Demography*, p. 357). Hollingsworth, in a study of plague mortality, takes the following figures for granted. Although the figures are a simplification of a complex pattern, they show clearly one aspect of the difference between the pneumonic and bubonic forms of the plague:

	Infective	Morbidity
Pneumonic plague	2 days	96%
Bubonic plague	3 days	50%

(*Ibid.*, p. 365.)

36. L. Fabian Hirst, *The Conquest of Plague* (Oxford University Press, Oxford, 1953), p. 34.
37. Dols, *The Black Death*, pp. 250–2.
38. Udovitch, "England to Egypt", p. 119.
39. Albert Hourani, "Introduction: The Islamic City in the Light of New Research", in A. H. Hourani and S. M. Stern, eds., *The Islamic City* (Bruno Cassirer, Oxford, 1970), p. 19.
40. Shawkani, *Nail al-awtar*, vol. 6, p. 350.
41. Ibn al-Humam, *Sharh*, vol. 11, p. 76.
42. Tahtawi, *Hashiyat*, vol. 2, p. 76.
43. Ibn Nujaim, *Bahr*, vol. 3, p. 214.
44. Ibn 'Abidin, *Radd*, pp. 622–3.
45. The following is more or less a literal translation of Ghazali's passage:

    [Coitus interruptus] is also practised in fear of the multiplication of material difficulties which result from an increase in the number of dependents. The consequent need for extra toil to earn a living, and the possibility of being driven by necessity to engage in immoral or illegal transactions, are matters for concern. Material well-being is an aid to a good Islamic life (*qillat al-haraj mu'in 'ala al-din*). It is true that there is perfection and nobility in total reliance on God, and that, with the practice of contraception, there is a fall from the pinnacle of perfection and a failure to do the very best; but the consideration of consequences, and the safeguarding and saving of money, although contrary to total reliance on God, is not forbidden (Ghazali, *Ihya'*, vol. 2, p. 41).

It would be a mistake to assume that Ghazali's view was unique to him, or that my reading of his text is arbitrary. See Ibn 'Abd Rabbihi, *'Iqd*, vol. 3, pp. 28–9, 34, 37. In the generation following Ghazali, Ibn al-Jawzi expressed the same point of view eloquently in *Said al-khatir*, returning to it frequently (vol. 1, p. 97; vol. 3, pp. 510–12, 585), and also explicitly making the connection between bad times and family limitation: "I have never seen the like of these ugly times, no one is lef̣t to whom one could turn for aid or a loan, so a man may be forced to engage in transactions that are beneath him . . . therefore it is necessary to limit the [size of the] family, etc." (*fa yanbaghi taqlil al-'a'ila*) (vol. 3, p. 511).

46. Hourani, "The Islamic City", p. 24.
47. For the Flagellant movement and the persecution of the Jews see Philip Ziegler, *The Black Death* (London, 1969), pp. 87ff. and 97–109. For the psychological impact of the plague disaster on the Europeans see William L. Langer, "The Next Assignment", *American Historical Review*, vol. 63 (January 1958), pp. 283–304, and *idem*, "The Black Death", *Scientific American* (February, 1964), pp. 114–22. For the reaction of the Egyptians and Syrians to the plague, see Dols, *The Black Death*, pp. 109–21.
48. Ibn al-Wardi, *Risalat*, pp. 184–8. See Michael Dols' translation in *Studies in Honor of George C. Miles*, ed. Dickran K. Kouymijian (Beirut, 1974) pp. 443–55 (the quotation used above is from p. 451). The association between political tyranny and the plague is an old medieval theme. The Abbasid Caliph al-Mansur is reported to have said that one of the blessings of his rule over the Muslims was that the plague had disappeared in his days. Someone observed that "God has refused to add the plague to the plague" (Bahrani, *Kashkul*, vol. 2, p. 184).
49. Hourani, "The Islamic City", p. 13.
50. *Ibid.*, p. 24.
51. Ibn Qudama, *Mughni*, vol. 3, p. 133; Mardawi, *Tanqih*, p. 230; Ibn al-Najjar, *Muntaha*, part 2, p. 227; Ibn Abi Bakr, *Ghayat*, vol. 3, p. 91; Bahuti, *Kashshaf*, vol. 5, p. 189; Ruhaibani, *Matalib*, vol. 5., p. 263; and Maqdisi, *Sharh*, vol. 3, p. 133.
52. See the critique of this approach in J. A. Banks, *Prosperity and Parenthood* (Routledge and Kegan Paul, London, 1954), pp. 1–11.
53. *Ibid.*; also J. A. and Olive Banks, *Feminism and Family Planning in Victorian England* (Schocken Books, New York, first published 1964, second printing 1972). See also David Glass, "Population Growth and Population Policy", in M. C. Sheps and J. C. Ridley, *Public Health and Population Change* (University of Pittsburgh Press, Pittsburgh, 1965), pp. 18–20; D. Glass and E. Grebenik, "World Population", p. 116; and J. M. Beshers, *Population Processes in Social Systems* (New York, 1967), pp. 44–7.
54. For example, E. Lewis-Fanning, "Family Limitation and Its Influence on Human Fertility During the Past Fifty Years", *Papers of the Royal Commission on Population* (London, 1949), vol. 1, chapter 12, especially Tables 123 and 125.

Sources

This is a list of the references which appear in the notes. Names of authors and titles of books are given first in the abbreviated form of the notes, and then followed by the complete bibliographical detail. In most cases, the author's date (year of death) is given between brackets immediately following his name.

'Abd al-Ghaffār (1911), *Aḥkām*: Muḥammad Sa'īd 'Abd al-Ghaffār, *Kitāb al-sa'īdiyyat fī aḥkām al-mu'āmālat*, 2 vols. (Cairo, A.H. 1327).

Abū al-Ḥasan al-Ṭabīb (1101), *Khalq al-insān*: Abū al-Ḥasan Sa'īd Ibn Hibatallah al-Ṭabib, *Kitab khalq al-insan*, Bodleian MS. Pococke 66.

Abū Shuja' and al-Sabī, *Kitāb tajārib al-umara', The Eclipse of the Abbasid Caliphate*, ed. D. S. Margoliouth and H. F. Amedroz (Oxford, 1920–1).

Abū al-Su'ūd (1574), *Irshād*: Abū al-Su'ūd Ibn Muḥammad, *Irshād al-'aql al-salīm ilā mazāyā al-kitāb al-karīm*, 5 vols. (Maktabat al-Riyad al-Haditha, Riyad, n.d.).

Afghānī (1908), *Kashf*: 'Abd al-Ḥakīm al-Afghānī, *Kitāb kashf al-ḥaqā'iq*, 2 vols. (Al-Matba'a al-Adabiyya, Cairo, A. H. 1318).

'Ainī (1451), *Ramz*: Maḥmūd Ibn Aḥmad al-'Ainī, *Ramz al-ḥaqā'iq*, 2 vols. (Matba'at al-Nil, Cairo, A. H. 1299).

'Umdat al-qārī: *'Umdat al-qārī sharh ṣaḥīḥ al-Bukhārī*, 25 vols. (Beirut reprint of A. H. 1348 Cairo edn).

'Ajalī (1202), *Sarā'ir*: Maḥmūd Ibn Idrīs al-'Ajalī, *Sarā'ir al-ḥāwī fī taḥrīr al-fatāwī* (no pagination, Tehran, A. H. 1270).

Āl Ḥusain (1961), *Zawā'id*: Muḥammad Ibn 'Abdallah Āl Ḥusain, *Al-Zawā'id fī fiqh imām al-sunna Aḥmad Ibn Ḥanbal* (Al-Matba'a al-Salafiyya, Cairo, 196–).

'Āmilī (1621), *Mukhlāt*: Bahā' al-Dīn Muḥammad Ibn al-Ḥusain al-'Āmilī, *Kitāb al-mukhlāt* (Beirut reprint of A. H. 1317 Cairo edn).

'Āmilī, al-Ḥurr (1692), *Wasā'il*: Muḥammad Ibn al-Ḥasan al-Ḥurr al-'Āmilī, *Wasā'il al-shī'a ilā taḥṣil masā'il al-sharī'a*, 9 vols. (2nd edn, Tehran, A. H. 1388).

'Āmilī (1558), *Masālik*: Zain al-Dīn Ibn 'Alī al-'Āmilī, *Masālik al-afhām sharḥ sharā'i' al-islām* (no pagination, Tehran, A. H. 1283).

Rawḍa: *Al-Rawḍa al-bahiyya fī sharḥ al-lum'a al-dimashqiyya*, 7 vols. (1st edn, Matba'at al-Adab, Najaf, n.d.).

Anonymous (attributed to Ghazālī), *Ḥikma*: *Al-Ḥikma fī makhlūqāt Allah*, edited by Muḥammad Rashīd Qabbānī (Beirut, 1978). An abbreviation of Ibn Qayyim's *Miftāḥ*.

Anonymous (attributed to Jāḥiẓ), *Dalā'il*: *Kitāb al-dalā'il wa al-i'tibār 'alā al-khalq wa al-tadbīr*, ed. Muḥammad Rāghib Tabbākh (Aleppo, 1928). Another, different abbreviation of Ibn Qayyim's *Miftah*, done before the eighteenth century.

Anṭākī (1599), *Tadhkirat*: Dāwūd Ibn 'Umar al-Anṭākī: *Tadhkirat ūlī al-albāb*, 3 vols. (Cairo, 1952).

Tazyīn: *Tazyīn al-ashwāq fī akhbār al-'ushshāq*, 2 vols. in 1 (Beirut, 1972).

'Arīb Ibn Sa'īd (10th century, fl. 961–76), *Khalq al-janīn*: 'Arīb Ibn Sa'īd al-Kātib al-Qurṭubī, *Kitāb khalq al-janīn wa tadbīr al-ḥabālā wa al-mawlūdīn* (Algiers, 1965).

Aristotle, *GA*: *Generation of Animals*, English translation by A. L. Peck (Loeb Classical Library, H.U.P., Cambridge, Mass., 1942). For the medieval Arabic translation see under Brugman.

Aṭfiyash (1914), *Sharḥ al-nīl*: Muḥammad Ibn Yūsuf Aṭfiyasḥ, *Sharḥ kitāb al-nīl wa shifā' al-'alīl* (Al-Matba'a al-Adabiyya, Cairo, n.d.).

Azraqī (15th century), *Tashīl*: Ibrāhīm Ibn 'Abd al-Raḥmān Ibn Abī Bakr al-Azraqī, *Tashīl al-manāfi' fī al-ṭibb wa al-ḥikma* (Cairo, 1963).

Bābartī (1384), *Sharḥ*: Muḥammad Ibn Mahmūd al-Bābartī al-Rūmī, *Sharḥ al-'ināya 'alā al-hidāya* (printed on the margin of Ibn al-Humām's *Sharḥ*).

Baghawī (1122), *Ma'ālim*: Abū Muḥammad al-Ḥusain Ibn Mas'ūd al-Farrā' al-Baghawī, *Ma'ālim al-tanzīl*, 7 vols. (printed on the margin of Khāzin, *Lubāb al-ta'wīl*).

Baḥrānī (d. circa 1695), *Burhān*: Hāshim Ibn Sulaimān al-Ḥusainī al-Baḥrānī, *Kitāb al-burhān fī tafsīr al-qur'ān*, 4 vols. (2nd edn, Tehran, 1956).

Baḥrānī (1772), *Kashkūl*: Yūsuf Ibn Aḥmad Ibn Ibrāhīm al-Baḥrānī, *Al-Kashkūl*, 3 vols. (Karbala, 1961).

Bahūtī (1641), *Sharḥ*: Manṣūr Ibn Yūnus al-Bahūtī, *Al-Rawḍ al-murbi' sharḥ zād al-mustanqi'*, 2 parts in 1 vol. (6th edn, al-Matba'a al-Salafiyya, Cairo, A.H. 1380).

Kashshāf: *Kashshāf al-qinā' 'an matn al-iqnā'*, 6 vols. (Maktabat al-Nasr al-Haditha, Riyad, n.d.).

Baiḍāwī (1286), *Tafsir*: 'Abd Allah Ibn 'Umar al-Baiḍāwī: *Tafsir al-Baiḍāwī, Anwār al-tanzīl wa asrār al-ta'wīl*, 8 vols. (printed on the margin of Khafajī's *'Ināyat*).

Balkhī (934), *Bad'*: Aḥmad Ibn Sahl al-Balkhī, *Kitāb al-bad' wa al-ta'rīkh*, 6 vols. (Paris, 1901).

Brūsawī (1725), *Rūḥ al-bayān*: Ismā'īl Ḥaqqī al-Brūsawī, *Rūḥ al-bayān*, 10 vols. (Istanbul, A.H. 1331).

Bujairimī (1806), *Iqnā'*: Sulaimān Ibn Muḥammad Al-Bujairimī, *Al-Iqnā' 'alā sharḥ Abī Shujā'* (Cairo, A.H. 1294).

Bukhārī (1413), *Sharḥ al-'ain*: Muḥammad Ibn Mubārak Shāh al Bukhārī, *Sharḥ ḥikmat al-'ain* (of Qazwīnī) (Mashad, 1974).

Dardīr (1786), *Sharḥ*: Aḥmad Ibn Muḥammad Abū al-Barakāt al-Dardīr, *Al-Sharḥ al-kabīr* (printed on the margin of Dasūqī's *Ḥāshiyat*).

Dasūqī (1815), *Ḥāshiyat*: Muḥammad Ibn 'Arafa al-Dasūqī, *Ḥāshiyat al-Dasūqī 'alā al-sharḥ al-kabīr*, 4 vols. (Cairo, A.H. 1373).

Dimashqī (fl. 1378), *Ikhtilāf*: Muḥammad Ibn 'Abd al-Rahmān al-Dimashqī (al-Khatīb al-'Uthmānī), *Kitāb raḥmāt al-umma fī ikhtilāf al-a'imma* (Al-Matba'a al-Bahiyya, Cairo, A.H. 1304).

Faiḍ al-Kāshī (1679), *Ṣāfī*: Muḥammad Ibn al-Murtaḍā Faiḍ al-Kāshī, *Kitāb al-ṣāfī fī tafsīr al-qur'ān*, 4 parts in 2 vols. (Tehran, A.H. 1387).

Tahdhīb: *Al-Mahajja al-baiḍā' fī tahdhīb al-Ihyā'*, 8 vols. (Tehran, A.H. 1340).

Fatāwā al-ʻĀlamgīriyya, 6 vols. (2nd edn, Cairo, A.H. 1310).
Galen, *De Semine*, in C. G. Kuhn, ed., *Claudii Galeni Opera Omnia*, 20 vols. (Leipzig, 1822), vol. IV, pp. 512–651.
Ghazālī (1111), *Iḥyā'*: Abū Ḥāmid Muḥammad al-Ghazālī, *Iḥyā' ʻulūm al-dīn* (Al-Matbaʻa al-Azhariyya al-Misriyya, Cairo, A.H. 1302).
Wajīz: *Al-Wajīz fī fiqh al-imām al-Shāfiʻī*, 2 vols. (Matbaʻat al-Adib, Cairo, A.H. 1317).
Ḥajāwī (1553), *Rawḍ*: Mūsā Ibn Aḥmad al-Ḥajāwī, *Al-Rawḍ al-murbiʻ bi sharḥ zād al-mustaqniʻ*, 2 parts in 1 vol. (Cairo, A.H. 1380).
Ḥalabī (1550), *Multaqā*: Ibrāhīm Ibn Muḥammad al-Ḥalabī, *Multaqā al-abḥur* (Dar al-Tibaʻa al-Misriyya, Cairo, A.H. 1363).
Ḥaṭṭāb (1547) *Mawāhib*: Muḥammad Ibn Muḥammad al-Ḥaṭṭāb, *Mawāhib al-jalīl li sharḥ Mukhtaṣar Khalīl*, 6 vols. (Tripoli, Libya reprint of A.H. 1329 Cairo edn).
Ḥillī (1277), *Mukhtaṣar*: Jaʻfar Ibn al-Ḥasan al-Ḥillī, *Al-Mukhtaṣar al-nāfiʻ fī fiqh al-imāmiyya* (Dār al-Kitab al-ʻArabi, Cairo, n.d.).
Sharā'iʻ: *Sharā'iʻ al-islām fī masā'il al-ḥalāl wa al-ḥarām* (Matbaʻat al-Adab, Najaf, 1969).
Ḥillī (al-Muṭahhar) (1325), *Sharḥ*: Ḥasan Ibn Yūsuf Ibn al-Muṭahhar al-Ḥillī, *Sharḥ tabṣirat al-mutaʻallimīn fī aḥkām al-dīn* (Najaf, 1962).
Tadhkirat: *Kitāb tadhkirat al-fuqahā'*, 2 vols. (lithograph, Tehran, n.d.).
Hippocrates, *The Seed* and *The Nature of the Child*, translated by I. M. Lonie, in G. E. R. Lloyd, ed., *Hippocratic Writings* (Penguin, London, 1978), pp. 317–47.
Ibn ʻAbbās (994), *Kāmil*: ʻAlī Ibn ʻAbbās al-Majūsī, *Kāmil al-ṣināʻa al-ṭibbiyya* (Bulaq, Cairo, A.H. 1294).
Ibn ʻAbd Rabbihi (940), *ʻIqd*: Abū ʻUmar Aḥmad Ibn Muḥammad Ibn ʻAbd Rabbihi al-Andalusī, *Kitāb al-ʻiqd al-farīd*, 7 vols. (Cairo, 1949).
Ibn Abī Bakr (1624), *Ghāyat*: Marʻī Ibn Yūsuf al-Karmī Ibn Abī Bakr, *Ghāyat al-muntahā fī al-jamʻ bain al-iqnāʻ wa al-muntahā*, 3 vols. (Damascus, A.H. 1378).
Ibn ʻĀbidīn (1889), *Hadiyya*: ʻAlā' al-Dīn Ibn ʻĀbidīn, *Al-Hadiyya al-ʻalā'iyya* (3rd edn, Damascus, 1965).
Ibn ʻĀbidīn (1836), *Minḥat*: Muḥammad Amīn Ibn ʻUmar Ibn ʻĀbidīn, *Minḥat al-khāliq* (printed on the margin of Ibn Nujaim's *Baḥr*).
Radd: *Radd al-muḥtār ʻalā al-durr al-mukhtār fī sharḥ tanwīr al-abṣār* (Bulaq, Cairo, 1870).
Ibn Abī Uṣaibiʻa (1270), *Ṭabaqāt*: Aḥmad Ibn Yūnus al-Saʻdī Ibn Abī Uṣaibiʻa, *ʻUyūn al-anbā' fī tabaqāt al-atibbā'*, 2 vols. (Cairo and Königsberg, 1882–4).
Ibn al-ʻArabī (1148), *Aḥkām al-qur'ān*: Abū Bakr Muḥammad Ibn ʻAbdallah Ibn al-ʻArabī, *Aḥkām al-qur'ān*, 4 vols. (Cairo, 1957–9).
Ibn al-Baiṭār (1248), *Mufradāt*: ʻAbdallah Ibn Aḥmad Ibn al-Baiṭār al-Māliqī, *Al-Jāmiʻ li mufradāt al-adwiya wa al-aghdhiya*, 4 vols. (Bulaq, Cairo, 1874–5).
Ibn Ḍūyān, *Manār*: Ibrāhīm Ibn Muḥammad Ibn Ḍūyān, *Kitāb manār al-sabīl fī sharḥ al-dalīl*, 2 vols. (Damascus, A.H. 1378).
Ibn Ḥajar (1449), *Fatḥ al-bārī*: Aḥmad Ibn ʻAlī Ibn Ḥajar al-ʻAsqalānī, *Fatḥ al-bārī bi sharḥ al-Bukhārī*, 17 vols. (Mustafa al-Babi al-Halabi, Cairo, 1959).
Zawā'id: *Al-Maṭālib al-āliya bi zawā'id al-masānīd al-thamāniya*, 4 vols. (Kuwait, 1973).
Ibn Ḥazm (1063), *Muḥallā*: ʻAlī Ibn Aḥmad Ibn Ḥazm, *Al-Muhalla*, 11 vols. in 8 (Cairo, A.H. 1352).

Ibn Hubal (1213), *Mukhtārāt*: Abū al-Ḥasan 'Alī Ibn Aḥmad Ibn 'Alī Ibn Hubal al-Baghdādī, *Kitāb al-mukhtārāt fī al-ṭibb*, 4 vols. in 2 (Haydarabad, A.H. 1364).
Ibn al-Humām (1457), *Sharḥ*: Kamāl al-Dīn Muḥammad Ibn al-Humām, *Sharḥ fatḥ al-qadīr* (Bulaq, Cairo, A.H. 1315).
Ibn al-Jawzī (1201), *Adhkiyā'*: Abū al-Faraj 'Abd al-Raḥmān Ibn 'Alī Ibn al-Jawzī, *Al-Adhkiyā'* (Damascus, 1971).
Akhbār al-nisā', ed. Nizar Rida and mistakenly attributed to Ibn Qayyim (Beirut, 1964).
Iltiqāṭ: *Kitāb iltiqāṭ al-manāfi'*, Bodleian MS. Hunt. Donat. 31, ff. 178–207.
Ṣaid al khāṭir, 3 vols. (Damascus, 1960).
Wafā: *Al-Wafā bi aḥwāl al-Muṣṭafā*, 2 vols. (Cairo, 1966).
Zād al-masīr: *Zād al-masīr fī 'ilm al-tafsīr*, 9 vols. (Al-Maktab al-Islami, Damascus/Beirut, 1965).
Ibn Jumai' (1198), *Irshād*: Hibatallah Ibn Jumai' al-Isrā'īlī, *Kitāb al-irshād li maṣāliḥ al-anfus wa al-ajsād*, Bodleian MS. Marsh 106, Bodleian MS. Hunt. 19, and Egyptian Library, Cairo No. Medicine 345.
Ibn Juzaiy (1340), *Qawānīn*: Muḥammad Ibn Aḥmad Ibn Juzaiy al-Kalbī, *Kitāb al-qawānīn al-fiqhiyya* (Matba'at al-Nahda, Fez, 1935).
Tashīl: *Kitāb al-tashīl li 'ulūm al-tanzīl*, 4 vols in 1 (2nd edn, Beirut, 1973).
Ibn Kathīr (1372), *Tafsīr*: Ismā'īl Ibn Kathīr, *Tafsīr al-qur'ān al-'aẓīm*, 4 vols. (Beirut, 1969).
Ibn Khaldūn (1406), *Muqaddimah*: *The Muqaddimah, An Introduction to History*, translated by Franz Rosenthal (Pantheon Books, New York, 1958).
Ibn al-Khaṭīb (1374), *'Amal man ṭabba*: Muḥammad Ibn 'Abdallah Ibn al-Khaṭīb, *Kitāb 'amal man ṭabba li man ḥabba*, ed. Maria Concepcion Vazquez De Benito (Acta Salmanticensia, Filosofia y Letras 66, Universidad De Salamanca, 1972).
Ibn al-Madanī (17th cent?), *Jawāhir*: *Al-Jawāhir al-manẓūma fī sharḥ al-Manẓūma fī ādāb al-nikāḥ*, printed on the margin of Ibn Yāmūn, *Ādāb al-nikāḥ* (Fez, 1900). Irregular pagination.
Ibn Maimūn (1204), *Al-Ṭibb al-qadīm*: Mūsā Ibn 'Ubaidallah al-Isrā'īlī al-Qurṭubī, *Kitāb al-ṭibb al-qadīm* (Matba'at Misr, Cairo, 1908).
Ibn Malkā (1165), *Mu'tabar*: Abū al-Barakāt Hibatallah Ibn 'Alī Ibn Malkā al-Baghdādī, *Al-Kitāb al-mu'tabar fī al-ḥikma*, 3 vols. (Haydarabad, A.H. 1358).
Ibn al-Nadīm (ca. 1000), *Fihrist*: Muhammad Ibn Isḥāq Ibn al-Nadīm, *The Fihrist of al-Nadim*, ed. Bayard Dodge (Columbia University Press, New York, 1970).
Ibn al-Najjār (1564), *Muntahā*: Muḥammad Ibn Aḥmad Ibn al-Najjār, *Muntahā al-irādāt fī jam' al-muqanni'* (Dar al-'Uruba, Cairo, 1962).
Ibn Nujaim (1562), *Bahr*: Zain al-'Ābidīn Ibn Ibrāhīm Ibn Nujaim al-Miṣrī, *Al-Baḥr al-rā'iq sharḥ kanz al-daqā'iq*, 4 vols. (printed on the margin of Marghinānī's *Hidāya*).
Ibn Qayyim (1350), *Badā'i'*: Muḥammad Ibn Abī Bakr al-Zaur'i, Ibn Qayyim al-Jawziyya, *Badā'i' al-fawā'id*, 4 vols. (Dar al-Kitab al-'Arabi, Beirut, n.d.).
Ighāthat: *Ighāthat al-lahfān min maṣāyid al-shaiṭān*, 2 vols. (Cairo, 1961).
Miftāḥ: *Miftāḥ dār al-sa'āda wa manshūr wilāyat al-'ilm wa al-irāda*, 2 vols. (Dar al Kutub al-'Ilmiyya, reprint of Egyptian edition, Beirut, n.d.).
Rawḍat: *Rawḍat al-muḥibbīn wa nuzhat al-mushtāqīn* (ed. Ahmad 'Ubaid, Cairo, 1956).

Rūḥ: *Kitāb al-rūḥ* (Haydarabad, A.H. 1357).
Shifā': *Shifā' al-'alīl fī masā'il al qaḍā' wa al-qadr wa al-ḥikma wa al-ta'līl* (Cairo, 1975).
Tibyān: *Al-Tibyān fī aqsām al-qur'ān* (1st edn, Cairo, 1933).
Tuḥfat: *Tuḥfat al-mawdūd bi aḥkām al-mawlūd* (Damascus, 1971).
Ṭuruq: *Al-Ṭuruq al-hikmiyya fī al-siyāsa al-shar'iyya* (Cairo, A.H. 1317).
Zād: *Zād al-ma'ād*, 4 vols. (Al-Matba'a al-Misriyya Cairo, n.d.).

Ibn Qudāma (1223), *Mughnī*: Abdallah Ibn Aḥmad Ibn Qudāma al-Maqdisī, *Al-Mughnī fī sharḥ mukhtaṣar al-Khiraqi*, 9 vols. (Matba'at al-Manar, Cairo, A.H. 1348).
Muqanni': *Al-Muqanni' fī fiqh Ibn Ḥanbal*, 3 vols. (Al-Matba'a al-Salafiyya, Cairo, n.d.).

Ibn al-Quff (1286), *'Umda*: Ya'qūb Ibn Ishāq Ibn al-Quff al-Masīḥī, *Kitāb al-'umda fī al-jirāha*, 2 vols. (Haydarabad, A.H. 1356).

Ibn Qutaiba (889), *Ta'wīl*: 'Abdallah Ibn Muslim Ibn Qutaiba al-Dīnawarī, *Kitāb ta'wīl mukhtalaf al-ḥadīth* (Cairo, A.H. 1326).
'Uyūn: *'Uyūn al-akhbār*, 4 vols. (reprint of 1925–30 edn, Cairo, 1963).

Ibn Rajab (1393), *Dhail*: Abu al-Faraj 'Abd al-Raḥmān Ibn Aḥmad Ibn Rajab, *Al-Dhail 'alā tabaqāt al-Ḥanābila*, 8 vols. (Matba'at al-Sunna al-Muhammadiyya, Cairo, 1953).
Jāmi': *Jāmi' al-'ulūm wa al-ḥikam*, 2 vols. (Cairo, 1969).
Qawā'id: *Al-Qawā'id fī al-fiqh al-islāmī* (Cairo, 1971).

Ibn Rushd (1198), *Kulliyāt*: Muḥammad Ibn Aḥmad Ibn Rushd, *Al-Kulliyāt*, ed. Alfredo Bustani (Spanish Morocco, 1939).

Ibn Sīnā (1037), *Ḥayawān*: Abū 'Alī al-Husain Ibn 'Alī Ibn Sīnā, *Al-Ḥayawān*, section 8 of *Al-Shifā'* (1) Tehran edn: *Al-Shifā'*, lithograph (1886), pp. 507 ff., and (2) Cairo edition: *Al-Shifā'*, vol. 8, *Al-Ḥayawān*, ed. Muntaṣir, Zāyid, and Ismā'īl, (1970).
Qānūn: *Kitāb al-qānūn fī al-ṭibb*, 3 vols. (reprint of Bulaq Cairo edition, Dar Sadir, Beirut, n.d.).

Ibn Taghrī-Birdī (1469), *Nujūm*: Jamāl al-Dīn Ibn Taghrī-Birdī, *Al-Nujūm al-zāhira fī mulūk miṣr wa al-qāhira*, 12 vols., William Popper, ed. (Dar al-Kutub al-Misriyya, Cairo).

Ibn Taimiya (1328), *Fatāwā*: Taqī al-Dīn Aḥmad Ibn 'Abd al-Ḥālim Ibn Taimiya, *Al-Fatāwā al-kubrā*, 5 vols. (Dar al-Kutub al-Haditha, Cairo, 1966).
'Ilm al-sulūk: *Kitāb 'ilm al-sulūk*, in *Majmū' fatāwā Ibn Taimiya*, ed. 'Abd al-Rahman Ibn Qasim (Riyad, A.H. 1381).

Ibn 'Ubaidān (1342), *Zawā'id*: 'Abd al-Raḥmān Ibn 'Ubaidan, *Kitāb zawā'id al-kāfī* (Al-Maktab al-Islami, Damascus, A.H. 1379).

Ibn al-Wardī (1349), *Risalat*: 'Umar Ibn al-Muẓaffar Ibn al-Wardī, *Risalāt al-naba' 'an al-wabā'* in Aḥmad Fāris al-Shidyāq, ed., *Majmū'at al-Jawā'ib* (Istanbul, A.H. 1300).

Ibn Yāmūn (1615), *Ādāb al-nikāḥ*: Abū al-Qāsim Ibn Aḥmad Ibn Yāmūn, *Manẓūma fī ādāb al-nikāḥ*, irregular pagination (Fez, 1900).

Ikhwān al-Ṣafā' (10th century), *Rasā'il*: *Rasā'il Ikhwān al-Ṣafā'*, 2 vols. (Beirut, 1957).

'Irāqī (1404), *Ṭarḥ al-tathrīb*: 'Abd al-Raḥīm Ibn al-Ḥusain al-'Irāqī, *Kitāb ṭarḥ al-tathrīb fī sharḥ al-taqrīb*, 8 vols. The book was finished after his death by the author's son, Abū Zur'a al-'Irāqī (Dar al-Ma'arif, Aleppo, n.d.).

Iṣfahānī (1108), *Mūhāḍarāt*: Ḥusain Ibn Muḥammad al-Rāghib al-Iṣfahānī, *Muhaḍarāt al-udabā'*, 4 vols. (Maktabat al-Hayat, Beirut, 1961).

Jāḥiẓ (868), *Ḥayawān*: Abū 'Uthmān 'Amr Ibn Baḥr al-Jāhiẓ, *Al-Ḥayawān*,

8 vols., ed. A. Hārūn (2nd edn, Cairo, 1966); also Beirut edn: 7 vols. in 2 (2nd edn, Dar Saab, Beirut, 1978).
Jamal (1789), *Futūḥāt*: Sulaimān Ibn ʻUmar al-Jamal, *Al-Futūḥāt al-ilāhiyya*, 4 vols. (Cairo, n.d.).
Karmānī (d. ca. 1017), *Rāḥat*: Aḥmad Ḥamid al-Dīn al-Karmānī, *Rāḥat al-ʻaql* (Dar al-Andalus, Beirut, n.d.).
Kasādāwī, *Badr*: Abū Bakr al-Kasādāwī, *Badr al-zawjain* (Cairo, A.H. 1367).
Kāsānī (1191), *Badā'iʻ al-sanā'iʻ*: ʻAlā' al-Dīn Ibn Masʻūd al-Kāsānī, *Kitāb badā'iʻ al-ṣanā'iʻ fī tartīb al-sharā'iʻ*, 2 vols. (Cairo, A.H. 1322).
al-Kātib (987), *Jawāmiʻ*: Abū al-Ḥasan ʻAlī Ibn Nasr al-Kātib, *Kitāb Jawāmiʻ al-ladhdha*, MS., Suleymaniye Library, Tasnif No. 61, 258.
Kāzarūnī (fl. ca. 1344), *Mughnī*: Mawlānā Sadīd al-Kāzarūnī, *Al-Sharḥ al-mughnī* (Calcutta, 1832).
Khafājī (1659), *ʻInāyat*: Aḥmad Ibn Muḥammad al-Khafājī, *ʻInāyat al-qāḍī wa kifāyat al-rāḍī*, 8 vols. (reprint, Dar Sadir, Beirut, n.d.).
Khāzin (1341), *Lubāb*: ʻAlā' al-Dīn ʻAlī Ibn Muḥammad al-Khāzin, *Lubāb al-ta'wīl fī maʻānī al-tanzīl*, 7 vols. (2nd edn, Cairo, 1955).
Khuwārizmī (1257), *Jāmiʻ*: Muḥammad Ibn Maḥmūd Ibn Muḥammad al-Khuwārizmī, *Jāmiʻ masānīd al-imām al-aʻẓam Abī Hanīfā*, 2 vols. (Haydarabad, A.H. 1332).
al-Kūhīn al-ʻAṭṭār (ca. 1260), *Minhāj al-dukkān*: Abū al-Munā Ibn Abī Naṣr al-Kūhīn al-ʻAṭṭār, *Minhāj al-dukkān wa dastūr al-aʻyān* (Cairo, 1912).
Majlīsī (1700), *Biḥār al-anwār*: Muḥammad Bāqir al-Majlīsī, *Biḥār al-anwār*, 25 vols. (Tabriz, A.H. 1275).
Mālik (795), *Muwaṭṭa'*: Mālik Ibn Anas, *Al-Muwaṭṭa'*, 2 vols. (Cairo, 1951).
Manqūr, *Masā'il*: Aḥmad Ibn Muḥammad al-Manqūr al-Tamīmī, *Al-Fawākih al-ʻadīda fī al-masā'il al-mufīda*, 2 vols. in 1 (Damascus, 1960).
Maqdisī (1283), *Sharḥ*: ʻAbd al-Raḥmān Ibn Qudāma al-Maqdisī, *Al-Sharḥ al-kabīr ʻala matn al-muqanniʻ* (Matbaʻat al-Manar, Cairo, A.H. 1348).
Mardāwī (1299), *ʻIqd*: Muḥammad Ibn ʻAbd al-Qawī al-Mardāwī, *ʻIqd al-farā'id wa kanz al-fawā'id*, 2 vols. (Damascus, 1964).
Mardāwī (1480), *Inṣāf*: ʻAlī Ibn Sulaimān al-Mardāwī, *Al-Inṣāf fī maʻrifat al-rājiḥ min al-khilāf*, 12 vols. in 6 (1st edn, Cairo, 1955–8).
Tanqīḥ: *Al-Tanqīḥ al-mushabbiʻ fī taḥrīr aḥkām al-muqanniʻ* (Al-Matbaʻa al-Salafiyya, Cairo, 1962).
Marghīnānī (1197), *Hidāya*: ʻAlī Ibn Abī Bakr al-Marghīnānī, *Al-Hidāya sharḥ bidāyat al-mubtadī*, 4 vols. (Matbaʻat al-Halabi, Cairo, 1937).
Masʻūdī (956), *Murūj*: Abū al-Hasan al-Masʻūdī, *Murūj al-dhahab wa maʻādin al-jawhar* (Beirut, 1965).
Maṭbaʻī, *Majmūʻ*: Muḥammad Najīb al-Maṭbaʻī, *Al-Majmūʻ sharḥ al-muhadhdhab*, the two major authors of this important Shāfiʻī work, in many volumes, are Nawawī (1277) and Subkī (1355) (Matbaʻat al-Imam, Cairo, 1966–9).
Mawla Khusraw (1480), *Durar*: Muḥammad Mawla Khusraw, *Al-Durar al-ḥukkām* (Dar al-Saʻada, Cairo, A.H. 1329).
Minhājī (1475), *Jawāhir*: Muḥammad Ibn Aḥmad al-Minhājī al-Asyūtī, *Jawāhir al-ʻuqūd wa muʻīn al-quḍāt wa al-muwaqqiʻīn wa al-shuhūd*, 2 vols. (Matbaʻat al-Sunna al-Muhammadiyya, Cairo, 1955).
Mullā Ṣadrā (1640), *Asfār*: Ṣadr al-Dīn Muḥammad Ibn Ibrāhīm al-Shīrāzī, *Al-Ḥikma al-mutaʻāliya fī al-asfār al-ʻaqliyya al-arbaʻa*, 8 vols. (Tehran, A.H. 1378).
Mabda': *Al-Mabda' wa al-maʻād* (Tehran, 1976).
Murtaḍā (1437), *Al-Baḥr al-zakhkhār*: Aḥmad Ibn Yahyā Ibn al-Murtaḍā, *Al-Baḥr*

al-zakhkhār al-jāmi' li madhāhib 'ulamā' al-amṣār (Matba'at al-Sunna al-Muhammadiyya, Cairo, 1948).
Nābulsī (1731), *Ta'bīr*: 'Abd al-Ghanī Ibn Ismā'īl al-Nābulsī, *Ta'ṭīr al-anām fī ta'bīr al-manām*, 2 vols. (Dar Ihya' al-Kutub al-'Arabiyya, Cairo, n.d.).
Nafzāwī (15/16th century), *Rawḍ*: Muhammad Ibn Muḥammad al-Nafzāwī, *Al-Rawḍ al-'aṭtr fī nuzhat al-khāṭir* (Maktabat al-Manar, Tunis, n.d.). English translation by Sir Richard Burton, *The Perfumed Garden of the Sheykh Nefzawi* (Castle Books, New York, 1964).
Najdī (1688), *Hidāyat*: 'Uthmān Aḥmad al-Najdī, *Hidāyat al-rāghib li sharḥ 'umdat al-ṭālib* (Cairo, 1960).
Nawawī (1277), *Rawḍat al-ṭālibīn*: Abū Zakariya Yaḥyā Ibn Sharaf al-Nawawī, *Rawḍat al-ṭālibīn*, 8 vols. (Damascus, 196?).
Sharḥ: *Sharḥ ṣaḥīḥ Muslim* (printed on the margin of Qastallani's, *Irshad al-sari*).
Nuwairī (ca. 1332), *Nihāyat al-arab*: Aḥmad Ibn 'Abd al-Wahhāb al-Nuwairī, *Nihāyat al-arab fī funūn al-adab*, 20 vols. (Dar al-Kutub, Cairo, n.d.).
al-Qāḍī al-Nu'mān (974), *Da'ā'im*: Abū Hanīfa al-Qāḍī al-Nu'mān Ibn Muḥammad, *Da'ā'im al-islām* (Cairo, 1960).
Qālī (967), *Amālī*: Abū 'Alī Ismā'il Ibn al-Qāsim al-Qālī, *Kitāb al-amālī*, 3 vols. (Cairo, 1926).
Qastallānī (1517), *Irshād al-sārī*: Aḥmad Ibn Muḥammad al-Qastallānī, *Irshād al-sārī li sharḥ ṣaḥīḥ al-Bukhārī*, 10 vols. (Bulaq, Cairo, A.H. 1305).
Qazwīnī (1283), *'Ajā'ib*: Zakariya Ibn Muḥammad al-Qazwīnī, *Kitāb 'ajā'ib al-makhlūqāt*, 2 vols. (Göttingen, 1849).
Qazwīnī (d. ca. 1276–94), *Ḥikmat al-'ain*: 'Alī Ibn 'Umar al-Kātibi al-Qazwīnī, *Ḥikmat al-'ain* (Mashad, 1974), with the commentary of *Bukhārī* (1413).
Qudūrī (1037), *Jawhara*: Aḥmad Ibn Ḥamdān al-Qudūrī, *Al-Jawhara al-nayyira*, 2 vols. (Al-Matba'a al-Khairiyya, Cairo, A.H. 1322).
Qurṭubī (1272), *Jāmi'*: Abū 'Abdallah Muḥammad Ibn Aḥmad al-Anṣārī al-Qurṭubī, *Al-Jāmi' li aḥkām al-qur'ān*, 18 vols. (reprint, Cairo, 1967).
Qushairī (1074), *Laṭā'if*: Abū al-Qāsim al-Qushairī, *Laṭā'if al-ishārāt*, 6 vols. (Dar al-Kitab al-'Arabi, Cairo, n.d.).
Rāzī (981), *Aḥkām al-qur'ān*: Aḥmad Ibn 'Alī al-Rāzī al-Jaṣṣāṣ, *Kitāb aḥkām al-qur'ān*, 3 vols. (Al-Matba'a al-Bahiyya, Cairo, A.H. 1347).
Rāzī (940), *Kāfī*: Muḥammad Ibn Ya'qūb al-Rāzī, *Al-Furū' min al-kāfī*, 7 vols. (Tehran, A.H. 1377–81).
Rāzī, Fakhr al-Dīn (1209), *Mabāḥith*: Fakhr al-Dīn al-Rāzī, *Kitāb Al-mabāḥith al-mashriqiyya*, 2 vols. (Haydarabad, A.H. 1343).
Tafsīr: *Al-Tafsīr al-kabīr (or) Mafātīh al-ghaib*, 32 vols. (1st edn, Cairo, 1934–62).
Rāzī, Abū Bakr (932), *Manṣūrī*: Abū Bakr Muḥammad Ibn Zakariya' al-Rāzī, *Kitāb al-ṭibb al-Manṣūrī*, Bodleian MS. Marsh 376.
Ḥāwī: *Kitāb al-ḥāwī fī al-ṭibb*, 17 vols. in 8, especially vols. 9 and 10 (Osmania Oriental Publications Bureau, Haydarabad, 1960).
Ruḥaibānī, *Maṭālib*: Muṣṭafā Ibn Sa'd al-Ruḥaibānī, *Maṭālib fī sharḥ ghāyat al-muntaha*, 6 vols. (Damascus, 1961).
Ṣaffūrī (15th century), *Nuzhat*: 'Abd al-Raḥmān Ibn 'Abd al-Salām al-Ṣaffūrī al-Shāfi'ī, *Nuzhat al-majālis wa muntakhab al-nafā'is*, 2 vols. (3rd edn, Cairo, 1967).
Ṣan'ānī, *Subul*: Muḥammad Ismā'īl al-San'ānī, *Subul al-salām sharḥ bulūgh al-marām* (Matba'at Subaih, Azhar Cairo, n.d.).

Ṣanawbarī (1412), *Raḥma*: Muḥammad al-Mahdāwī Ibn 'Alī Ibn Ibrāhīm al-Ṣanawbarī, *Kitāb al-raḥma fī al-ṭibb wa al-ḥikma*, all the printed editions attribute the book, wrongly, to Suyuti (Cairo, n.d.).
Sarakhsī (1090), *Sharḥ al-siyar*: Muḥammad Ibn Aḥmad Ibn Abī Sahl al-Sarakhsī, *Sharḥ al-siyar al-kabīr*, 4 vols. (Haydarabad, A.H. 1335).
Shāfi'ī (820), *Umm*: Muḥammad Ibn Idrīs al-Shāfi'ī, *Al-Umm*, 8 vols. (Matba'at al-Kulliyya al-Azhariyya, Cairo, 1961).
Aḥkām: *Aḥkām al-qur'ān*, as collected by al-Baihaqī al-Nīsābūrī (1066), 2 vols. (reprint, Dar al-Kutub al-'Ilmiyya, Beirut, n.d.).
Shaibānī (ca. 804), *Āthār*: Muḥammad Ibn al-Ḥasan al-Shaibānī, *Kitāb al-āthār* (Haydarabad, 1965).
Muwaṭṭa': *Muwaṭṭa' al-imām Mālik* (2nd edn, Cairo, 1967).
Sha'rānī (1565), *Kashf al-ghimma*: 'Abd al-Wahhāb al-Sha'rānī, *Kitāb kashf al-ghimma 'an jamī' al-umma*, 2 vols. (Cairo, A.H. 1281).
Mīzān: *Kitāb al-mīzān*, 2 vols. (Matba'at al-Taqqadum, Cairo, A.H. 1321).
Tadhkirat: *Mukhtaṣar tadhkirat al-Suwaidī fī al-ṭibb* (printed on the margin of Ibn 'Abbas, *Kamil*).
Shawkānī (1839), *Fawā'id*: Muḥammad Ibn 'Alī al-Shawkānī, *Al-Fawā'id al-majmū'a fī al-aḥādith al-mawḍu'a* (Cairo, 1960).
Nail al-awṭār: *Nail al-awṭār sharḥ muntaqā al-akhbār* (Cairo, A.H. 1344).
Sail: *Kitāb al-sail al-jarrār al-mutadaffiq 'alā ḥadā'iq al-azhār*, 2 vols. (Cairo, 1971).
Shihāb al-Dīn, Abū Firās (1478), *Īḍāḥ*: Shihāb al-Dīn Ibn al-Qāḍī Naṣr al-Dailamī, *Kitāb al-īḍāḥ* (Beirut, 1964).
Shīrazī (1083), *Muhadhdhab*: Abū Iṣḥāq Ibrāhīm Ibn 'Alī al-Shīrāzī, *Al-Muhadhdhab fī fiqh al-imām al-Shāfi'ī* (Matba'at al-Halabi, Cairo, n.d.).
Sijistānī (889), *Masā'il*: Abū Dāwūd Sulaimān Ibn al-Ash'ath al-Sijistānī, *Kitāb masā'il al-imām Aḥmad* (Cairo, A.H. 1353).
Sindī (16th century), *Matāna*: Muḥammad Ibn Ja'far Ibn 'Abd al-Karīm al-Sindī, *Al-Matāna fī al-marma 'an al-khazāna* (Karachi, 1962).
Suyūṭī (1505), *Tafsīr*: Jalāl al-Dīn 'Abd al-Raḥmān Ibn Abī Bakr al-Suyūṭī, *Kitāb al-durr al-manthūr fī al-tafsīr bi al-ma'thūr*, 5 vols. (reprint, Beirut, n.d.).
Ṭabarī (861), *Firdaws*: 'Alī Ibn Rabbān al-Ṭabarī, *Firdaws al-ḥikma* (Berlin, 1928).
Ḥifẓ al-ṣiḥḥa: *Kitāb ḥifẓ al-ṣiḥḥa*, Bodleian MS. Marsh 413.
Ṭabarī (923), *Jāmi'*: Muḥammad Ibn Jarīr al-Ṭabarī, *Jāmi' al-bayān 'an ta'wīl āi al-qur'an*, 30 vols. (2nd edn, Cairo, 1954).
Ta'rīkh: *Ta'rīkh al-rusul wa al-mulūk* (E. J. Brill, Leiden, 1879–81).
Ṭabarsī (1153), *Majma' al-bayān*: Abū 'Alī al-Faḍl Ibn al-Ḥasan al-Ṭabarsī, *Majma' al-bayān fī tafsīr al-qur'ān*, 10 vols. in 5 (reprint, Beirut, of A.H. 1379 Iran edn).
Ṭahāwī (933), *Mukhtaṣar*: Aḥmad Ibn Muḥammad al-Azdī al-Ṭaḥāwī, *Al-Mukhtaṣar fī al-fiqh* (Dar al-Kitab al'Arabi, Cairo, A.H. 1370).
Ṭahṭāwī (1816), *Ḥāshiyat*: Aḥmad Ibn Muḥammad al-Ṭahṭāwī, *Ḥāshiyat al-durr al-mukhtar*, 4 vols. (Cairo, 1838).
Tawḥīdī (1023), *Imtā'*: Abū Hayyān al-Tawḥīdī, *Kitāb al-imtā' wa al-mu'ānasa*, 3 vols. (2nd edn, Cairo, 1953).
Tha'ālibī (1037), *Tamthīl*: Abū Manṣūr 'Abd al-Mālik Ibn Muḥammad al-Tha'ālibī, *Al-Tamthīl wa al-muḥāḍara* (Cairo, 1961).
Thābit Ibn Qurra (901), *Dhakhīra*: Thābit Ibn Qurra al-Ḥarrānī, *Kitāb al-dhakhīra fī 'ilm al-ṭibb* (Cairo, 1928).

Tifāshī (1253), *Rujū'*: Aḥmad Ibn Yūsuf al-Tifāshī, *Rujū' al-shaykh ilā ṣibāh fī al-quwwa 'alā al-bāh* (Mustafa Fihmi, Cairo, 1319). The book is wrongly ascribed to Ibn Kamāl Pasha, Aḥmad Ibn Sulaimān.
Tījānī (ca. 1310), *Tuḥfat*: Muḥammad Ibn Aḥmad al-Tījānī, *Tuḥfat al-'arūs wa nuzhat al-nufūs* (Cairo, A.H. 1301).
Ṭūsī (1067), *Mabsūṭ*: Abū Ja'far Muḥammad Ibn al-Ḥasan al-Ṭūsī, *Al-Mabsūṭ fī fiqh al-imāmiyya*, 6 vols. (Tehran, A.H. 1387).
Nihāya: *Al-Nihāya fī mujarrad al-fiqh wa al-fatāwā* (Beirut, 1970).
Tibyān: *Tafsīr al-tibyān*, 10 vols. (Najaf, 1962).
'Ulaish (1881), *Fatḥ*: Muḥammad Ibn Aḥmad 'Ulaish, *Fatḥ al-'alī al-mālik fī al-fatwā 'alā madhhab al-imām Mālik*, 2 vols. (Cairo, 1937).
Wazzānī (1730), *Mi'yār*: Al-Mahdī Ibn Muḥammad al-Wazzānī, *Al-Mi'yār al-jadīd al-mu'rib 'an fatāwā al-muta'akhkhirīn min 'ulamā' al-maghrib*, 11 vols. (Fez, A.H. 1318).
Yazdī, *'Urwa*: Muḥammad Kāẓim al-Ṭabāṭabā'ī al-Yazdī, *Al-'Urwa al-wuthqā*, 2 vols. (Tehran, A.H. 1384).
Zabīdī (1790), *Itḥāf*: Muḥammad Ibn Muḥammad al-Murtaḍā al-Zabīdī, *Itḥāf al-sāda al-muttaqīn bi sharḥ ihya' 'ulūm al-dīn* (reprint, Dar Ihya' al-Turath al-'Arabi, Beirut, n.d.).
Zamakhsharī (1144), *Kashshāf*: Maḥmūd Ibn 'Umar al-Zamakhsharī, *Al-Kashshāf 'an ḥaqa'iq ghawāmiḍ al-tanzīl*, 4 vols. (Beirut, reprint of 1947 edn).
Zurqānī (1710), *Sharḥ*: Abū 'Abdallah Muḥammad Ibn 'Abd al-Bāqī al-Zurqānī, *Sharḥ muwaṭṭa' al-imām Mālik*, 4 vols. (Cairo, 1962).

Other works cited in the text

Adelmann, Howard B., *Marcello Malpighi and the Evolution of Embryology*, 5 vols. (Cornell University Press, Ithaca, 1966).

Arnaldez, R., "Ibn Hazm", *Encyclopaedia of Islam*, new edn, vol. 3, pp. 790–9.

Ashtor, Eliyahu, *Histoire des prix et des salaires dans l'Orient mediéval* (Paris, 1969).

"The Karimi Merchants", *Journal of the Royal Asiatic Society*, London (1956), pp. 45–56.

Banks, J. A., "Historical Sociology and the Study of Population", *Daedalus* (Spring 1968), pp. 397–414.

Prosperity and Parenthood, A Study of Family Planning among the Victorian Middle Classes (Routledge and Kegan Paul, London, 1954; 2nd impression, 1965).

and Olive Banks, *Feminism and Family Planning in Victorian England* (Schocken Books, New York, first published 1964; 2nd impression, 1972).

Bean, J. M. W., "Plague, Population, and Economic Decline in England in the Later Middle Ages", *The Economic History Review*, 2nd series, vol. 15 (1962–3), pp. 423–37.

Belgueds, S., "La Collection Hippocratique et l'embryologie Coranique", in *La Collection Hippocratique et son role dans l'histoire de la medicine* (E. J. Brill, Leiden, 1975), pp. 321–33.

Beshers, J. M., *Population Processes in Social Systems* (New York, 1967).

Borrie, W. D., *The Growth and Control of World Population* (Weidenfeld and Nicolson, London, 1970).

Bouhdiba, Adbelwahab, *La Sexualité en Islam* (Paris, 1975).

Bousquet, G. H., *L'ethique sexuelle de l'Islam* (Paris, 1966).

Brockelmann, Carl, *Geschichte der Arabischen Litteratur* (Weimar, 1898).

Browne, Edward G., *Arabian Medicine* (Cambridge, University Press, 1921).

Brugman, J. and Drossart Lulofs, H. J., eds., *Aristotle's Generation of Animals, the Arabic Translation* (E. J. Brill, Leiden, 1971).

Brunschvig, Robert, "'Abd", in *Encyclopaedia of Islam*, new edn, vol. 1, pp. 24–40.

"Perspectives", in G. E. von Grunebaum, ed., *Unity and Variety in Muslim Civilization* (University of Chicago Press, Chicago, 1955), pp. 47–62.

Carlsson, Gosta, "The Decline of Fertility: Innovation or Adjustment Process", *Population Studies*, vol. 20, no. 2 (1966), pp. 149–74.

Churchill, Frederick B., "The History of Embryology as Intellectual History", *Journal of the History of Biology*, vol. 3, no. 1 (1970), pp. 65–86.

Clark, G. K., *The Critical Historian* (London, 1967).

Coale, A. J., "The Demographic Transition Re–considered", *International Population Conference* (Liège, 1973).
Cole, F. J., *Early Theories of Sexual Generation* (Oxford University Press, Oxford, 1930).
Cook, M. A., ed., *Studies in the Economic History of the Middle East from the Rise of Islam to the Present Day* (Oxford University Press, London, 1970).
Coulson, N. J., *A History of Islamic Law* (Edinburgh University Press, Edinburgh, 1964).
Daniel, Norman, *Islam and the West, The Making of an Image* (Edinburgh University Press, Edinburgh, 1960).
Darwin, Charles, *The Variation of Animals and Plants under Cultivation*, 2 vols. (2nd edn, New York, 1897).
Deane, Phyllis, *The First Industrial Revolution* (Cambridge, University Press, 1965).
Demeny, Paul, "Early Fertility Decline in Austria–Hungary: A lesson in Demographic Transition", in Glass and Revelle, eds., *Population and Social Change*.
Devereux, George, *A Study of Abortion in Primitive Societies* (revised edn, International Universities Press, New York, 1976).
Dols, Michael Walters, *The Black Death in the Middle East* (Princeton, 1977).
Elgood, Cyril, *A Medical History of Persia and the Eastern Caliphate* (Cambridge University Press, Cambridge, 1951).
Encyclopedia of Islam, New Edition (E. J. Brill, Leiden, 1960–).
Eversley, D. E. C., "Population, Economy, and Society", in Glass and Chambers, eds., *Population in History*.
Fagley, Richard M., "Doctrines and Attitudes of Major Religions in Regard to Fertility", *Proceedings of the World Population Conference*, vol. 2 (United Nations, New York, 1967).
Feldman, D. M., *Birth Control in Jewish Law* (University Press, New York, 1968).
Fischel, Walter J., "The Spice Trade in Mamluk Egypt", *Journal of the Economic and Social History of the Orient*, vol. 1 (1958), pp. 502–14.
Freedman, Ronald, ed., *Population, The Vital Revolution* (Anchor Books, New York, 1964).
Gasking, Elizabeth, *Investigations into Generation 1651–1828* (London, 1967).
Gibb, H. A. R., "Islamic Biographical Literature", in B. Lewis and P. M. Holt, eds., *Historians of the Middle East* (Oxford University Press, London, 1962).
Mohammedanism (2nd edn, Oxford University Press, New York 1962; first published 1953).
and Kramers, J. H., eds., *Shorter Encyclopedia of Islam* (E. J. Brill, Leiden, 1961).
Glass, David, "Population Growth and Population Policy", in Sheps and Ridley, eds., *Public Health and Population Change*.
and Eversley, D. E. C., eds., *Population in History* (Chicago, 1965).
and Grebenik, E., "World Population 1800–1950", in *Cambridge Economic History of Europe*, vol. 6, part 1 (Cambridge University Press, Cambridge, 1965).
and Revelle, Roger, eds., *Population and Social Change* (London, 1972).
Goitein, S. D., "From the Mediterranean to India", *Speculum*, vol. 39 (1954), pp. 181–97.
A Mediterranean Society, vol. 1, *Economic Foundations* (University of California Press, Berkeley, 1967).
Goubert, Pierre, "Legitimate Fecundity and Infant Mortality in France During the

Eighteenth Century: A Comparison", *Daedalus* (Spring 1968), pp. 593–603.
Hanley, Susan B., "Fertility, Mortality, and Life Expectancy in Pre-Modern Japan", in *Population Studies*, vol. 28, no. 1 (March 1974).
Harvey, William, "On Animal Generation", in *The Works of William Harvey*, trans. R. Willis (London, 1847).
Hauser, Philip M., "The Population of the World: Recent Trends and Prospects", in R. Freedman, ed., *Population, the Vital Revolution*.
Henry, Louis, "Europe's Fertility Transition", in *Population Bulletin*, vol. 34, no. 6 (1980).
"Some Data on Natural Fertility", *Eugenics Quarterly*, vol. 8, no. 2 (June 1961).
Hilton-Simpson, M. W., *Arab Medicine and Surgery* (Oxford University Press, London, 1922).
Himes, Norman E., *The Medical History of Contraception* (Baltimore, 1936; reprinted New York, 1963).
Hirst, L. Fabian, *The Conquest of Plague* (Oxford University Press, Oxford, 1953).
Hollingsworth, T. H., *Historical Demography* (Cornell University Press, Ithaca, 1969).
Horowitz, Maryanne Cline, "Aristotle and Women", *Journal of the History of Biology*, vol. 9, no. 2 (1976), pp. 183–214.
Hourani, Albert, "Introduction: the Islamic City in the Light of Recent Research", in A. H. Hourani and S. M. Stern, eds., *The Islamic City* (Bruno Cassirer, Oxford, 1970).
Ibn al-Sharīf, Mahmūd, *Al-Islām wa al-ḥayāt al-jinsiyya* (Anglo-Egyptian Bookstore, Cairo, n.d.).
Iskandar, A. Z., *Arabic Manuscripts on Medicine and Science*, in the Wellcome Historical Medical Library (London, 1967).
Issawi, Charles, "The Decline of Middle Eastern Trade, 1100–1850", in D. S. Richards, ed., *Islam and the Trade of Asia*, pp. 245–66.
The Economic History of the Middle East 1800–1914 (University of Chicago Press, 1966).
"Middle East Economic Development, 1815–1914: The General and the Specific", in M. A. Cook, ed., *Studies in the Economic History of the Middle East*, pp. 395–411.
Khan, A. Hamed, *Islamic Opinions on Contraception* (Dacca, 1963).
Kindelberger, C. P., *Economic Growth in France and Britain 1851–1950* (Harvard University Press, Cambridge, Mass., 1964).
Kopp, Marie K., *Birth Control in Practice* (McBridge, New York, 1934).
Langer, William L., "The Black Death", *Scientific American* (February 1964), pp. 114–22.
"The Next Assignment", *American Historical Review*, vol. 63 (January 1958), pp. 283–304.
Laoust, Henry, "Ibn al-Djawzi", *Encyclopedia of Islam*, new edn.
Lapidus, Ira, *Muslim Cities in the Later Middle Ages* (Harvard University Press, Cambridge, Mass., 1967).
Lesky, Erna, *Die Zeugungs-und Vererbungslehren der Antike und ihr Nachwirken* (Abhandlungen der Geistes- und Sozial-wissenschaftlichen Klasse, Akademie der Wissenschaften und der Literatur in Mainz, no. 19, 1950).
Lewis, Bernard, "Egypt and Syria", in P. M. Holt, Ann Lampton and Bernard Lewis, eds., *The Cambridge History of Islam* (Cambridge University Press, Cambridge, 1970), part 2, chapter 2, pp. 175–230.
Lewis, Bernard, and Holt, P. M., eds., *Historians of the Middle East* (Oxford, University Press, 1962).

Lewis-Fanning, E., "Family Limitation and Its Influence on Human Fertility during the Past Fifty Years", *Papers of the Royal Commission on Population* (London, 1949), vol. 1, chapter 12.

Livi-Bacci, Massimo, "Fertility and Population Growth in Spain in the Eighteenth and Nineteenth Centuries", in Glass and Revelle, eds., *Population and Social Change*.

Madkūr, Muḥammad Salām, *Al-janīn wa al-aḥkām al-muta'alliqa bihi fī al-fiqh al-islāmī* (Cairo, 1969).

Naẓrat al-islām ilā taḥdīd al-naṣl (Dar al-Nahda al-'Arabiyya, Cairo, 1965).

Mawsū'at Jamāl 'Abd al-Nāṣir fī al-fiqh al-Islāmī (Cairo, A. H. 1388).

McKeown, Thomas, "Medicine and World Population", in Sheps and Ridley, eds., *Public Health and Population Change*.

The Modern Rise of Population (New York, 1967).

Morsnick, Johannes, "Was Aristotle's Biology Sexist?", *Journal of the History of Biology*, vol. 12, no. 1 (1979) pp. 83–112.

Mottahedeh, Roy P., *Loyalty and Leadership in an Early Islamic Society* (Princeton, 1980).

Munajjid, Ṣalāḥ al-Dīn, *Al-Ḥayāt al-jinsiyya 'ind al-'arab* (Beirut, 1958).

Needham, Joseph, *A History of Embryology* (Cambridge, 1934).

Noonan, John T., Jr, *Contraception, A History of Its Treatment by the Catholic Theologians and Canonists* (Harvard University Press, Cambridge, Mass., 1966).

"Intellectual and Demographic History", in Glass and Revelle, eds., *Population and Social Change*.

Notestein, Frank W., "Economic Problems of Population Change", in *Proceedings of the Eighth International Conference of Agricultural Economists* (Oxford University Press, London, 1953).

Peel, John and Potts, Malcolm, *Textbook of Contraceptive Practice* (Cambridge University Press, 1969).

Perkins, Dwight H., *Agriculture Development in China 1368–1968* (Aldine Publishing Company, Chicago, 1969).

Potter, R. G., New, M. L., Wyon, J. B., and Gordon, J. E., "Lactation and its Effects upon Birth Intervals in Eleven Punjab Villages, India", *Journal of Chronic Diseases*, vol. 18, pp. 1125–40.

Preus, Anthony, "Galen's Criticism of Aristotle's Conception Theory", *Journal of the History of Biology*, vol. 10, no. 1 (1977), pp. 65–86.

"Science and Philosophy in Aristotle's *Generation of Animals*", *Journal of the History of Biology*, vol. 3, no. 1 (1970) pp. 1–52.

Richards, D. S., ed., *Islam and the Trade of Asia* (Bruno Cassirer, Oxford, 1970).

Roger, Jacques, *Les Sciences de la vie dans la pensée francaise du XVIIIe siecle* (2nd edn, Paris, 1971).

Rosenthal, Franz, *A History of Muslim Historiography* (2nd edn, Leiden, 1968).

"Fiction and Reality: Sources for the Role of Sex in Medieval Muslim Society", in A. L. al-Sayyid-Marsot, ed., *Society and the Sexes in Medieval Islam* (Undena Publications, Malibu, California, 1979), pp. 3–22.

Russell, J. C., "Late Ancient and Medieval Populations", *Transactions of the American Philosophical Society*, new series, vol. 48, no. 3, (1958).

"The Population of Medieval Egypt", *Journal of the American Research Center in Egypt*, vol. 5 (1966), pp. 69–82.

Sarton, George, *Introduction to the History of Science*, 5 vols. (Baltimore, 1927–48).

Schacht, Joseph, *An Introduction to Islamic Law* (Oxford University Press, Oxford, 1964).
The Origins of Muhammadan Jurisprudence (Oxford University Press, Oxford, 1950).
Sharabassy, Ahmad, *Islam and Family Planning* (Al-Ahram Printing House, Cairo, 1969).
Sheps, Mindel C., and Ridley, J. C., eds., *Public Health and Population Change* (University of Pittsburgh Press, 1965).
Spengler, Joseph J., "Demographic Factors and Early Modern Economic Development", in Glass and Revelle, eds., *Population and Social Change*.
Southern, R. W., *Western Views of Islam in the Middle Ages* (Harvard University Press, Cambridge, Mass., 1962).
Stolnitz, George J., "The Demographic Transition: From High to Low Birth Rates and Death Rates", in Ronald Freedman, ed., *Population, The Vital Revolution*.
Stiks, R. K., and Notestein, F. W., *Controlled Fertility, An Evaluation of Clinical Service* (The Williams and Wilkins Company, Baltimore, 1940).
Temkin, Owsei, *Galenism: Rise and Decline of a Medical Philosophy* (Cornell University Press, Ithaca, 1973).
Tyan, E., "Fatwa", Encyclopaedia of Islam, new edn, vol. 2, pp. 886–7.
Udovitch, Abraham, Lopez, Robert, and Miskimin, Harry, "England to Egypt: Long-Term Trends and Long Distance Trade", in M. A. Cook, ed., *Studies in the Economic History of the Middle East*, pp. 93–128.
Ullman, Manfred, *Die Medizin im Islam* (E. J. Brill, Leiden, 1970).
Die Natur und Geheimwissenschaften im Islam (E. J. Brill, Leiden, 1972).
Islamic Medicine (Edinburgh University Press, 1978).
Van de Walle, Etienne, "Marriage and Marital Fertility", in Glass and Revelle, eds., *Population and Social Change*.
"Motivations and Technology in the Decline of French Fertility", in R. Wheaton and T. Haraven, eds., *Family and Sexuality in French History* (Philadelphia, 1980).
and Knodel, John, "Europe's Fertility Transition: New Evidence and Lessons for Today's Developing World", *Population Bulletin*, vol. 34, no. 6 (Population Reference Bureau, Inc., Washington D.C., 1980).
Von Grunebaum, G. E., ed., *Unity and Variety in Muslim Civilization* (Chicago, 1955).
Watt, W. Montgomery, "Al-Ghazali", *Encyclopedia of Islam*, new edn, vol. 2, pp. 1038–41.
Weisheipl, James A., ed., *Albertus Magnus and the Sciences* (Pontifical Institute of Medieval Studies, Toronto, 1980).
Wensinck, A. J., *Handbook of Early Muhammadan Tradition* (E. J. Brill, Leiden, 1960).
Wiet, Gaston, "Les Marchands d'épices sous les Sultans Mamlouks", *Cahiers d'Histoire Egyptienne*, vol. 7 (Cairo, 1955), pp. 81–147.
Wrigley, E. A., "Family Limitation in Pre-Industrial England", *Economic History Review*, 2nd series, vol. 19, no. 1 (1966), pp. 82–109.
Ziadeh, Nicola A., *Urban Life in Syria under the Early Mamluks* (Beirut, 1953).
Ziegler, Philip, *The Black Death* (Collins, London, 1969).

Index

In the alphabetical order the Arabic article (al-) is neglected